3rd Workshop on Innovative Use of NLP for Building Educational Applications 2008

Held in conjunction with ACL-HLT 2008

Columbus, Ohio, USA
19 June 2008

ISBN: 978-1-61738-552-0

Printed from e-media with permission by:

Curran Associates, Inc.
57 Morehouse Lane
Red Hook, NY 12571

CURRAN ASSOCIATES INC. proceedings.com

Some format issues inherent in the e-media version may also appear in this print version.

Printed by Curran Associates, Inc. (2010)

Association for Computational Linguistics
209 N. Eighth Street
Stroudsburg, Pennsylvania 18360

Phone: 1-570-476-8006
Fax: 1-570-476-0860

acl@aclweb.org

Additional copies of this publication are available from:

Curran Associates, Inc.
57 Morehouse Lane
Red Hook, NY 12571 USA
Phone: 845-758-0400
Fax: 845-758-2634
Email: curran@proceedings.com
Web: www.proceedings.com

Introduction

The use of NLP in educational applications is becoming increasingly widespread and sophisticated. Such applications are intended to fulfil a variety of needs, from automated scoring of essays and short-answer responses, to grammatical error detection, to assisting learners in the development of their writing, reading, and speaking skills, in both their native and non-native languages.

The rapid growth of this area of research is evidenced by the number of topic-specific workshops in recent years. This workshop is the next in a series which began at ACL 1997 and continued on with HTL/NAACL 2003 and ACL 2005. Since 1997, there have also been other related meetings such as the InSTIL/ICALL Symposium at COLING 2004, and most recently the CALICO 2008 workshop entitled *Automatic Analysis of Learner Language: Bridging Foreign Language Teaching Needs and NLP Possibilities*.

In keeping with previous workshops, our aim is to bring together the ever-growing community of researchers from both academic institutions and industry, and foster communication on issues regarding the broad spectrum of instructional settings, from K-12 to university level to EFL/ESL and professional contexts. In this endeavor, we are assisted by the wide variety of topics and languages covered by the papers presented.

For this workshop, we received 18 submissions, and accepted 13 papers: 8 were accepted as long presentations (20 minutes) and 5 as short presentations (15 minutes). All accepted papers are published in these proceedings as full-length papers of up to 9 pages. Each paper was reviewed by two members of the Program Committee.

The papers in this workshop fall under several main themes:

- **Second Language Learner Systems** Several papers detail work on systems aimed at helping students learn. [Dickinson et al.] describe an ICALL system for learners of Russian; the *King Alfred* system [Michaud] provides a translation environment to assist learners of Anglo-Saxon English; [Pendar et al.]'s approach to the identification of discourse moves aims to improve students' scientific writing; and [Hldaka et al.] present a corpus-based approach to help Czech students in their study of syntax. [Nagata et al.] present work on detecting romanized Japanese words in written learner English. Finally, [Bernhard et al] describe a method for answering a student's question via paraphrasing.

- **Automatic Assessment** There are also several papers on automatic assessment, including scoring the semantic content of student responses [Bailey et al.] [Nielsen et al.] and automatically scoring speech fluency [Zechner et al.].

- **Readability** Another concern is the readability of materials presented to students, and how to identify materials at appropriate difficulty levels for the intended audience. The issue of retrieval is discussed by [Heilman et al. (b)], while the prediction of reading difficulty is the topic of [Miltsakaki et al.] and [Heilman et al. (a)]

- **Intelligent Tutoring** [Boyer er al.] discuss ways to improve feedback given to students in a tutorial dialogue setting.

We wish to thank all of the authors for participating, and the members of the Program Committee for reviewing the submissions on a very tight schedule.

Joel Tetreault, Educational Testing Service
Jill Burstein, Educational Testing Service
Rachele De Felice, Oxford University

Organizers:

Joel Tetreault, Educational Testing Service
Jill Burstein, Educational Testing Service
Rachele De Felice, Oxford University

Program Committee:

Martin Chodorow, Hunter College, CUNY, USA
Mark Core, ICT/USC, USA
Bill Dolan, Microsoft, USA
Jennifer Foster, Dublin City University, Ireland
Michael Gamon, Microsoft, USA
Na-Rae Han, Korea University, Korea
Derrick Higgins, ETS, USA
Emi Izumi, NICT, Japan
Ola Knutsson, KTH Nada, Sweden
Claudia Leacock, Butler Hill Group, USA
John Lee, MIT, USA
Kathy McCoy, University of Delaware, USA
Detmar Meurers, OSU, USA
Lisa Michaud, Wheaton College, USA
Mari Ostendorf, University of Washington, USA
Stephen Pulman, Oxford, UK
Mathias Schulze, University of Waterloo, Canada
Stephanie Seneff, MIT, USA
Richard Sproat, UIUC, USA
Jana Sukkarieh, ETS, USA

Table of Contents

Workshop Program

Thursday, June 19, 2008

9:00–9:15 Opening Remarks

9:15–9:40 *Developing Online ICALL Resources for Russian*
Markus Dickinson and Joshua Herring

9:40–10:05 *Classification Errors in a Domain-Independent Assessment System*
Rodney D. Nielsen, Wayne Ward and James H. Martin

10:05–10:30 *King Alfred: A Translation Environment for Learners of Anglo-Saxon English*
Lisa N. Michaud

10:30–11:00 Break

11:00–11:20 *Recognizing Noisy Romanized Japanese Words in Learner English*
Ryo Nagata, Jun-ichi Kakegawa, Hiromi Sugimoto and Yukiko Yabuta

11:20–11:40 *An Annotated Corpus Outside Its Original Context: A Corpus-Based Exercise Book*
Barbora Hladka and Ondrej Kucera

11:40–12:00 *Answering Learners' Questions by Retrieving Question Paraphrases from Social Q&A Sites*
Delphine Bernhard and Iryna Gurevych

12:00–12:20 *Learner Characteristics and Feedback in Tutorial Dialogue*
Kristy Boyer, Robert Phillips, Michael Wallis, Mladen Vouk and James Lester

12:20–1:55 Lunch

1:55–2:20 *Automatic Identification of Discourse Moves in Scientific Article Introductions*
Nick Pendar and Elena Cotos

2:20–2:45 *An Analysis of Statistical Models and Features for Reading Difficulty Prediction*
Michael Heilman, Kevyn Collins-Thompson and Maxine Eskenazi

2:45–3:10 *Retrieval of Reading Materials for Vocabulary and Reading Practice*
Michael Heilman, Le Zhao, Juan Pino and Maxine Eskenazi

Thursday, June 19, 2008 (continued)

3:10–3:30 *Real Time Web Text Classification and Analysis of Reading Difficulty*
Eleni Miltsakaki and Audrey Troutt

3:30–4:00 Break

4:00–4:25 *Towards Automatic Scoring of a Test of Spoken Language with Heterogeneous Task Types*
Klaus Zechner and Xiaoming Xi

4:25–4:50 *Diagnosing Meaning Errors in Short Answers to Reading Comprehension Questions*
Stacey Bailey and Detmar Meurers

Developing Online ICALL Exercises for Russian

Markus Dickinson
Department of Linguistics
Indiana University
md7@indiana.edu

Joshua Herring
Department of Linguistics
Indiana University
jwherrin@indiana.edu

Abstract

We outline a new ICALL system for learners of Russian, focusing on the processing needed for basic morphological errors. By setting out an appropriate design for a lexicon and distinguishing the types of morphological errors to be detected, we establish a foundation for error detection across exercises.

1 Introduction and Motivation

Intelligent computer-aided language learning (ICALL) systems are ideal for language pedagogy, aiding learners in the development of awareness of language forms and rules (see, e.g., Amaral and Meurers, 2006, and references therein) by providing additional practice outside the classroom to enable focus on grammatical form. But such utility comes at a price, and the development of an ICALL system takes a great deal of effort. For this reason, there are only a few ICALL systems in existence today, focusing on a limited range of languages.

In fact, current systems in use have specifically been designed for three languages: German (Heift and Nicholson, 2001), Portuguese (Amaral and Meurers, 2006, 2007), and Japanese (Nagata, 1995). Although techniques for processing ill-formed input have been developed for particular languages (see Vandeventer Faltin, 2003, ch. 2), many of them are not currently in use or have not been integrated into real systems. Given the vast array of languages which are taught to adult learners, there is a great need to develop systems for new languages and for new types of languages.

There is also a need for re-usability. While there will always be a significant amount of overhead in developing an ICALL system, the effort involved in producing such a system can be reduced by reusing system architecture and by adapting existing natural language processing (NLP) tools. ICALL systems to date have been developed largely independently of each other (though, see Felshin, 1995), employing system architectures and hand-crafted NLP tools specific to the languages they target. Given the difficulty involved in producing systems this way for even a single language, multilingual systems remain a distant dream. Rather than inefficiently "reinventing the wheel" each time we develop a new system, however, a sensible strategy is to adapt existing systems for use with other languages, evaluating and optimizing the architecture as needed, and opening the door to eventual shared-component, multilingual systems. Furthermore, rather than handcrafting NLP tools specific to the target language of individual systems, it makes sense to explore the possibility of adapting existing tools to the target language of the system under construction, developing resource-light technology that can greatly reduce the effort needed to build new ICALL systems. In this light, it is important to determine where and how reuse of technology is appropriate.

In this spirit, we are developing an ICALL system for beginning learners of Russian based on the TAGARELA system for Portuguese, reusing many significant components. The first priority is to determine how well and how much of the technology in TAGARELA can be adapted for efficient and accurate use with Russian, which we outline in section 2.

Proceedings of the Third ACL Workshop on Innovative Use of NLP for Building Educational Applications, pages 1–9,
Columbus, Ohio, USA, June 2008.

Focusing on Russian requires the development of techniques to parse ill-formed input for a morphologically-rich language. Compared with other languages, a greater bulk of the work in processing Russian is in the morphological analysis. As there are relatively few natural language processing tools freely available for Russian (though, see Sharoff et al., 2008), we are somewhat limited in our selection of components.

In terms of shaping an underlying NLP system, though, the first question to ask for processing learner input is, what types of constructions need to be accounted for? This can be answered by considering the particular context of the activities. We therefore also need to outline the types of exercises used in our system, as done in section 3, since constraining the exercises appropriately (i.e., in pedagogically and computationally sound ways) can guide processing. Based on this design, we can outline the types of errors we expect to find for morphologically-rich languages, as done in section 4. Once these pieces are in place, we can detail the type of processing system(s) that we need and determine whether and how existing resources can be reused, as discussed in section 5.

2 System architecture

Our system is based on the TAGARELA system for learners of Portuguese (Amaral and Meurers, 2006, 2007), predominantly in its overall system architecture. As a starting point, we retain its modularity, in particular the separation of activities from analysis. Each type of activity has its own directory, which reflects the fact that each type of activity loads different kinds of external files (e.g., sound files for listening activities), and that each type of activity could require different processing (Amaral, 2007).

In addition to the modular design, we also retain much of the web processing code - including the programming code for handling things like user logins, and the design of user databases, for keeping track of learner information. In this way, we minimize the amount of online overhead in our system and are able to focus almost immediately on the linguistic processing.

In addition to these more "superficial" aspects of TAGARELA, we also carry over the idea of using annotation-based processing (cf. Amaral and Meurers, 2007). Before any error detection or diagnosis is performed, the first step is to annotate the learner input with the linguistic properties which can be automatically determined. From this annotation and from information about, e.g., the activity, a separate error diagnosis module can determine the most likely error.

Unfortunately, the "annotator" (or the *analysis model*) cannot be carried over, as it is designed specifically for Portuguese, which differs greatly from Russian in terms of how it encodes relevant syntactic and morphological information. With an annotation-based framework, the focus for processing Russian is to determine which information can provide the linguistic properties relevant to detecting and diagnosing ill-formed input and thus which NLP tools will provide analyses (full or partial) which have a bearing on detecting the errors of interest.

3 Exercise design

A perennial question for ICALL systems in general is what types of errors are learners allowed to make? This is crucially dependent upon the design of the activities. We want the processing of our system to be general, but we also take as a priority making the system usable, and so any analysis done in an annotation-based framework must be relevant for what learners are asked to do.

The goal of our system is to cover a range of exercises for students enrolled in an eight-week "survival" Russian course. These students start the course knowing nothing about Russian and finish it comfortable enough to travel to Russia. The exercises must therefore support the basics of grammar, but also be contextualized with situations that a student might encounter. To aid in contextualization, we plan to incorporate both audio and video, in order to provide additional "real-life" listening (and observing) practice outside of the classroom.

The exercises we plan to design include: listening exercises, video-based narrative exercises, reading practice, exercises centered around maps and locations, as well as more standard fill-in-the-blank (FIB) exercises. These exercises allow for variability in difficulty and in learner input.

From the processing point of view, each will have

its own hurdles, but all require some morphosyntactic analysis of Russian. To constrain the input for development and testing purposes, we are starting with an FIB exercise covering verbal morphology. Although this is not the ideal type of exercise for displaying the full range of ICALL benefits and capabilities, it is indispensible from a pedagogical point of view (given the high importance of rapid recognition of verbal forms in a morphologically rich language like Russian) and allows for rapid development, testing, and perfection of the crucial morphological analysis component, as it deals with complicated morphological processing in a suitably constrained environment. The successes and pitfalls of this implementation are unlikely to differ radically for morphological processing in other types of exercises; the techniques developed for this exercise thus form the basis of a reusable framework for the project as a whole.

A simple example of a Russian verbal exercise is in (1), where the verb needs to be past tense and agree with third person singular masculine noun.

(1) Вчера он __ (видеть) фильм.
Yesterday he __ (to see) a film

4 Taxonomy for morphological errors

When considering the integration of NLP tools for morphological error detection, we need to consider the nature of learner language. In this context, an analyzer cannot simply reject unrecognized or ungrammatical strings, as does a typical spell-checker, for example, but must additionally recognize what was intended and provide meaningful feedback on that basis. Formulating an error taxonomy delineates what information from learner input must be present in the linguistic analysis.

Our taxonomy is given in figure 1. As can be seen at a glance, the errors become more complex and require more information about the complete syntax as we progress in the taxonomy.

To begin with, we have inappropriate verb stems. For closed-form exercises, the only way that a properly-spelled verb stem can be deemed appropriate or inappropriate is by comparing it to the verb that the student was asked to use. Thus, errors of type #1b are straightforward to detect and to provide feedback on; all that needs to be consulted is

1. Inappropriate verb stem
   (a) Always inappropriate
   (b) Inappropriate for this context
2. Inappropriate verb affix
   (a) Always inappropriate
   (b) Always inappropriate for verbs
   (c) Inappropriate for this verb
3. Inappropriate combination of stem and affix
4. Well-formed word in inappropriate context
   (a) Inappropriate agreement features
   (b) Inappropriate verb form (tense, perfective/imperfective, etc.)

Figure 1: Error taxonomy for Russian verbal morphology

the activity model.[1] Errors of type #1a (and #2a) are essentially misspellings and will thus require spell-checking technology, which we do not focus on in this paper, although we discuss it briefly in section 5.3.

Secondly, there are inappropriate verb affixes, which are largely suffixes in Russian. Other than misspellings (#2a), there are two ways that affixes can be incorrect, as shown in example (2). In example (2a), we have the root for 'begin' (pronounced *nachina*) followed by an ending (*ev*) which is never an appropriate ending for any Russian verb, although it is a legitimate nominal suffix (#2b). The other subtype of error (#2c) involves affixes which are appropriate for different stems within the same POS category. In example (2b), a third person singular verb ending was used (*it*), but it is appropriate for a different conjugation class. The appropriate form for 'he/she/it begins' is начинает.

(2) a. *начина-ев
begin-??
b. *начина-ит
begin-3s

The third type of error is where the stem and affix

[1]Note that if one were allowing free input, this error type could be the most difficult, in that the semantics of the sentence would have to be known to determine if a verb was appropriate.

may both be correct, but they were put together inappropriately. In a sense, these are a specific type of misspelling. For example, the infinitive мочь (*moch*, 'to be able to') can be realized with different stems, depending upon the ending, i.e., мог-у (*mogu* 'I can') мож-ем (*mozhem* 'we can'). Thus, we might expect to see errors such as *мож-у (*mozhu*), where both the stem and the affix are appropriate—and appropriate for this verb—but are not combined in a legitimate fashion. The technology needed to detect these types of errors is no more than what is needed for error type #2, as we discuss in section 5.

The final type of error is the one which requires the most attention in terms of NLP processing. This is the situation when we have a well-formed word appearing in an inappropriate context. In other words, there is a mismatch between the morphological properties of the verb and the morphological properties dictated by the context for that verb.

There are of course different ways in which a verb might display incorrect morphological features. In the first case (#4a), there are inappropriate agreement features. Verbs in Russian agree with the properties of their subject, as shown in example (3). Thus, as before, we need to know the morphological properties of the verb, but now we need not just the possible analyses, but the best analysis in this context. Furthermore, we need to know what the morphological properties of the subject noun are, to be able to check whether they agree. Access to the subject is something which can generally be determined by short context, especially in relatively short sentences.

(3) a. Я думаю
I think-1sg

b. Он думает
He think-3sg

c. *Я думает
I think-3sg

In the second case (#4b), the verb could be in an inappropriate form: the tense could be inappropriate; the verbal form (gerund, infinitive, etc.) could be inappropriate; the distinction between perfective and imperfective verbs could be mistakenly realized; and so forth. Generally speaking, this kind of contextual information comes from two sources: 1) The activity model can tell us, for example, whether a perfective (generally, a completed action) or an imperfective verb is required. 2) The surrounding sentence context can tell us, for example, whether an infinitive verb is governed by a verb selecting for an infinitive. Thus, we need the same tools that we need for agreement error detection.

By breaking it down into this taxonomy, we can more clearly delineate when we need external technology in dealing with morphological variation. For error types #1 through #3, we make no use of context and only need information from an activity model and a lexicon to tell us whether the word is valid. For these error types, the processing can proceed in a relatively straightforward fashion, provided that we have a lexicon, as outlined in section 5. Note also that our error taxonomy is meant to range over the space of logically possible error types for learners from any language background of any language's morphological system. In this way, it differs from the more heuristic approaches of earlier systems such as Athena (Murray, 1995), which used taxonomies tailored to the native languages of the system's users.

That leaves category #4. These errors are morphological in nature, but the words are well-formed, and the errors have to do with properties conditioned by the surrounding context. These are the kind for which we need external technology, and we sketch a proposed method of analysis in section 5.4.

Finally, we might have considered adding a fifth type of error, as in the following:

5. Well-formed word appropriate to the sentence, used inappropriately
   (a) Inappropriate position
   (b) Inappropriate argument structure

However, these issues of argument structure and of pragmatically-conditioned word order variation do not result in morphological errors of the verb, but rather clearly syntactic errors. We are currently only interested in morphological errors, given that in certain exercises, as in the present cases, syntactic errors are not even possible. With an FIB design, even though we might still generate a complete analysis of the sentence, we know which word has the potential for error. Even though we are not currently concerned with these types of errors, we can note that argument structure errors can likely be handled through the activity model and through a similar analysis to what described is in section 5.4 since both context-dependent morphological errors (e.g., agreement errors) and argument structure errors rely on relations between the verb and its arguments.

5 Linguistic analysis

Given the discussion of the previous section, we are now in a position to discuss how to perform morphological analysis in a way which supports error diagnosis.

5.1 The nature of the lexicon

In much syntactic theory, sentences are built from feature-rich lexical items, and grammatical sentences are those in which the features of component items agree in well-defined ways. In morphologically-rich languages like Russian, the heavy lifting of feature expression is done by overt marking of words in the form of affixes (mainly prefixes and suffixes in the case of Russian). To be able to analyze words with morphological errors, then, we need at least partially successful morphological analysis of the word under analysis (as well as the words in the context).

The representation of words, therefore, must be such that we can readily obtain accurate partial information from both well-formed and ill-formed input. A relatively straightforward approach for analysis is to structure a lexicon such that we can build up partial (and competing) analyses of a word as the word is processed. As more of the word is (incrementally) processed, these analyses can be updated. But how is this to be done exactly?

In our system, we plan to meet these criteria by using a fully-specified lexicon, implemented as a Finite State Automaton (FSA) and indexed by both word edges. Russian morphological information is almost exclusively at word edges—i.e., is encoded in the prefixes and suffixes—and thus an analysis can proceed by working inwards, one character at a time, beginning at each end of an input item.[2]

By *fully-specified*, we mean that each possible form of a word is stored as a separate entity (path). This is not as wasteful of memory as it may sound. Since the lexicon is an FSA, sections shared across forms need be stored only once with diversion represented by different paths from the point where the shared segment ends. In fact, representing the lexicon as an FSA ensures that this process efficiently encodes the word possibilities. Using an FSA over all stored items, regular affixes need to be stored only once, and stems which require such affixes simply point to them (Clemenceau, 1997). This gives the analyzer the added advantage that it retains explicit knowledge of state, making it easy to simultaneously entertain competing analyses of a given input string (Ćavar, 2008), as well as to return to previous points in an analysis to resolve ambiguities (cf., e.g., Beesley and Karttunen, 2003).

We also need to represent hypothesized morpheme boundaries within a word, allowing us to segment the word into its likely component parts and to analyze each part independently of the others. Such segmentation is crucial for obtaining accurate information from each morpheme, i.e., being able to ignore an erroneous morpheme while identifying an adjoining correct morpheme. Note also that because an FSA encodes competing hypotheses, multiple segmentations can be easily maintained.

Consider example (4), for instance, for which the correct analysis is the first person singular form of the verb *think*. This only becomes clear at the point where segmentation has been marked. Up to that point, the word is identical to some form of дума (*duma*), 'parliament' (alternatively, 'thought'). Once the system has seen дума, it automatically entertains the competing hypotheses that the learner intends 'parliament,' or any one of many forms of 'to think,' as these are all legal continuations of what it has seen so far. Any transition to ю after дума carries with it the analysis that there is a morpheme boundary here.

(4) дума|ю
think-1sg

Obviously this bears non-trivial resemblance to spell-checking technology. The crucial difference

[2] See Roark and Sproat (2007) for a general overview of implementational strategies for finite-state morphological analysis.

comes in the fact that an ICALL morphological analyzer must be prepared to do more than simply reject strings not found in the lexicon and thus must be augmented with additional, morphological information. Transitions in the lexicon FSA will need to encode more information than just the next character in the input; they also need to be marked with possible morphological analyses at points where it is possible that a morpheme boundary begins.

Maintaining hypothesized paths through a lexicon based on erroneous input must obviously be constrained in some way (to prevent all possible paths from being simultaneously entertained), and thus we first developed the error taxonomy above. Knowing what kinds of errors are possible is crucial to keeping the whole process workable.

5.2 FSAs for error detection

But why not use an off-the-shelf morphological analyzer which returns all possible analyses, or a more traditional paradigm-based lexicon? There are a number of reasons we prefer exploring an FSA implementation to many other approaches to lexical storage for the task of supporting error detection and diagnosis.

First, traditional mophological analyzers generally assume well-formed input. And, unless they segment a word, they do not seem to be well-suited to providing information relevant to context-independent errors.

Secondly, we need to readily have access to alternative analyses, even for a legitimate word. With phonetically similar forms used as different affixes, learners can accidentally produce correct forms, and thus multiple analyses are crucial. For example, -у can be either a first person singular marker for certain verb classes or an accusative marker for certain noun classes. Suppose a learner attempts to make a verb out of the noun душ (*dush*), meaning 'shower' and thus forms the word душу. It so happens that this incorrect form is identical to an actual Russian word: the accusative form of the noun 'soul.' A more traditional morphological analysis will likely only find the attested form. Keeping track of the history from left-to-right records that the 'shower' reading is possible; keeping track of the history from right-to-left records that a verbal ending is possible. Compactly representing such ambiguity—especially when the ambiguity is not in the language itself but in the learner's impression of how the language works—is thus key to identifying errors.

Finally, and perhaps most importantly, morphological analysis over a FSA lexicon allows for easy implementation of activity-specific heuristics. In the current example, for instance, an activity might prioritize a 'shower' reading over a 'soul' one. Since entertained hypotheses are all those which represent legal continuations (or slight alterations of legal continuations) through the lexicon from a given state in the FSA, it is easy to bias the analyzer to return certain analyses through the use of weighted paths. Alternatively, paths that we have strong reason to believe will not be needed can be "disconnected." In the verbal morphology exercise, for example, suffix paths for non-verbs can safely be ignored.

The crucial point about error detection in ICALL morphological analysis is that the system must be able to speculate, in some broadly-defined sense, on what learners *might have meant* by their input, rather than simply evaluating the input as correct or incorrect based on its (non)occurrence in a lexicon. For this reason, we prefer to have a system where at least one component of the analyzer has 100% recall, i.e., returns a set of all plausible analyses, one of which can reasonbly be expected to be correct. Since an analyzer based on an FSA lexicon has full access to the lexicon at all stages of analysis, it efficiently meets this requirement, and it does this without anticipating specific errors or being tailored to a specific type of learner (cf., e.g., Felshin, 1995).

5.3 Error detection

Having established that an FSA lexicon supports error detection, let us outline how it will work. Analysis is a process of attempting to form independent paths through the lexicon - one operating "forward" and the other operating "backward." For grammatical input, there is generally one unique path through the lexicon that joins both ends of the word. Morphological analysis is found by reading information from the transitions along the chain (cf. Beesley and Karttunen, 2003). For ungrammatical input, the analyzer works by trying to build a connecting path based on the information it has.

Consider the case of the two ungrammatical verbs in (5).

(5) a. *начина-ев
begin-??

b. *начина-ит
begin-3s

In (5a) (error type #2b) the analysis proceeding from the end of the word would fail to detect that the word is intended to be a verb. But it would, at the point of reaching the е in ев, recognize that it had found a legitimate nominal suffix. The processing from the beginning of the word, however, would recognize that it has seen some form of *begin*. We thus have enough information to know what the verbal stem is and that there is probably a morpheme boundary after начина-. These two hypotheses do not match up to form a legitimate word (thereby detecting an error), but they provide crucial partial information to tell us how the word was misformed.

Detecting the error in (5b) (type #2c) works similarly, and the diagnosis will be even easier. Again, analyses proceeding from each end of the word will agree on the location of the morpheme boundary and that the type of suffix used (third person singular) is a type appropriate to verbs, just not for this conjugation class. Having a higher-level rule recognize that all features match, merely the form is wrong, is easily achieved in a system with an explicit taxonomy of expected error types coded in.

Errors of type #3 are handled in exactly the same fashion: information about which stem or which affix is used is readily available, even if there is no complete path to form a whole word.

Spelling errors within a stem or an affix (error types #1a and #2a) require additional technology in order to find the intended analysis—which we only sketch here—but it is clear that such spell-checking should be done separately on each morpheme.[3] In the above examples, if the stem had been misspelled, that should not change the analysis of the suffix. Integrating spell-checking by calculating edit distances between a realized string and a morpheme in the lexicon should be relatively straightforward, as that technology is well-understood (see, e.g., Mitton, 1996) and since we are already analyzing subparts of words.

Obviously, in many cases there will be lingering ambiguity, either because there are multiple grammatical analyses in the lexicon for a given input form, or because the learner has entered an ungrammatical form, the intention behind which cannot entirely be determined from the input string alone. It is for such cases that the morphological analyzer we propose is most useful. Instead of returning the most likely path through the analyzer (e.g., the GPARS system of Loritz, 1992), our system proposes to follow *all plausible* paths through the lexicon *simultaneously*—including those that are the result of string edit "repair" operations.[4] In short, we intend a system that entertains competing hypotheses "online" as it processes input words.[5]

This results in a set of analyses, providing sentence-level syntactic and semantic analysis modules quick access to competing hypotheses, from which the the analysis most suitable to the context can be chosen, including those which are misspelled. The importance of this kind of functionality is especially well demonstrated in Pijls et al. (1987), which points out that in some languages—Dutch, in this case—minor, phonologically vacuous spelling differences are syntactically conditioned, making spell checking and syntactic analysis mutually dependent. Such cases are rarer in Russian, but the functionality remains useful due to the considerable interdependence of morphological and syntactic analysis.

5.4 Morphological analysis in context

For the purposes of the FIB exercise currently under development, the finite-state morphological analyzer we are building will of course be sufficient, but as exercises grow in complexity, it will be necessary to use it in conjunction with other tools. It is worth briefly sketching how the components of this integrated system will work together to provide useful error feedback to our learners.

If the learner has formed a legitimate word, the task becomes one of determining whether or not it

[3]Clearly, we will be able to determine whether a word is correctly spelled or not; the additional technology is needed to determine the candidate corrections.

[4]These include transitions to states on no input symbol (INSERTION), transitions to states on a different symbol from the next input symbol (SUBSTITUTION), and consumption of an input symbol without transition to a new state (DELETION).

[5]It is worth noting here that GPARS was actually a sentence-level system; it is for the word-level morphological analysis discussed here that we expect the most gain from our approach.

is appropriate to the context. The FSA analyzer will provide a list of possible analyses (i.e., augmented POS tags) for each input item (ranked, if need be). We can explore using a third-party tagger to narrow down this output list to analyses that make sense in context. We are considering both the Hidden Markov Model tagger TnT (Brants, 2000) and the Decision Tree Tagger (Schmid, 1997), with parameter files from Sharoff et al. (2008). Both of these taggers use local context, but, as they provide potentially different types of information, the final system may use both in parallel, weighing the output of each to the degree which each proves useful in trial runs to make its decision.

Since POS tagging does not capture every syntactic property that we might need access to, we are not sure how accurate error detection can be. Thus, to supplement its contextual information, we intend to use shallow syntactic processing methods, perhaps based on a small set of constraint grammar rules (cf, e.g., Bick, 2004). This shallow syntactic recognizer can operate over the string of now-annotated tags to resolve any remaining ambiguities and point out any mismatches between the items (for example, a noun-adjective pair where the gender does not match), thereby more accurately determining the relations between words.

6 Summary and Outlook

We have outlined a system for Russian ICALL exercises, the first of its kind for a Slavic language, and we have specifically delineated the types of errors to which need to be analyzed for such a morphologically-rich language. In that process, we have proposed a method for analyzing the morphology of learner language and noted where external NLP tools will be useful, making it clear how all these tools can be optimized for learning environments where the priority is to obtain a correct analysis, over obtaining any analysis.

The initial challenge is in creating the FSA lexicon, given that no such resource exists. However, unsupervised approaches to calculating the morphology of a language exist, and these can be directly connected to FSAs (Goldsmith and Hu, 2004). Thus, by using a tool such as Linguistica[6] on a corpus such as the freely available subset of the Russian Internet Corpus (Sharoff et al., 2008),[7] we can semi-automatically construct an FSA lexicon, pruning it by hand.

Once the lexicon is constructed—for even a small subset of the language covering a few exercises—the crucial steps will be in performing error detection and error diagnosis on top of the linguistic analysis. In our case, linguistic analysis is provided by separate (levels of) modules operating in parallel, and error detection is largely a function of either noticing where these modules disagree, or in recognizing cases where ambiguity remains after one has been used to constrain the output of the other.

We have also tried to advance the case that this and future ICALL systems do better to build on existing technologies, rather than building from the bottom up for each new language. We hope that the approach we are taking to morphological analysis will prove to be just such a general, scalable system, one applicable—with some tweaking and to various levels—to morphologically-rich languages and isolating languages alike.

Acknowledgments We would like to thank Detmar Meurers and Luiz Amaral for providing us with the TAGARELA sourcecode, as well as for valuable insights into the workings of ICALL systems; and to thank Anna Feldman and Jirka Hana for advice on Russian resources. We also thank two anonymous reviewers for insightful comments that have influenced the final version of this paper. This research was supported by grant P116S070001 through the U.S. Department of Education's Fund for the Improvement of Postsecondary Education.

References

Amaral, Luiz (2007). Designing Intelligent Language Tutoring Systems: integrating Natural Language Processing technology into foreign language teaching. Ph.D. thesis, The Ohio State University.

Amaral, Luiz and Detmar Meurers (2006). Where does ICALL Fit into Foreign Language Teaching? Talk given at CALICO Conference. University of Hawaii, http:

[6] http://linguistica.uchicago.edu/

[7] http://corpus.leeds.ac.uk/mocky/

//purl.org/net/icall/handouts/calico06-amaral-meurers.pdf.

Amaral, Luiz and Detmar Meurers (2007). Putting activity models in the driver's seat: Towards a demand-driven NLP architecture for ICALL. Talk given at EUROCALL. University of Ulster, Coleraine Campus, http://purl.org/net/icall/handouts/eurocall07-amaral-meurers.pdf.

Beesley, Kenneth R. and Lauri Karttunen (2003). *Finite State Morphology*. CSLI Publications.

Bick, Eckhard (2004). PaNoLa: Integrating Constraint Grammar and CALL. In Henrik Holmboe (ed.), *Nordic Language Technology*, Copenhaguen: Museum Tusculanum, pp. 183–190.

Brants, Thorsten (2000). TnT – A Statistical Part-of-Speech Tagger. In *Proceedings of the Sixth Applied Natural Language Processing Conference (ANLP 2000)*. Seattle, WA, pp. 224–231.

Ćavar, Damir (2008). The Croatian Language Repository: Quantitative and Qualitative Resources for Linguistic Research and Language Technologies. Invited talk, Indiana University Department of Lingistics, January 2008.

Clemenceau, David (1997). Finite-State Morphology: Inflections and Derivations in a Singl e Framework Using Dictionaries and Rules. In Emmanuel Roche and Yves Schabes (eds.), *Finite State Language Processing*, The MIT Press.

Felshin, Sue (1995). The Athena Language Learning Project NLP System: A Multilingual System for Conversation-Based Language Learning. In *Intelligent Language Tutors: Theory Shaping Technology*, Lawrence Erlbaum Associates, chap. 14, pp. 257–272.

Goldsmith, John and Yu Hu (2004). From Signatures to Finite State Automata. In *Midwest Computational Linguistics Colloquium (MCLC-04)*. Bloomington, IN.

Heift, Trude and Devlan Nicholson (2001). Web delivery of adaptive and interactive language tutoring. *International Journal of Artificial Intelligence in Education* 12(4), 310–325.

Loritz, D. (1992). Generalized Transition Network Parsing for Language Study: the GPARS system for English, Russian, Japanese and Chinese. *CALICO Journal* 10(1).

Mitton, Roger (1996). *English Spelling and the Computer*. Longman.

Murray, Janet H. (1995). Lessons Learned from the Athena Language Learning Project: Using Natural Language Processing, Graphics, Speech Processing, and Interactive Video for Communication-Based Language Learning. In V. Melissa Holland, Michelle R. Sams and Jonathan D. Kaplan (eds.), *Intelligent Language Tutors: Theory Shaping Technology*, Lawrence Erlbaum Associates, chap. 13, pp. 243–256.

Nagata, Noriko (1995). An Effective Application of Natural Language Processing in Second Language Instruction. *CALICO Journal* 13(1), 47–67.

Pijls, Fieny, Walter Daelemans and Gerard Kempen (1987). Artificial intelligence tools for grammar and spelling instruction. *Instructional Science* 16, 319–336.

Roark, Brian and Richard Sproat (2007). *Computational Approaches to Morphology and Syntax*. Oxford University Press.

Schmid, Helmut (1997). Probabilistic part-of-speech tagging using decision trees. In D.H. Jones and H.L. Somers (eds.), *New Methods in Language Processing*, London: UCL Press, pp. 154–164.

Sharoff, Serge, Mikhail Kopotev, Tomaž Erjavec, Anna Feldman and Dagmar Divjak (2008). Designing and evaluating Russian tagsets. In *Proceedings of LREC 2008*. Marrakech.

Vandeventer Faltin, Anne (2003). Syntactic error diagnosis in the context of computer assisted language learning. Thèse de doctorat, Université de Genève, Genève.

Classification Errors in a Domain-Independent Assessment System

Rodney D. Nielsen[1,2], Wayne Ward[1,2] and James H. Martin[1]
[1] Center for Computational Language and Education Research, University of Colorado, Boulder
[2] Boulder Language Technologies, 2960 Center Green Ct., Boulder, CO 80301
Rodney.Nielsen, Wayne.Ward, James.Martin@Colorado.edu

Abstract

We present a domain-independent technique for assessing learners' constructed responses. The system exceeds the accuracy of the majority class baseline by 15.4% and a lexical baseline by 5.9%. The emphasis of this paper is to provide an error analysis of performance, describing the types of errors committed, their frequency, and some issues in their resolution.

1 Introduction

Assessment within state of the art Intelligent Tutoring Systems (ITSs) generally provides little more than an indication that the student's response expressed the target knowledge or it did not. There is no indication of exactly what facets of the concept a student contradicted or failed to express. Furthermore, virtually all ITSs are developed in a very domain-specific way, with each new question requiring the handcrafting of new semantic extraction frames, parsers, logic representations, or knowledge-based ontologies (c.f., Graesser et al., 2001; Jordan et al., 2004; Peters et al., 2004; Roll et al., 2005; VanLehn et al., 2005). This is also true of research in the area of scoring constructed response questions (e.g., Callear et al., 2001; Leacock, 2004; Mitchell et al., 2002; Pulman and Sukkarieh, 2005). The present paper analyzes the errors of a system that was designed to address these limitations.

Rather than have a single expressed versus not-expressed assessment of the reference answer as a whole, we instead break the reference answer down into what we consider to be approximately its lowest level compositional facets. This roughly translates to the set of triples composed of labeled (typed) dependencies in a dependency parse of the reference answer. Breaking the reference answer down into fine-grained facets permits a more focused assessment of the student's response, but a simple yes or no entailment at the facet level still lacks semantic expressiveness with regard to the relation between the student's answer and the facet in question, (e.g., did the student contradict the facet or just fail to address it?). Therefore, it is also necessary to break the annotation labels into finer levels in order to specify more clearly the relationship between the student's answer and the reference answer facet.

In this paper, we present an error analysis of our system, detailing the most frequent types of errors encountered in our implementation of a domain-independent ITS assessment component and discuss plans for correcting or mitigating some of the errors. The system expects constructed responses of a phrase to a few sentences, but does not rely on technology developed specifically for the domain or subject matter being tutored – without changes, it should handle history as easily as science. We first briefly describe the corpus used, the knowledge representation, and the annotation. In section 3, we describe our assessment system. Then we present the error analysis and discussion.

2 Assessing Student Answers

2.1 Corpus

We acquired grade 3-6 responses to 287 questions from the Assessing Science Knowledge (ASK) project (Lawrence Hall of Science, 2006). The responses, which range in length from moderately

Proceedings of the Third ACL Workshop on Innovative Use of NLP for Building Educational Applications, pages 10–18,
Columbus, Ohio, USA, June 2008.

short verb phrases to several sentences, cover all 16 diverse teaching and learning modules, spanning life science, physical science, earth and space science, scientific reasoning, and technology. We generated a corpus by transcribing a random sample (approx. 15400) of the students' handwritten responses.

2.2 Knowledge Representation

The ASK assessments included a reference answer for each of their constructed response questions. We decomposed these reference answers into low-level facets, roughly extracted from the relations in a syntactic dependency parse and a shallow semantic parse. However, we use the word *facet* to refer to any fine-grained component of the reference answer semantics. The decomposition is based closely on these well-established frameworks, since the representations have been shown to be learnable by automatic systems (c.f., Gildea and Jurafsky, 2002; Nivre et al., 2006). These facets are the basis for assessing learner answers. See (Nielsen et al., 2008b) for details on extracting the facets; here we simply sketch the makeup of the final assessed reference answer facets.

Example 1 presents a reference answer from the Magnetism and Electricity module and illustrates the facets derived from its dependency parse (shown in Figure 1), along with their glosses. These facets represent the fine-grained knowledge the student is expected to address in their response.

(1) The brass ring would not stick to the nail because the ring is not iron.

(1a) NMod(ring, brass)
(1a') The ring is brass.
(1b) Theme_not(stick, ring)
(1b') The ring does not stick.
(1c) Destination_to_not(stick, nail)
(1c') Something does not stick to the nail.
(1d) Be_not(ring, iron)
(1d') The ring is not iron.
(1e) Cause_because(1b-c, 1d)
(1e') 1b and 1c are caused by 1d.

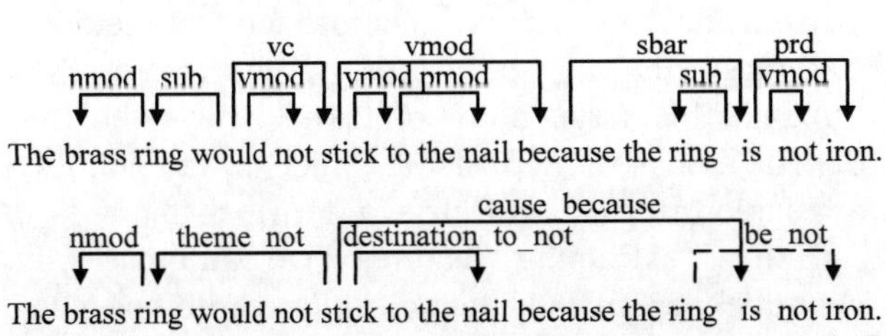

Figure 1. Reference answer representation revisions

Typical facets, as in (1a), are derived directly from a dependency parse, in this case retaining its dependency type label, NMod (noun modifier). Other facets, such as (1b-e), are the result of combining multiple dependencies, VMod(*stick*, *to*) and PMod(*to*, *nail*) in the case of (1c). When the head of the dependency is a verb, as in (1b,c), we use Thematic Roles from VerbNet (Kipper et al., 2000) and adjuncts from PropBank (Palmer et al., 2005) to label the facet relation. Some copulas and similar verbs were themselves used as facet relations, as in (1d). Dependencies involving determiners and many modals, such as *would*, in ex. 1, are discarded and negations, such as *not*, are incorporated into the associated facets.

We refer to facets that express relations between higher-level propositions as *inter-propositional facets*. An example of such a facet is (1e) above, connecting the proposition the brass ring did not stick to the nail to the proposition the ring is not iron. In addition to specifying the headwords of inter-propositional facets (*stick* and *is*, in 1e), we also note up to two key facets from each of the propositions that the relation is connecting (b, c, and d in ex. 1). Reference answer facets that are assumed to be understood by the learner a priori, (generally because they are part of the information given in the question), are also annotated to indicate this.

There were a total of 2878 reference answer facets, with a mean of 10 facets per reference answer (median of 8). Facets that were assumed to be understood a priori by students accounted for 33% of all facets and inter-propositional facets accounted for 11%. The experiments in automated annotation of student answers (section 3) focus on the facets that are not assumed to be understood a priori (67% of all facets); of these, 12% are inter-propositional.

2.3 Annotating Student Understanding

After defining the reference answer facets, we annotated each student answer to indicate whether and how they addressed each reference answer facet. We settled on the annotation labels in Table 1. For a given student answer, one label is assigned for each facet in the associated reference answer. These labels and the annotation process are detailed in (Nielsen et al., 2008a).

Assumed: Reference answer facets that are assumed to be understood a priori based on the question
Expressed: Any reference answer facet directly expressed or inferred by simple reasoning
Inferred: Reference answer facets whose understanding is inferred by pragmatics or nontrivial logical reasoning
Contra-Expr: Reference answer facets directly contradicted by negation, antonymous expressions, and their paraphrases
Contra-Infr: Reference answer facets contradicted by pragmatics or complex reasoning
Self-Contra: Reference answer facets that are both contradicted and implied (self contradictions)
Diff-Arg: Reference answer facets whose core relation is expressed, but it has a different modifier or argument
Unaddressed: Reference answer facets that are not addressed at all by the student's answer

Table 1. Facet Annotation Labels

Example 2 shows a fragment of a question and associated reference answer broken down into its constituent facets with an indication of whether the facet is assumed to be understood a priori. A corresponding student answer is shown in (3) along with its final annotation in 2a'-c'. It is assumed that the student understands that the pitch is higher (facet 2b), since this is given in the question and similarly it is assumed that the student will be explaining what has the causal effect of producing this higher pitch (facet 2c). Therefore, unless the student explicitly addresses these facets they are labeled *Assumed*. The student phrase *the string is long* is aligned with reference answer facet 2a, since they are both expressing a property of the string, but since the phrase neither contradicts nor indicates an understanding of the facet, the facet is labeled *Diff-Arg*, 2a'. The causal facet 2c' is labeled *Expressed*, since the student expresses a causal relation and the cause and effect are each properly aligned. In this way, the automated tutor will know the student is on track in attempting to address the cause and it can focus on remediating the student's understanding of that cause.

(2) Question: ... Write a note to David to tell him why the pitch gets higher rather than lower. Reference Answer: The string is tighter, so the pitch is higher...

(2a) Be(string, tighter), ---
(2b) Be(pitch, higher), Assumed
(2c) Cause(2b, 2a), Assumed

(3) David this is why because you don't listen to your teacher. If the string is long, the pitch will be high.

(2a')Be(string, tighter), Diff-Arg
(2b')Be(pitch, higher), Expressed
(2c')Cause(2b', 2a'), Expressed

A tutor will treat the labels Expressed, Inferred and Assumed all as Understood by the student and similarly Contra-Expr and Contra-Infr are combined as Contradicted. These labels are kept separate in the annotation to facilitate training different systems to detect these different inference relationships, as well as to allow evaluation at that level. The consolidated set of labels, comprised of Understood, Contradicted, Self-Contra, Diff-Arg and Unaddressed, are referred to as the *Tutor Labels*.

3 Automated Classification

A high level description of the assessment procedure is as follows. We start with the hand generated reference answer facets. We generate automatic parses for the reference answers and the student answers and automatically modify these parses to match our desired representation. Then for each reference answer facet, we extract features indicative of the student's understanding of that facet. Finally, we train a machine learning classifier on our training data and use it to classify unseen test examples, assigning a Tutor Label (described in the preceding paragraph), for each reference answer facet.

3.1 Preprocessing and Representation

Many of the features utilized by the machine learning algorithm here are based on document co-occurrence counts. We use three publicly available corpora (English Gigaword, The Reuters corpus, and Tipster) totaling 7.4M articles and 2.6B terms. These corpora are all drawn from the news domain, making them less than ideal sources for assessing student's answers to science questions. We utilized these corpora to generate term relatedness statistics primarily because they comprised a readily available large body of text. They were indexed and searched using Lucene, a publicly available Information Retrieval tool.

Before extracting features, we automatically generate dependency parses of the reference answers and student answers using MaltParser (Nivre et al., 2006). These parses are then *automatically* modified in a way similar to the manual revisions made when extracting the reference answer facets, as sketched in section 2.2. We reattach auxiliary verbs and their modifiers to the associated regular verbs. We incorporate prepositions and copulas into the dependency relation labels, and similarly append negation terms onto the associated dependency relations. These modifications, all made automatically, increase the likelihood that terms carrying significant semantic content are joined by dependencies that are utilized in feature extraction. In the present work, we did not make use of a thematic role labeler.

3.2 Machine Learning Features & Approach

We investigated a variety of linguistic features and chose to utilize the features summarized in Table 2, informed by training set cross validation results. The features assess the facets' lexical similarity via lexical entailment probabilities following (Glickman et al., 2005), part of speech (POS) tags, and lexical stem matches. They include syntactic information extracted from the modified dependency parses such as relevant relation types and path edit distances. Remaining features include information about polarity among other things. The revised dependency parses described earlier are used in aligning the terms and facet-level information for feature extraction, as indicated in the feature descriptions.

The data was split into a training set and three test sets. The first test set, *Unseen Modules*, consists of *all* the data from three of the 16 science modules, providing a domain-independent test set. The second, *Unseen Questions*, consists of all the student answers associated with 22 randomly selected questions from the 233 questions in the remaining 13 modules, providing a question-independent test set. The third test set, *Unseen Answers*, was created by randomly assigning all of the facets from approximately 6% of the remaining learner answers to a test set with the remainder comprising the training set. In the present work, we utilize only the facets that were not assumed to be understood a priori. This selection resulted in a total of 54,967 training examples, 30,514 examples in the Unseen Modules test set, 6,699 in the Unseen Questions test set and 3,159 examples in the Unseen Answers test set.

Lexical Features

Gov/Mod_MLE: The lexical entailment probabilities (LEPs) for the reference answer facet governor (Gov; e.g., *string* in 2a) and modifier (Mod; e.g., *tighter* in 2a) following (Glickman et al., 2005; c.f., Turney, 2001). The LEP of a reference answer word w is defined as:

(1) $LEP(w) = \max_{v \in l}(n_{w,v}/n_v)$,

where v is a word in the student answer, n_v is the # of docs (see section 3.1) containing v, and $n_{w,v}$ is the # of docs where w & v cooccur. {Ex. 2a: the LEPs for *string→string* and *tension→ tighter*, respectively}†

Gov/Mod_Match: True if the Gov (Mod) stem has an exact match in learner answer. {Ex. 2a: True for Gov: *string*, and (False for Mod: no stem match for *tighter*)}†

Subordinate_MLEs: The lexical entailment probabilities for the primary constituent facets' Govs and Mods when the facet represents a relation between higher-level propositions (see inter-propositional facet definition in section 2.2). {Ex. 2c: the LEPs for *pitch→pitch*, *up→higher*, *string→string*, and *tension→tighter*}†

Syntactic Features

Gov/Mod_POS: POS tags for the facet's Gov and (Mod). {Ex. 2a: NN for *string* and (JJR for *tighter*)}†

Facet/AlignedDep_Reltn: The labels of the facet and aligned learner answer dependency – alignments were based on co-occurrence MLEs as with words, (i.e., they estimate the likelihood of seeing the reference answer dependency in a document given it contains the learner answer dependency – replace words with dependencies in equation 1 above). {Ex. 2a: Be is the facet label and Have is the aligned student answer dependency}†

Dep_Path_Edit_Dist: The edit distance between the dependency path connecting the facet's Gov and Mod (not necessarily a single step due to parser errors) and the path connecting the aligned terms in the learner answer. Paths include the dependency relations generated in our modified parse with their attached prepositions, negations, etc, the direction of each dependency, and the POS tags of the terms on the path. The calculation applies heuristics to judge the similarity of each part of the path (e.g., dropping a subject had a much higher cost than dropping an adjective). Alignment for this feature was made based on which set of terms in an *N*-best list (*N*=5 in the present experiments) for the Gov and Mod resulted in the smallest edit distance. The *N*-best list was generated based on the lexical entailment values (see Gov/Mod_MLE). {Ex. 2b: *Distance*(*up*:VMod> *went*:V<*pitch*:Subject, *pitch*:Be>*higher*)}†

Other Features

Consistent_Negation: True if the facet and aligned student dependency path had the same number of negations. {Ex. 2a: True: neither one have a negation}†

RA_CW_cnt: The number of content words (non-function words) in the reference answer. {Ex. 2: 5 = count(*string, tighter, so, pitch & higher*)}†

† Examples within {} braces are based on reference answer Ex. 2 and the learner answer:
The pitch went up because the string has more tension

Table 2. Machine Learning Features

We evaluated several machine learning algorithms (rules, trees, boosting, ensembles and an svm) and C4.5 (Quinlan, 1993) achieved the best results in cross validation on the training data. Therefore, we used it to obtain all of the results presented here. A number of classifiers performed comparably and Random Forests outperformed C4.5 with a previous feature set and subset of data. A thorough analysis of the impact of the classifier chosen has not been completed at this time.

3.3 System Results

Given a student answer, we generate a separate Tutor Label (described at the end of section 2.3) for each associated reference answer facet to indicate the level of understanding expressed in the student's answer (similar to giving multiple marks on a test). Table 3 shows the classifier's Tutor Label accuracy over all reference answer facets in cross validation on the training set as well as on each of our test sets. The columns first show two simpler baselines, the accuracy of a classifier that always chooses the most frequent class in the training set – Unaddressed, and the accuracy based on a lexical decision that chooses Understood if both the governing term and the modifier are present in the learner's answer and outputs Unaddressed otherwise, (we also tried placing a threshold on the product of the governor and modifier lexical entailment probabilities following Glickman et al. (2005), who achieved the best results in the first RTE challenge, but this gave virtually the same results as the word matching baseline). The column labeled Table 2 Features presents the results of our classifier. (Reduced Training is described in the Discussion section, which follows.)

	Majority Label	Lexical Baseline	Table 2 Features	Reduced Training
Training Set CV	54.6	59.7	**77.1**	
Unseen Answers	51.1	56.1	**75.5**	
Unseen Questions	58.4	63.4	61.7	**66.5**
Unseen Modules	53.4	62.9	61.4	**68.8**

Table 3. Classifier Accuracy

4 Discussion and Error Analysis

4.1 Results Discussion

The accuracy achieved, assessing learner answers within this new representation framework, represent an improvement of 24.4%, 3.3%, and 8.0% over the majority class baseline for Unseen Answers, Questions, and Modules respectively. Accuracy on Unseen Answers is also 19.4% better than the lexical baseline. However, this simple baseline outperformed the classifier on the other two test sets. It seemed probable that the decision tree over fit the data due to bias in the data itself; specifically, since many of the students' answers are very similar, there are likely to be large clusters of identical feature-class pairings, which could result in classifier decisions that do not generalize as well to other questions or domains. This bias is not problematic when the test data is very similar to the training data, as is the case for our Unseen Answers test set, but would negatively affect performance on less similar data, such as our Unseen Questions and Modules.

To test this hypothesis, we reduced the size of our training set to about 8,000 randomly selected examples, which would result in fewer of these dense clusters, and retrained the classifier. The result for Unseen Questions, shown in the *Reduced Training* column, was an improvement of 4.8%. Given this promising improvement, we attempted to find the optimal training set size through cross-validation on the training data. Specifically, we iterated over the science modules holding one module out, training on the other 12 and testing on the held out module. We analyzed the learning curve varying the number of randomly selected examples per facet. We found the optimal accuracy for training set cross-validation by averaging the results over all the modules and then trained a classifier on that number of random examples per facet in the training set and tested on the Unseen Modules test set. The result was an increase in accuracy of 7.4% over training on the full training set. In future work, we will investigate other more principled techniques to avoid this type of overfitting, which we believe is somewhat atypical.

4.2 Error Analysis

In order to focus future work on the areas most likely to benefit the system, an error analysis was performed based on the results of 13-fold cross-validation on the training data (one fold per science module). In other words, 13 C4.5 decision tree classifiers were built, one for each science module in the training set; each classifier was trained, utilizing the feature set shown in Table 2, on all of the data from 12 science modules and then tested on the data in the remaining, held-out module. This effectively simulates the Unseen Modules test condition. To our knowledge, no prior work has analyzed the assessment errors of such a domain-independent ITS.

Several randomly selected examples were analyzed to look for patterns in the types of errors the system makes. However, only specific categories of data were considered. Specifically, only the subsets of errors that were most likely to lead to short-term system improvements were considered. This included only examples where all of the annotators agreed on the annotation, since if the annotation was difficult for humans, it would probably be harder to construct features that would allow the machine learning algorithm to correct its error. Second, only Expressed and Unaddressed facets were considered, since Inferred facets represent the more challenging judgments, typically based on pragmatic inferences. Contradictions were excluded since there was almost no attempt to handle these in the present system. Third, only facets that were not inter-propositional were considered, since the inter-propositional facets are more complicated to process and only represent 12% of the non-Assumed data. We discuss Expressed facets in the next section of the paper and Unaddressed in the following section.

4.3 Errors in Expressed Facets

Without examining each example relative to the decision tree that classified it, it is not possible to know exactly what caused the errors. The analysis here simply indicates what factors are involved in inferring whether the reference answer facets were understood and what relationships exist between the student answer and the reference answer facet. We analyzed 100 random examples of errors where annotators considered the facet Expressed and the system labeled it Unaddressed, but the analysis only considered one example for any given reference answer facet. Out of these 100 examples, only one looked as if it was probably incorrectly annotated. We group the potential error factors seen in the data, listed in order of frequency, according to issues associated with paraphrases, logical inference, pragmatics, and preprocessing errors. In the following paragraphs, these groups are broken down for a more fine-grained analysis. In over half of the errors considered, there were two or more of these fine-grained factors involved.

Paraphrase issues, taken broadly, are subdivided into three main categories: coreference resolution, lexical substitution, syntactic alternation and phrase-based paraphrases. Our results in this area are in line with (Bar-Haim et al., 2005), who considered which inference factors are involved in proving textual entailment. Three coreference resolution factors combined are involved in nearly 30% of the errors. Students use on average 1.1 pronouns per answer and, more importantly, the pronouns tend to refer to key entities or concepts in the question and reference answer. A pronoun was used in 15 of the errors (3 personal pronouns – *she*, 11 uses of *it*, and 1 use of *one*). It might be possible to correct many of these errors by simply aligning the pronouns to essentially all possible nouns in the reference answer and then choosing the single alignment that gives the learner the most credit. In 6 errors, the student referred to a concept by another term (e.g., substituting *stuff* for *pieces*). In another 6 errors, the student used one of the terms in a noun phrase from either the question or reference answer to refer to a concept where the reference answer facet included the other term as its modifier or vice versa. For example, one reference answer was looking for NMod(*particles*, *clay*) and Be(*particles*, *light*) and the student said *Because clay is the lightest*, which should have resulted in an Understood classification for the second facet (one could argue that there is an important distinction between the answers, but requiring elementary school students to answer at this level of specificity could result in an overwhelming number of interactions to clarify understanding).

As a group, the simple lexical substitution categories (synonymy, hypernymy, hyponymy, meronymy, derivational changes, and other lexical paraphrases) appear more often in errors than any of the other factors with around 35 occurrences. Roughly half of these relationships should be detectable using broad coverage lexical resources. For example, substituting *tiny* for *small*, CO_2 for *gas*, *put* for *place*, *pen* for *ink* and *push* for *carry* (WordNet entailment). However, many of these lexical paraphrases are not necessarily associated in lexical resources such as WordNet. For example, in the substitution of *put the pennies* for *distribute the pennies*, these terms are only connected at the top of the WordNet hierarchy at the Synset (*move*, *displace*). Similarly, WordNet appears not to have any connection at all between *have* and *contain*. VerbNet also does not show a relation between either pair of words. Concept definitions account for an additional 14 issues that could potentially be addressed by lexical resources such as WordNet.

Vanderwende et al. (2005) found that 34% of the Recognizing Textual Entailment Challenge test data could be handled by recognizing simple syntactic variations. However, while syntactic variation is certainly common in the kids' data, it did not appear to be the primary factor in any of the system errors. Most of the remaining paraphrase errors were classified as involving phrase-based paraphrases. Examples here include *...it will heat up faster* versus *it got hotter faster* and *in the middle* versus *halfway between.* Six related errors essentially involved negation of an antonym, (e.g., substituting *not a lot* for *little* and *no one has the same fingerprint* for *everyone has a different print*). Paraphrase recognition is an area that we intend to invest significant time in future research (c.f., Lin and Pantel, 2001; Dolan et al., 2004). This research should also reduce the error rate on lexical paraphrases.

The next most common issues after paraphrases were deep or logical reasoning and then pragmatics. These two factors were involved in nearly 40% of the errors. Examples of logical inference include recognizing that two cups have the same amount of water given the following student response, *no, cup 1 would be a plastic cup 25 ml water and cup 2 paper cup 25 ml and 10 g sugar*, and that two sounds must be *very different* in the case that *...it is easy to discriminate...* Examples of pragmatic issues include recognizing that saying *Because the vibrations* implies that a rubber band is vibrating given the question context, and that *the earth* in the response *...the fulcrum is too close to the earth* should be considered to be *the load* referred to in its reference answer. It is interesting that these are all examples that three annotators unanimously considered to be Expressed versus Inferred facets.

Finally, the remaining errors were largely the result of preprocessing issues. At least two errors would be eliminated by simple data normalization (*3→three* and *g→grams).* Semantic role labeling has the potential to provide the classifier with information that would clearly indicate the relationships between the student and the reference answer, but there was only one error in which this came to mind as an important factor and it was not due to the role labels themselves, but because MaltParser labels only a single head. Specifically, in the sentence *She could sit by the clothes and check every hour if one is dry or not*, the pronoun *She* is attached as the subject of *could sit*, but *check* is left without a subject.

In previous work, analyzing the dependency parses of fifty one of the student answers, many had what were believed to be minor errors, 31% had significant errors, and 24% had errors that looked like they could easily lead to problems for the answer assessment classifier. Over half of the more serious dependency parse errors resulted from inopportune sentence segmentation due to run-on student sentences conjoined by *and.* To overcome these issues, the text could be parsed once using the original sentence segmentation and then again with alternative segmentations under conditions to be determined by further dependency parser error analysis. One partial approach could be to split sentences when two noun phrases are conjoined and they occur between two verbs, as is the case in the preceding example, where the alternative segmentation results in correct parses. Then the system could choose the parse that is most consistent with the reference answer. While we believe improving the parser output will result in higher accuracy by the assessment classifier, there was little evidence to support this in the small number of parses examined in the assessment error analysis. We only checked the parses when the dependency path features looked wrong and it was somewhat surprising that the classifier made an error (for example, when there were simple lexical substitutions involving very similar words) – this was the case for only about 10-15 examples. Only two of these classification errors were associated with parser errors. However, better parses should lead to more reliable (less noisy) features, which in turn will allow the machine learning algorithm to more easily recognize which features are the most predictive.

It should be emphasized that over half of the errors in Expressed facets involved more than one of the fine-grained factors discussed here. For example, to recognize the child understands a tree is blocking the sunlight based on the answer *There is a shadow there because the sun is behind it and light cannot go through solid objects. Note, I think that question was kind of dumb*, requires resolving *it* to the *tree* and the *solid object* mentioned to the *tree*, and then recognizing that *light cannot go through* [*the tree*] entails the tree blocks the light.

4.4 Errors in Unaddressed Facets

Unlike the errors in Expressed facets, a number of the examples here appeared to be questionable annotations. For example, given the student answer fragment *You could take a couple of cardboard houses and... 1 with thick glazed insulation...*, all three annotators suggested they could not infer the student meant the insulation should be installed in one of the houses. Given the student answer *Because the darker the color the faster it will heat up*, the annotators did not infer that the student believed the sheeting chosen was the *darkest color*.

One of the biggest sources of errors in Unaddressed facets is the result of ignoring the context of words. For example, consider the question *When you make an electromagnet, why does the core have to be iron or steel?* and its reference answer *Iron is the only common metal that can become a temporary magnet. Steel is made from iron.* Then, given the student answer *It has to be iron or steel because it has to pick up the washers*, the system classified the facet Material_from(*made*, *iron*) as Understood based on the text *has to be iron*, but ignores the context, specifically, that this should be associated with the production of steel, Product(*made*, *steel*). Similarly, the student answer *You could wrap the insulated wire to the iron nail and attach the battery and switch* leads to the classification of Understood for a facet indicating to *touch the nail* to a permanent magnet to turn it into a temporary magnet, but *wrapping* the wire *to the nail* should have been aligned to a different method of making a temporary magnet.

Many of the errors in Unaddressed facets appear to be the result of antonyms having very similar statistical co-occurrence patterns. Examples of errors here include confusing *closer* with *greater* distance and *absorbs energy* with *reflects energy*. However, both of these also may be annotation errors that should have been labeled Contra-Expr.

The biggest source of error is simply classifying a number of facets as Understood if there is partial lexical similarity and perhaps syntactic similarity as in the case of accepting *the balls are different* in place of *different girls*. However, there are also a few cases where it is unclear why the decision was made, as in an example where the system apparently trusted that the student understood a complicated electrical circuit based on the student answer *we learned it in class*.

The processes and the more informative features described in the preceding section describing errors in Expressed facets should allow the learning algorithm to focus on less noisy features and avoid many of the errors described in this section. However, additional features will need to be added to ensure appropriate lexical and phrasal alignment, which should also provide a significant benefit here. Future plans include training an alignment classifier separate from the assessment classifier.

5 Conclusion

To our knowledge, this is the first work to successfully assess constructed-response answers from elementary school students. We achieved promising results, 24.4% and 15.4% over the majority class baselines for Unseen Answers and Unseen Modules, respectively. The annotated corpus associated with this work will be made available as a public resource for other researches working on educational assessment applications or other textual entailment applications.

The focus of this paper was to provide an error analysis of the domain-independent (Unseen Modules) assessment condition. We discussed the common types of issues involved in errors and their frequency when assessing young students' understanding of the fine-grained facets of reference answers. This domain-independent assessment will facilitate quicker adaptation of tutoring systems (or general test assessment systems) to new topics, avoiding the need for a significant effort in hand-crafting new system components. It is also a necessary prerequisite to enabling unrestricted dialogue in tutoring systems.

Acknowledgements

We would like to thank the anonymous reviewers, whose comments improved the final paper. This work was partially funded by Award Number 0551723 from the National Science Foundation.

References

Bar-Haim, R., Szpektor, I. and Glickman, O. 2005. Definition and Analysis of Intermediate Entailment Levels. In *Proc. Workshop on Empirical Modeling of Semantic Equivalence and Entailment.*

Callear, D., Jerrams-Smith, J., and Soh, V. 2001. CAA of short non-MCQ answers. In *Proc. of the 5th International CAA conference*, Loughborough.

Dolan, W.B., Quirk, C, and Brockett, C. 2004. Unsupervised Construction of Large Paraphrase Corpora: Exploiting Massively Parallel News Sources. *Proceedings of COLING 2004*, Geneva, Switzerland.

Gildea, D. and Jurafsky, D. 2002. Automatic labeling of semantic roles. *Computational Linguistics, 28*:3, 245–288.

Glickman, O. and Dagan, WE., and Koppel, M. 2005. Web Based Probabilistic Textual Entailment. In *Proceedings of the PASCAL Recognizing Textual Entailment Challenge Workshop.*

Graesser, A.C., Hu, X., Susarla, S., Harter, D., Person, N.K., Louwerse, M., Olde, B., and the Tutoring Research Group. 2001. AutoTutor: An Intelligent Tutor and Conversational Tutoring Scaffold. In *Proceedings for the 10th International Conference of Artificial Intelligence in Education* San Antonio, TX, 47-49.

Jordan, P.W., Makatchev, M., and VanLehn, K. 2004. Combining competing language understanding approaches in an intelligent tutoring system. In J. C. Lester, R. M. Vicari, and F. Paraguacu, Eds.), *7th Conference on Intelligent Tutoring Systems*, 346-357. Springer-Verlag Berlin Heidelberg.

Kipper, K., Dang, H.T., and Palmer, M. 2000. Class-Based Construction of a Verb Lexicon. *AAAI Seventeenth National Conference on Artificial Intelligence*, Austin, TX.

Lawrence Hall of Science 2006. Assessing Science Knowledge (ASK), University of California at Berkeley, NSF-0242510

Leacock, C. 2004. Scoring free-response automatically: A case study of a large-scale Assessment. *Examens, 1*(3).

Lin, D. and Pantel, P. 2001. Discovery of inference rules for Question Answering. In *Natural Language Engineering, 7*(4):343-360.

Mitchell, T., Russell, T., Broomhead, P. and Aldridge, N. 2002. Towards Robust Computerized Marking of Free-Text Responses. In *Proc. of 6th International Computer Aided Assessment Conference*, Loughborough.

Nielsen, R., Ward, W., Martin, J. and Palmer, M. 2008a. Annotating Students' Understanding of Science Concepts. In *Proc. LREC.*

Nielsen, R., Ward, W., Martin, J. and Palmer, M. 2008b. Extracting a Representation from Text for Semantic Analysis. In *Proc. ACL-HLT.*

Nivre, J. and Scholz, M. 2004. Deterministic Dependency Parsing of English Text. In *Proceedings of COLING*, Geneva, Switzerland, August 23-27.

Nivre, J., Hall, J., Nilsson, J., Eryigit, G. and Marinov, S. 2006. Labeled Pseudo-Projective Dependency Parsing with Support Vector Machines. In *Proceedings of the Tenth Conference on Computational Natural Language Learning (CoNLL).*

Palmer, M., Gildea, D., and Kingsbury, P. 2005. The proposition bank: An annotated corpus of semantic roles. In *Computational Linguistics.*

Peters, S., Bratt, E.O., Clark, B., Pon-Barry, H., and Schultz, K. 2004. Intelligent Systems for Training Damage Control Assistants. In *Proc. of Interservice/Industry Training, Simulation, and Education Conference.*

Pulman, S.G. and Sukkarieh, J.Z. 2005. Automatic Short Answer Marking. In *Proc. of the 2nd Workshop on Building Educational Applications Using NLP, ACL.*

Quinlan, J.R. 1993. C4.5: *Programs for Machine Learning.* Morgan Kaufmann.

Roll, WE., Baker, R.S., Aleven, V., McLaren, B.M., and Koedinger, K.R. 2005. Modeling Students' Metacognitive Errors in Two Intelligent Tutoring Systems. In L. Ardissono, P. Brna, and A. Mitrovic (Eds.), *User Modeling*, 379–388.

Turney, P.D. 2001. Mining the web for synonyms: PMI-IR versus LSA on TOEFL. In *Proceedings of the Twelfth European Conference on Machine Learning (ECML-2001)*, 491–502.

Vanderwende, L., Coughlin, D. and Dolan, WB. 2005. What Syntax can Contribute in the Entailment Task. In *Proc. of the PASCAL Workshop for Recognizing Textual Entailment.*

VanLehn, K., Lynch, C., Schulze, K. Shapiro, J. A., Shelby, R., Taylor, L., Treacy, D., Weinstein, A., and Wintersgill, M. 2005. The Andes physics tutoring system: Five years of evaluations. In G. McCalla and C. K. Looi (Eds.), *Proceedings of the 12th International Conference on Artificial Intelligence in Education.* Amsterdam: IOS Press.

King Alfred: A Translation Environment for Learners of Anglo-Saxon English

Lisa N. Michaud
Computer Science Department
St. Anselm College
Manchester, NH 03102
lmichaud@anselm.edu

Abstract

King Alfred is the name of both an innovative textbook and a computational environment deployed in parallel in an undergraduate course on Anglo-Saxon literature. This paper details the ways in which it brings dynamically-generated resources to the aid of the language student. We store the feature-rich grammar of Anglo-Saxon in a bi-level glossary, provide an annotation context for use during the translation task, and are currently working toward the implementation of automatic evaluation of student-generated translations.

1 Introduction

Criticisms of the application of computational tools toward language learning have often highlighted the reality that the mainstays of modern language teaching—including dialogue and a focus on communicative goals over syntactic perfectionism—parallel the shortcomings of computational environment. While efforts continue to extend the state of the art toward making the computer a conversational partner, they nevertheless often fall short of providing the language learner with learning assistance in the task of communicative competence that can make a real difference within or without the classroom.

The modern learner of ancient or "dead" languages, however, has fundamentally different needs; learners are rarely asked to produce utterances in the language being learned (L2). Instead of communication or conversation, the focus is on translation from source texts into the learner's native language (L1). This translation task typically involves annotation of the source text as syntactic data in the L2 are decoded, and often requires the presence of many auxiliary resources such as grammar texts and glossaries.

Like many learners of ancient languages, the student of Anglo-Saxon English must acquire detailed knowledge of syntactic and morphological features that are far more complex than those of Modern English. Spoken between circa A.D. 500 and 1066, Anglo-Saxon or "Old" English comprises a lexicon and a grammar both significantly removed from that of what we speak today. We therefore view the task of learning Anglo-Saxon to be that of acquiring a foreign language even to speakers of Modern English.

In the Anglo-Saxon Literature course at Wheaton College[1], students tackle this challenging language with the help of *King Alfred's Grammar* (Drout, 2005). This text challenges the learner with a stepped sequence of utterances, both original and drawn from ancient texts, whose syntactic complexity complements the lessons on the language. This text has recently been enhanced with an electronic counterpart that provides the student with a novel environment to aid in the translation task. Services provided by the system include:

- A method to annotate the source text with grammatical features as they are decoded.
- Collocation of resources for looking up or querying grammatical- and meaning-related data.
- Tracking the student's successes and challenges in order to direct reflection and further study.

[1]Norton, Massachusetts

Proceedings of the Third ACL Workshop on Innovative Use of NLP for Building Educational Applications, pages 19–26,
Columbus, Ohio, USA, June 2008.

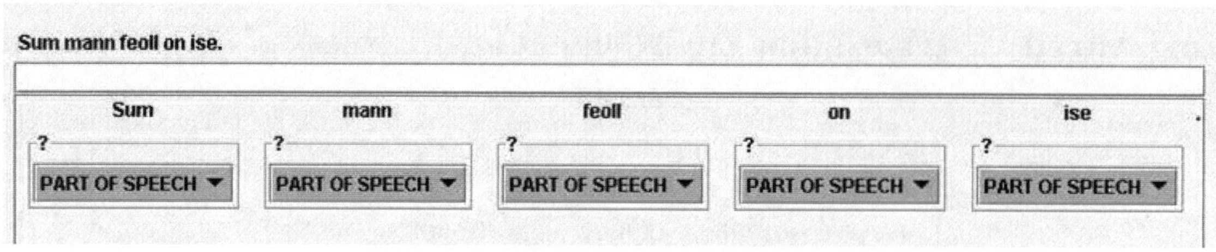

Figure 1: The main workspace for translation in King Alfred.

This paper overviews the current status of the King Alfred tutorial system and enumerates some of our current objectives.

2 System Overview

King Alfred is a web-accessible tutorial environment that interfaces with a central database server containing a curriculum sequence of translation exercises (Drout, 1999). It is currently implemented as a Java applet using the Connector/J class interface to obtain curricular, glossary, and user data from a server running MySQL v5.0.45.

When a student begins a new exercise, the original Anglo-Saxon sentence appears above a text-entry window in which the student can type his or her translation as seen in Figure 1. Below this window, a *scratch pad* interface provides the student with an opportunity to annotate each word with grammatical features, or to query the system for those data if needed. This simultaneously replaces traditional annotation (scribbling small notes in between lines of the source text) and the need to refer to auxiliary resources such as texts describing lexical items and morphological patterns. More on how we address the latter will be described in the next section.

When the student is finished with the translation, she clicks on a "Submit" button and progresses to a second screen in which her translation is displayed alongside a stored instructor's translation from the database. Based on the correctness of scratch pad annotations aggregated over several translation exercises, the system gives feedback in the form of a simple message, such as *King Alfred is pleased with your work on strong nouns and personal pronouns,* or *King Alfred suggests that you should review weak verbs.* The objective of this feedback is to give the students assistance in their own self-directed study. Additional, more detailed information about the student's recorded behavior is viewable through an open user model interface if the student desires.

3 Resources for the Translation Task

As part of the scratch pad interface, the student can annotate a lexical unit with the value of any of a wide range of grammatical features dependent upon the part of speech. After the student has indicated the part of speech, the scratch pad presents an interface for this further annotation as seen in Figure 2, which shows the possible features to annotate for the verb *feoll*.

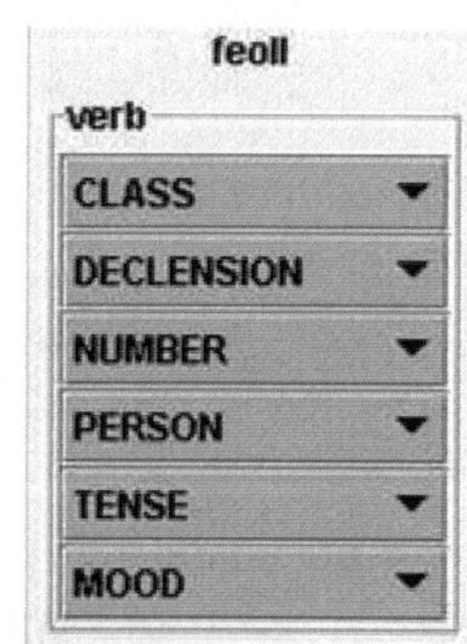

Figure 2: A scratch pad menu for the verb *feoll*.

The scratch pad provides the student with the opportunity to record data (either correctly, in which case the choice is accepted, or incorrectly, where the student is notified of having made a mistake) or to to query the system for the answer. While student users are strongly encouraged to make educated guesses based on the morphology of the word, thrashing blindly is discouraged; if the information is key to the translation, and the student does not have any idea, asking the system to *Tell me!* is preferable to continually guessing wrong and it allows the student to get "unstuck" and continue with the translation. None of the interaction with the scratch pad is mandatory; the translator can proceed without ever using it. It merely exists to simultaneously allow for recording data as it is decoded, or to query for data when it is needed.

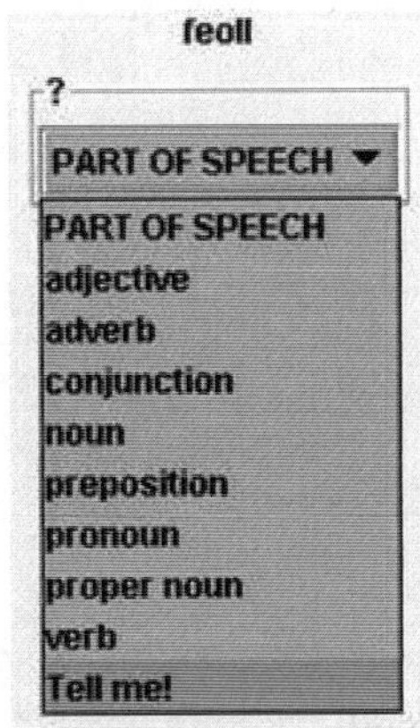

Figure 3: Querying King Alfred for help.

3.1 Lexical Lookup

Like most Anglo-Saxon texts, *King Alfred* also contains a glossary which comprises all of the Anglo-Saxon words in the exercise corpus. These glossaries typically contain terms in "bare" or "root" form, stripped of their inflection. A novice learner has to decode the root of the word she is viewing (no easy task if the inflection is irregular, or if she is unaware, for example, which of seven declensions a verb belongs to) in order to determine the word to search for in the glossary, a common stumbling block (Colazzo and Costantino, 1998). The information presented under such a root-form entry is also incomplete; the learner can obtain the meaning of the term, but may be hampered in the translation task by not knowing for certain how this particular instance is inflected (e.g., that this is the third person singular present indicative form), or which of the possible meanings is being used in this particular sentence.

Alternatively, a text can present terms in their surface form, exactly as they appear in the exercise corpus. This approach, while more accessible to the learner, has several drawbacks, including the fact that glossary information (such as the meaning of the word and the categories to which it belongs) is common to all the different inflected versions, and it would be redundant to include that information separately for each surface form. Also, in such an entry the user may not be able to discover the root form, which may make it more difficult to recognize other terms that share the same root. To avoid these issues, a glossary may contain both, with every surface form annotated with the information about its inflection and then the root entry shown so that the reader may look up the rest of the information.

We believe we can do better than this. In order to incorporate the advantages of both forms of glossary data, we have implemented two separate but interlinked glossaries, where each of the surface realizations is connected to the root entry from which it is derived. Because electronic media enable the dynamic assembly of information, the learner is not obligated to do two separate searches for the information; displaying a glossary entry shows both the specific, contextual information of the surface form and the general, categorical data of the root form in one presentation. This hybrid glossary view is shown in Figure 4.

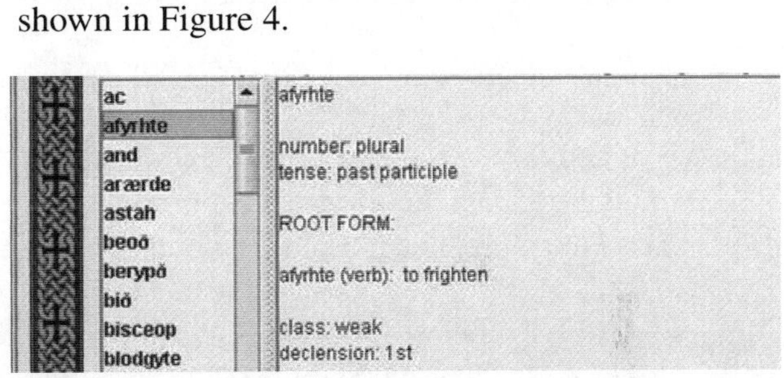

Figure 4: A partial screen shot of the King Alfred glossary browser.

3.2 Surface and Root Forms

To build this dual-level glossary, we have leveraged the *Entity-Relationship Model* as an architecture on which to structure King Alfred's curriculum of sentences and the accompanying glossary. Figure 5 shows a partial Entity-Relationship diagram for the relevant portion of the curriculum database, in which:

- *Sentences* are entities on which are stored various attributes, including a holistic *translation* of the entire sentence provided by the instructor.
- The relationship *has word* connects Sentences

to *Words*, the collection of which forms the surface level of our glossary. The instances of this relationship include the ordinality of the word within the sentence; the actual sentence is, therefore, not found as a single string in the database, but is constructed dynamically at need by obtaining the words in sequence from the glossary. Each instance of the relationship also includes the translation of the word *in the specific context of this sentence*.[2]

- The entity set *Words* contains the actual orthography of the word as it appears (*text*) and through an additional relationship set (not shown) is connected to all of the grammatical features specific to a surface realization (e.g. for a noun, *person*=third, *number*=singular, *case*=nominative).

- The relationship *has root* links entries from the surface level of the glossary to their corresponding entry at the root level.

- The *Roots* glossary has the orthography of the root form (*text*), possible definitions of this word, and through another relationship set not in the figure, data on other syntactic categories general to any realization of this word.

Since the root form must be displayed in some form in the glossary, we have adopted the convention that the root of a verb is its infinitive form, the roots of nouns are the singular, nominative forms, and the roots of determiners and adjectives are the singular, masculine, nominative forms.

Other related work does not explicitly represent the surface realization in the lexicon; the system described by (Colazzo and Costantino, 1998), for example, uses a dynamic word stemming algorithm to look up a surface term in a glossary of root forms by stripping off the possible suffixes; however, it is unable to recognize irregular forms or to handle ambiguous stems. GLOSSER (Nerbonne et al., 1998) for Dutch learners of French also automatically analyzes surface terms to link them to their stem entries and to other related inflections, but shares the same problem with handling ambiguity.

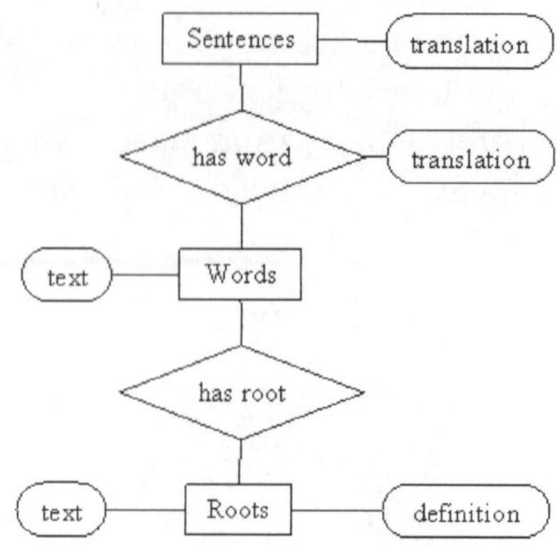

Figure 5: A piece of the Entity-Relationship diagram showing the relationships of Sentences, Words, and Roots.

Our approach ensures that no term is misidentified by an automatic process which may be confused by ambiguous surface forms, and none of these systems allows the learner access to which of the possible meanings of the term is being used in *this* particular context. The result of King Alfred's architecture is a pedagogically accurate glossary which has an efficiency of storage and yet dynamically pulls together the data stored at multiple levels to present the learner with all of the morphosyntactic data which she requires.

3.3 Adding to the Glossary

Because there is no pre-existing computational lexicon for Anglo-Saxon we can use and because creating new translation sentences within this database architecture via direct database manipulation is exceedingly time consuming—and inaccessible for the novice user—we have equipped King Alfred with an extensive instructor's interface which simultaneously allows for the creation of new sentences in the curriculum and the expansion of the glossary to accommodate the new material.[3]

The instructor first types in an Anglo-Saxon sentence, using special buttons to insert any non-ASCII characters from the Anglo-Saxon alphabet. A holis-

[2]This does not negate the necessity of the holistic translation of the sentence, because Anglo-Saxon is a language with very rich morphology, and therefore is far less reliant upon word order to determine grammatical role than Modern English. In many Anglo-Saxon sentences, particularly when set in verse, the words are "scrambled" compared to how they would appear in a translation.

[3]All changes created by this interface are communicated directly to the stored curriculum in the central server.

tic translation of the entire sentence is entered at this time as well. The interface then begins to process each word of the sentence in turn. At each step, the instructor views the entire sentence with the word currently being processed highlighted:

- Sum mann feoll on ise.

The essential process for each word is as follows:

1. The system searches for the word in the surface glossary to see if it has already occurred in a previous sentence. All matches are displayed (there are multiple options if the same realization can represent more than one inflection) and the instructor may indicate which is a match for this occurrence. If a match is found, the word has been fully processed; otherwise, the interface continues to the next step.

2. The instructor is prompted to create a new surface entry. The first step is to see if the root of this word already exists in the root glossary; in a process similar to the above, the instructor may browse the root glossary and select a match.

    (a) If the root for this word (*feallan* in our example) already exists, the instructor selects it and then provides only the additional information specific to this realization (e.g. *tense*=past, *person*=3rd, *number*=singular, and *mood*=indicative).

    (b) Otherwise, the instructor is asked to provide the root form and then is presented with an interface to select features for both the surface and root forms (the above, plus *class*=strong, *declension*=7th, *definition*="to fall").

When this process has been completed for each word, the sentence is finally stored as a sequence of indices into the surface glossary, which now contains entries for all of the terms in this sentence. The instructor's final input is to associate a contextual gloss (specific to this particular sentence) with each word (these are used as "hints" for the students when they are translating and need extra help).

4 Automatically Scoring a Translation

When initially envisioned, King Alfred did not aspire to automatic grading of the student-generated translation because of the large variation in possible translations and the risk of discouraging a student who has a perfectly valid alternative interpretation (Drout, 1999). We now believe, however, that King Alfred's greatest benefit to the student may be in providing accurate, automatic feedback to a translation that takes the variety of possible translation results into account.

Recent work on machine translation evaluation has uncovered methodologies for automatic evaluation that we believe we can adapt to our purposes. Techniques that analyze n-gram precision such as BLEU score (Papineni et al., 2002) have been developed with the goal of comparing candidate translations against references provided by human experts in order to determine accuracy; although in our application the candidate translator is a student and not a machine, the principle is the same, and we wish to adapt their technique to our context.

Our approach will differ from the n-gram precision of BLEU score in several key ways. Most importantly, BLEU score only captures potential *correct* translations but equally penalizes errors without regard to how serious these errors are. This is not acceptable in a pedagogical context; take, for example, the following source sentence[4]:

(1) *Sum mann feoll on ise.*

The instructor's translation is given as:

(2) One man fell on the ice.

Possible student translations might include:

(3) One man fell on **ice**.

(4) **Some** man fell on the ice.

In the case of translation (3), the determiner before the indirect object is implied by the case of the noun

[4]This example sentence, also used earlier in this paper, reflects words that are very well preserved in Modern English to help the reader see the parallel elements in translation; most sentences in Anglo-Saxon are not nearly so accessible, such as shown in example (5).

ise but not, in the instructor's opinion, required at all. Translation (3) is therefore as valid as the instructor's. Translation (4), on the other hand, reflects the presence of the *faux ami*, or false friend, in the form of *sum*, which looks like Modern English 'some' but should not be translated as such. This is a minor mistake which should be corrected but not seen as a reflection of a serious underlying grammatical misconception.

Adverbs that modify the main verb also have flexible placement:

(5) *Þa wurdon þa mynstermen miccle afyrhte.*

(6) **Then** the monks became greatly frightened.

(7) The monks **then** became greatly frightened.

(8) The monks became **then** greatly frightened.

(9) The monks became greatly frightened **then**.

And there are often many acceptable translations of a given word:

(10) Then the monks became greatly **afraid**.

What we wish to focus our attention on most closely are misinterpretations of the morphological markers on the source word, resulting in a misinflected translation:

(11) Then the monks **become** greatly frightened.

This is a difference which is most salient in a pedagogical context. Assuming that the student is unlikely to make an error in generating an utterance in her native language, it can be concluded that such an error reflects a misinterpretation of the source morphology.

A summary of the differences between our proposed approach and that of (Papineni et al., 2002) would include:

- The reliance of BLEU on the diversity of multiple reference translations in order to capture some of the acceptable alternatives in both word choice and word ordering that we have shown above. At this time, we have only one reference translation with which to compare the candidate; however, we have access to other resources which can be applied to the task, as discussed below.

- The reality that automatic MT scoring usually has little to no grammatical data available for either the source or target strings of text. We, however, have part of speech tags for each of the source words encoded as part of the curriculum database; we also have encoded the word or short phrase to which the source word translates, which for any target word occurring in the candidate translation essentially grants it a part of speech tag. This means that we can build in flexibility regarding such elements as adverbs and determiners when the context would allow for optional inclusion (in the case of determiners) or multiple placements (in the case of adverbs).

- Multiple possible translations of the word can come from a source other than multiple translators. We intend to attempt to leverage WordNet (Fellbaum, 1998) in situations where a candidate word does not occur in the reference translation to determine if it has a synonym that does. The idea of recognizing a word that does not match the target but nevertheless has a related meaning has previously been explored in a the context of answers to reading comprehension questions by (Bailey, 2007).

- Minor mistranslations such as *sum*/some due to *faux amis* can be captured in the glossary as a kind of "bug rule" capturing typical learner errors.

- Other mistranslations, including using the wrong translation of a source word for the context in which it occurs—a common enough problem whenever a novice learner relies on a glossary for translation assistance—can be caught by matching the multiple possible translations of a root form against an unmatched word in the candidate translation. Some morphological processing may have to be done to match a stem meaning against the inflected form occurring in the candidate translation.

- The primary focus of the automatic scoring would be the misinflected word which can be aligned with a word from the reference translation but is not inflected in the same way. Again, morphological processing will be required to be able to pair together mismatched surface forms, with the intention of achieving two goals:
  1. Marking in the student model that a misinterpretation has occurred.
  2. Giving the user targeted feedback on how the source word was mistranslated.

With this extension, King Alfred would be empowered to record much richer data on student competency in Anglo-Saxon by noting which structures and features she translates correctly, and which she has struggled with. Such a model of student linguistic mastery can be a powerful aid to provide instructional feedback, as discussed in (Michaud and McCoy, 2000; Michaud and McCoy, 2006; Michaud et al., 2001).

5 Other New Directions

Ongoing work with the glossary browser includes enhancements to include dynamically generated references to other occurrences of words from the same stem or root throughout the translation corpus in order to reflect other inflected forms in their contexts as many dictionaries do.

This, however, is a relatively simplistic attempt to illustrate the pattern of morphological inflection of a root to the learner. A long-term plan is to incorporate into King Alfred a full morphological engine encoding the inflection patterns of Anglo-Saxon English so that the surface glossary is only needed as a collection of the feature values active in a specific context; with the ability to dynamically generate fully inflected forms from the root forms, King Alfred would empower the learner to access lessons on inflection using the specific words occurring in a sentence currently being translated.

We are unaware of any existing efforts to encode Anglo-Saxon morphology in such a fashion, although in other learning contexts the system Word Manager (Hacken and Tschichold, 2001) displays a lexicon grouping other words applying the same inflection or formation rule in order to aid the learner in acquiring the rule, a similar goal.

6 Conclusion

King Alfred was deployed in the Anglo-Saxon literature course at Wheaton College in the Fall semesters of 2005 and 2007. Preliminary feedback indicates that the students found the hybrid glossary very useful and the collocation of translation resources to be of great benefit to them in completing their homework assignments. Ongoing research addresses the aggregation of student model data and how the system may best aid the students in their independent studies.

We are most excited, however, about how we may leverage the structuring of the curriculum database into our dual-level linguistic ontology toward the task of automatically evaluating translations. We believe strongly that this will not only enhance the student experience but also provide a rich stream of data concerning student mastery of syntactic concepts. The primary objective of student modeling within King Alfred is to provide tailored feedback to aid students in future self-directed study of the linguistic concepts being taught.

7 Acknowledgments

The Anglo-Saxon course at Wheaton College is taught by Associate Professor of English Michael Drout. Student/faculty collaboration on this project has been extensively supported by Wheaton grants from the Davis, Gebbie, and Mars Foundations, and the Emily C. Hood Fund for the Arts and Sciences. We would particularly like to thank previous undergraduate student collaborators David Dudek, Rachel Kappelle, and Joseph Lavoine.

References

Stacey Bailey. 2007. On automatically evaluating answers to reading comprehension questions. Presented at CALICO-2007, San Marcos, Texas, May 24-26.

Luigi Colazzo and Marco Costantino. 1998. Multi-user hypertextual didactic glossaries. *International Journal of Artificial Intelligence in Education*, 9:111–127.

Michael D. C. Drout. 1999. King Alfred: A teacher controlled, web interfaced Old English learning assistant. *Old English Newsletter*, 33(1):29–34, Fall.

Michael D. C. Drout. 2005. *King Alfred's Grammar*. Version 4.0.

Christiane Fellbaum, editor. 1998. *WordNet: An Electronic Lexical Database*. MIT Press.

Pius Ten Hacken and Cornelia Tschichold. 2001. Word manager and CALL: structured access to the lexicon as a tool for enriching learners' vocabulary. *ReCALL*, 13(1):121–131.

Lisa N. Michaud and Kathleen F. McCoy. 2000. Supporting intelligent tutoring in CALL by modeling the user's grammar. In *Proceedings of the Thirteenth International Florida Artificial Intelligence Research Society Conference (FLAIRS-2000)*, pages 50–54, Orlando, Florida, May 22-24. FLAIRS.

Lisa N. Michaud and Kathleen F. McCoy. 2006. Capturing the evolution of grammatical knowledge in a CALL system for deaf learners of English. *International Journal of Artificial Intelligence in Education*, 16(1):65–97.

Lisa N. Michaud, Kathleen F. McCoy, and Litza A. Stark. 2001. Modeling the acquisition of English: an intelligent CALL approach. In Mathias Bauer, Piotr J. Gmytrasiewicz, and Julita Vassileva, editors, *Proceedings of the 8th International Conference on User Modeling*, volume 2109 of *Lecture Notes in Artificial Intelligence*, pages 14–23, Sonthofen, Germany, July 13-17. Springer.

John Nerbonne, Duco Dokter, and Petra Smit. 1998. Morphological processing and Computer-Assisted Language Learning. *Computer-Assisted Language Learning*, 11(5):421–37.

Kishore Papineni, Salim Roukos, Todd Ward, and Wei-Jing Zhu. 2002. BLEU: a method for automatic evaluation of machine translation. In *Proceedings of the 40th Annual Meeting of the Association for Computational Linguistics*, pages 311–318, Philadelphia, PA, July 6-12. ACL.

Recognizing Noisy Romanized Japanese Words in Learner English

Ryo Nagata
Konan University
Kobe 658-8501, Japan
rnagata[at]konan-u.ac.jp

Jun-ichi Kakegawa
Hyogo University of Teacher Education
Kato 673-1421, Japan
kakegawa[at]hyogo-u.ac.jp

Hiromi Sugimoto
The Japan Institute for
Educational Measurement, Inc.
Tokyo 162-0831, Japan
sugimoto[at]jiem.co.jp

Yukiko Yabuta
The Japan Institute for
Educational Measurement, Inc.
Tokyo 162-0831, Japan
yabuta[at]jiem.co.jp

Abstract

This paper describes a method for recognizing romanized Japanese words in learner English. They become noise and problematic in a variety of tasks including Part-Of-Speech tagging, spell checking, and error detection because they are mostly unknown words. A problem one encounters when recognizing romanized Japanese words in learner English is that the spelling rules of romanized Japanese words are often violated by spelling errors. To address the problem, the described method uses a clustering algorithm reinforced by a small set of rules. Experiments show that it achieves an F-measure of 0.879 and outperforms other methods. They also show that it only requires the target text and a fair size of English word list.

1 Introduction

Japanese learners of English frequently use romanized Japanese words in English writing, which will be referred to as Roman words hereafter; examples of Roman words are: SUKIYAKI[1], IPPAI (*many*), and GANBARU (*work hard*). Approximately 20% of different words are Roman words in a corpus consisting of texts written by Japanese second and third year junior high students. Part of the reason is that they are lacking in English vocabulary, which leads them to using Roman words in English writing.

Roman words become noise in a variety of tasks. In the field of second language acquisition, researchers often use a Part-Of-Speech (POS) tagger to analyze learner corpora (Aarts and Granger, 1998; Granger, 1998; Granger, 1993; Tono, 2000). Since Roman words are romanized Japanese words and thus are unknown to POS taggers, they degrades the performance of POS taggers. In spell checking, they are a major source of false positives because they are unknown words as just mentioned. In error detection, most methods such as Chodorow and Leacock (2000), Izumi et al. (2003), Nagata et al. (2005; 2006), and Han et al. (2004; 2006) use a POS tagger and/or a chunker to detect errors. Again, Roman words degrades their performances.

When viewed from another perspective, Roman words play an interesting role in second language acquisition. It would be interesting to see what Roman words are used in the writing of Japanese learners of English. A frequency list of Roman words should be useful in vocabulary learning and teaching. English words corresponding to frequent Roman words should be taught because learners do not know the English words despite the fact that they frequently use the Roman words.

To the best knowledge, there has been no method for recognizing Roman words in the writing of learners of English as Sect. 2 will discuss. Therefore, this paper explores a novel method for the purpose. At first sight, it might appear to be trivial to recognize Roman words in English writing since the spelling system of Roman words is very different from that of English words. On the contrary, it is not because spelling errors occur so frequently that the rules in both spelling systems are violated in many cases. To address spelling errors, the described method uses a clustering algorithm reinforced with a small set of

[1] For consistency, we print Roman words in all capitals.

Proceedings of the Third ACL Workshop on Innovative Use of NLP for Building Educational Applications, pages 27–35,
Columbus, Ohio, USA, June 2008.

rules. One of the features of the described method is that it only requires the target text and a fair size of an English word list. In other words, it does not require sources of knowledge such as manually annotated training data that are costly to obtain.

The rest of this paper is structured as follows. Section 2 discusses related work. Section 3 introduces some knowledge of Roman words which is needed to understand the rest of this paper. Section 4 discusses our initial idea. Section 5 describes the method. Section 6 describes experiments conducted to evaluate the method and discusses the results.

2 Related Work

Basically, no methods for recognizing Roman words have been proposed in the past. However, there have been a great deal of work related to Roman words.

Transliteration and back-transliteration often involve romanization from Japanese Katakana words into their equivalents spelled in Roman alphabets as in Knight and Graehl (1998) and Brill et al. (2001). For example, Knight and Graehl (1998) back-transliterate Japanese Katakana words into English via Japanese romanized equivalents.

Transliteration and back-transliteration, however, are different tasks from ours. Transliteration and back-transliteration are a task where given English and Japanese Katakana words are put into their corresponding Japanese Katakana and English words, respectively, whereas our task is to recognize Roman words in English text written by learners of English.

More related to our task is loanword identification; our task can be viewed as loanword identification where loanwords are Roman words in English text. Jeong et al. (1999) describe a method for distinguishing between foreign and pure Korean words in Korean text. Nwesri et al.(2006) propose a method for identifying foreign words in Arabic text. Khaltar et al. (2006) extract loanwords from Mongolian corpora using a Japanese loanword dictionary.

These methods are fundamentally different from ours in the following two points. First, the target text in our task is full of spelling errors both in Roman and English words. Second, the above methods require annotated training data and/or other sources of knowledge such as a Japanese loanword dictionary that are hard to obtain in our task.

3 Roman Words

This section briefly introduces the spelling system of Roman words which is needed to understand the rest of this paper. For detailed discussion of Japanese-English romanization, see Knight and Graehl (1998).

The spelling system has five vowels: {a, i, u, e, o}. It has 18 consonants : {b, c, d, f, g, h, j, k, l, m, n, p, r, s, t, w, y, z}. Note that some alphabets such as *q* and *x* are not used in Roman words.

Roman words basically satisfy the following two rules:

1. Roman words end with either a vowel or *n*
2. A consonant is always followed by a vowel

The first rule implies that one can tell that a word ending with a consonant except *n* is not a Roman word without looking at the whole word. There are two exceptions to the second rule. The first is that the consonant *n* sometimes behaves like a vowel and is followed by other consonants such as *nb* as in GANBARU. The second is that some combinations of two consonants such as *ky* and *tt* are used to express gemination and contracted sounds. However, the second rule is satisfied if these combinations are regarded to function as a consonant to express gemination and contracted sounds. An implication from the second rule is that alternate occurrences of a consonant-vowel are very common to Roman words as in SAMURAI[2] and SUKIYAKI. Another is that a sequence of three consonants, such as *tch* and *btl* as in *watch* and *subtle*, respectively, never appear in Roman words excluding the exceptional consecutive consonants for gemination and contracted sounds.

In the writing of Japanese learners of English, the two rules are often violated because of spelling errors. For example, SHSHI, GZUUNOTOU, and MATHYA appear in corpora used in the experiments where the underline indicates where the violations of the rules exist; we believe that even native speakers of the Japanese language have difficulty guessing the right spellings (The answers are shown in Sect. 6.2).

[2]Well-known Japanese words such as SAMURAI and SUKIYAKI are used as examples for illustration purpose. In the writing of Japanese learners of English, however, a wide variety of Japanese words appear as exemplified in Sect. 1.

Also, English words are mis-spelled in the writing of Japanese learners of English. Mis-spelled English words often satisfy the two rules. For example, the word *because* is mis-spelled with variations in error such as *becaus*, *becose*, *becoue*, *becouese*, *becuse*, *becaes*, *becase*, and *becaues* where the underlines indicate words that satisfy the two rules.

In summary, the spelling system of Roman words is quite different from that of English. However, in the writing of Japanese learners of English, the two rules are often violated because of spelling errors.

4 Initial (but Failed) Idea

This section discusses our initial idea for the task, which turned out to be a failure. Nevertheless, this section discusses it because it will play an important role later on.

Our initial idea was as follows. As shown in Sect. 3, Roman words are based on a spelling system that is very different from that of English. The spelling system is so different that a clustering algorithm such as k-means clustering (Abney, 2007) is able to distinguish Roman words from English words if the differences are represented well in the feature vector.

A trigram-based feature vector is well-suited for capturing the differences. Each attribute in the vector corresponds to a certain trigram such as *sam*. The value corresponds to the number of occurrences of the trigram in a given word. For example, the value of the attribute corresponding to the trigram *sam* is 1 in the Roman word SAMURAI. The dummy symbols ^ and $ are appended to denote the beginning and end of a word, respectively. All words are converted entirely to lowercase when transformed into feature vectors. For example, the Roman word:

SAMURAI

would give the trigrams:

^^s ^sa sam amu mur ura rai ai$ i$$,

and be transformed into a feature vector where the values corresponding to the above trigrams are 1, otherwise 0.

The algorithm for recognizing Roman words based on this initial idea is as follows:

Input: target corpus and English word list

Output: lists of Roman words and English words

Step 1. make a word list from the target corpus

Step 2. remove all words from the list that are in the English word list

Step 3. transform each word in the resulting list into the feature vector

Step 4. run k-means clustering on the feature vectors with $k = 2$

Step 5. output the result

In *Step 1.*, the target corpus is turned into a word list. In *Step 2.*, words that are in the English word list are recognized as English words and removed from the word list. Note that at this point, there will be still English words on the list because an English word list is never comprehensive. More importantly, the list includes mis-spelled English words. In *Step 3.*, each word in the resulting list is transformed into the feature vector as just explained above. In *Step 4.*, k-means clustering is used to find two clusters for the feature vectors; $k = 2$ because there are two classes of words — one for Roman words and one for English words. In *Step 5.*, each word is outputted with the result of the clustering. This was our initial idea. It was unsupervised and easy to implement.

Contrary to our expectation, however, the results were far from satisfactory as Sect. 6 will show. The resulting clusters were meaningless in terms of Roman word recognition. For instance, one of the obtained two clusters was for gerunds and present participles (namely, words ending with *ing*) and the other was for the rest (including Roman words and other English words). The results reveal that it is impossible to represent all English words by one cluster obtained from a centroid that is initially randomly chosen. The algorithm was tested with different settings (different k and different numbers of instances to compute the initial centroids). It sometimes performed slightly better, but it was too ad hoc to be a reliable method.

This is why we had to take another approach. At the same time, this initial idea will play an important role soon as already mentioned.

5 Proposed Method

So far, we have seen that a clustering algorithm does not work well on the task. However, there is no doubt that the spelling system of Roman words is very different from that of English words. Because of the differences, the two rules described in Sect. 3 should almost perfectly recognize Roman words if there were no spelling errors.

To make the task simple, let us assume that there were no spelling errors in the target corpus for the time being. Under this assumption, the task is greatly simplified. As with the initial idea, known English words can easily be removed from the word list. Then, all Roman words will be retrieved from the list with few English words by pattern matching based on the two rules.

For pattern matching, words are first put into a Consonant Vowel (CV) pattern. It is simply done by replacing consonants and vowels as defined in Sect. 3 with dummy characters denoting consonants and vowels (C and V in this paper), respectively. For example, the Roman word:

SAMURAI

would be transformed into the CV pattern:

CVCVCVV

while the English word:

fighter

into the CV pattern:

CVCCCVC.

There are some notable differences between the two. An exception to the transformation is that the consonant *n* is replaced with C only when it follows one of the consonants since it sometimes behaves like a vowel (see Sect. 3 for details) and requires a special care. Before the transformation, the exceptional consecutive consonants for gemination and contract sounds are normalized by the following simple replacement rules:

> *double consonants* $\rightarrow$ *single consonant*
> (e.g, *tt* $\rightarrow$ *t*),
> ([bdfghjklmnstprz])y([auo]) $\rightarrow$ $1$2
> (e.g., *bya*$\rightarrow$*ba*),
> ([sc])h([aiueo]) $\rightarrow$ $1$2
> (e.g., *sha* $\rightarrow$ *sa*),
> tsu $\rightarrow$ tu

For example, the double consonant *tt* is replaced with the single consonant *t* using the first rule. Then, a word is recognized as a Roman word if its CV pattern matches:

^[Vn]*(C[Vn]+)*$

where the matcher is written in Perl or Java-like regular expression. Roughly, words that comprise sequences of a consonant-vowel, and end with a vowel or the consonant *n* are recognized as Roman words.

This method should work perfectly if we disregard spelling errors. We will refer to this method as the rule-based method, hereafter. Actually, it works surprisingly well even with spelling errors as the experiments in Sect. 6 will show. However, there is still room for improvement in handling mis-spelled words.

Now back to the real world. The sources of false positives and negatives in the rule-based method are spelling errors both in Roman and English words. For instance, the rule-based method recognizes mis-spelled English words such as *becose*, *becoue*, and *becouese*, which are correctly the word *because*, as Roman words. Likewise, mis-spelled Roman words are recognized as English words.

Here, the initial idea comes to play an important role. Like in the initial idea, each word can be transformed into a point in vector space as exemplified in a somewhat simplified manner in Fig. 1; R and E in Fig. 1 denote words recognized by the rule-based method as Roman and English words, respectively. Pale R and E correspond to false positives and negatives, (which of course is unknown to the rule-based method). Unlike in the initial idea, we now know plausible centroids for Roman and English words. We can compute the centroid for Roman words from the words recognized as Roman words by the rule-based method. Also, we can compute the centroid for English words from the words in the English word dictionary. This situation is shown in Fig. 2 where the centroids are denoted by +. False positives and negatives are expected to be nearer to the centroids for their true class, because even with spelling errors they share a structural similarly with their correctly-spelled counterparts. Taking this into account, all predictions obtained by the rule-based method are overridden by the class of their nearest centroid as shown in Fig. 3. The procedures for computing the centroids and overriding the predictions can be repeated until convergence. Then, this part is the same as the initial idea based on k-means clustering.

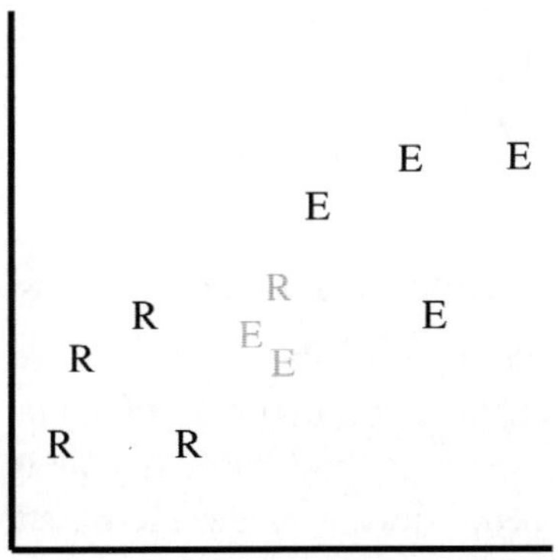

Figure 1: Roman and English words in vector space

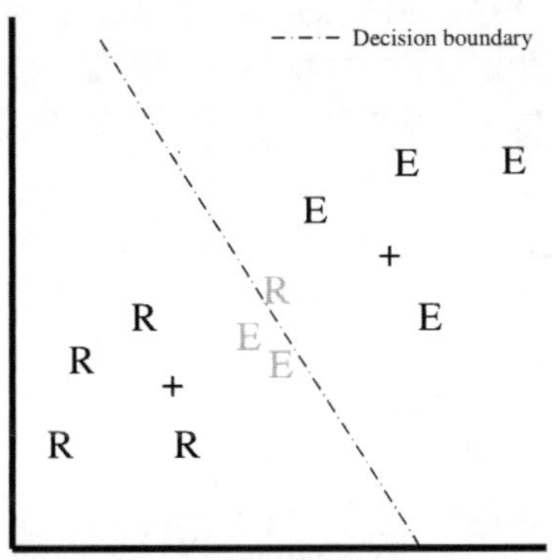

Figure 2: Plausible centroids

The algorithm of the proposed method is:
Input: target corpus and English word list
Output: list of Roman words

Step A. make a word list from the target corpus

Step B. remove all words from the list that are in the English word list

Step C. transform each word in the resulting list into the feature vector

Step D. obtain a tentative list of Roman words using the rule-based method

Step E. compute centroids for Roman and English words from the tentative list and the English word list, respectively

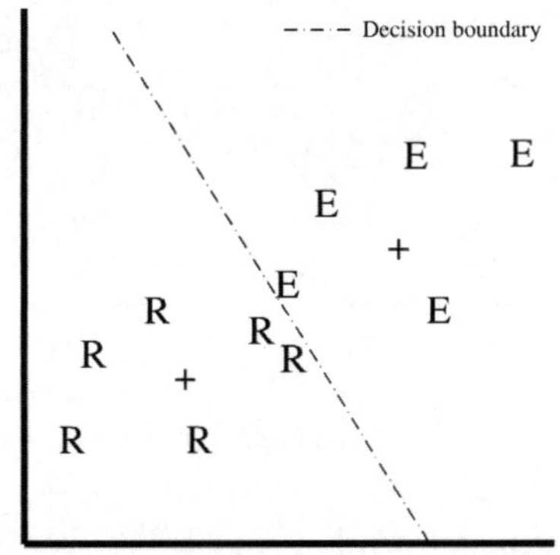

Figure 3: Overridden false positives and negatives

Step F. override the previous class of each word by the class of its nearest centroid

Step G. repeat *Step E* and *F* until convergence

Step H. output the result

Steps A to *C* are the same as in the algorithm of the initial idea. *Step D* then uses the rule-based method to obtain a tentative list of Roman words. *Step E* computes centroids for Roman and English words by taking averages of each value of the feature vectors. *Step F* overrides previous classes obtained by the rule-based method or previous iteration. The distances between each feature vector and the centroids are measured by the Euclidean distance. *Step G* computes centroids and overrides previous predictions until convergence. This step may be omitted to give a variation of the proposed method. *Step H* outputs words belonging to the centroid for Roman words.

6 Experiments

6.1 Experimental Conditions

Three sets of corpora were used for evaluation. The first consisted of essays on the topic *winter holiday* written by second year junior high students. It was used to develop the rule-based method. The second consisted of essays on the topic *school trip* written by third year junior high students. The third was the combination of the two. Table 1 shows the target corpora statistics[3]. Evaluation was done on only unknown words in the target corpora since known

Table 1: Target corpora statistics

Corpus	# sentences	# words	# diff. words	# diff. unknown words	# diff. Roman words
Jr. high 2	9928	56724	1675	1040	275
Jr. high 3	10441	60546	2163	1334	500
Jr. high 2&3	20369	117270	3299	2237	727

words can be easily recognized as English words by referring to an English word list.

As an English word list, the 7,726 words (Leech et al., 2001) that occur at least 10 times per million words in the British National Corpus (Burnard, 1995) were combined with the English word list in Ispell, the spell checker. The whole list consisted of 19816 words.

As already mentioned in Sect. 2, there has been no method for recognizing Roman words. Therefore, we set three baselines for comparison. In the first, all words that were not listed in the English word list were recognized as Roman words. In the second, k-means clustering was used to recognize Roman words in the target corpora as described in Sect. 4 (i.e., the initial idea). The k-means clustering-based method was tested on each target corpora five times and the results were averaged to calculate the overall performances. Five instances were randomly chosen to compute the initial centroids for each class. In the third, the rule-based method described in Sect. 5 was used as a baseline.

The performance was evaluated by recall, precision, and F-measure. Recall and precision were defined by

$$R = \frac{\text{\# Roman words correctly recognized}}{\text{\# diff. Roman words}} \qquad (1)$$

and

$$P = \frac{\text{\# Roman words correctly recognized}}{\text{\# words recognized as Roman words}}, \qquad (2)$$

respectively. F-measure was defined by

$$F = \frac{2RP}{R+P}. \qquad (3)$$

[3]From the Jr. high 2&3 corpus, we randomly took 200 sentences (1645 words) to estimate the spelling error rate. It was an error rate of 2.8% (46/1645). We also investigated if there was ambiguity between Roman and English words in the target corpora (for example, the word *sake* can be a Roman word (a kind of alcohol) and an English word (as in *God's sake*). It turned out that there were no such cases in the target corpora.

6.2 Experimental Results and Discussion

Table 2, Table 3, and Table 4 show the experimental results for the target corpora. In the tables, List-based, K-means, and Rule-based denote the English word list-based, k-means clustering-based, and rule-based baselines, respectively. Also, Proposed (iteration) and Proposed denote the proposed method with and without iteration, respectively.

Table 2: Experimental results for Jr. high 2

Method	R	P	F
List-based	**1.00**	0.268	0.423
K-means	0.737	0.298	0.419
Rule-based	0.898	0.737	0.810
Proposed (iteration)	0.855	**0.799**	0.826
Proposed	0.938	0.761	**0.840**

Table 3: Experimental results for Jr. high 3

Method	R	P	F
List-based	**1.00**	0.382	0.553
K-means	0.736	0.368	0.490
Rule-based	0.824	0.831	0.827
Proposed (iteration)	0.852	**0.916**	0.883
Proposed	0.914	0.882	**0.898**

Table 4: Experimental results for Jr. high 2&3

Method	R	P	F
List-based	**1.00**	0.331	0.497
K-means	0.653	0.491	0.500
Rule-based	0.849	0.794	0.820
Proposed (iteration)	0.851	**0.867**	0.859
Proposed	0.922	0.840	**0.879**

The results show that the English word list-based baseline does not work well. The reason is that mis-spelled words occur so frequently in the writing of Japanese learners of English that simply recognizing unknown words as Roman words causes a lot of false positives.

The k-means clustering-based baseline performs similarly or even worse in terms of F-measure. Section 4 has already discussed the reason. Namely, it is impossible to represent all English words by one cluster obtained by simple k-means clustering.

Unlike the other two, the rule-based baseline performs surprisingly well considering the fact that it is based on a simple (pattern matching) rule. This indicates that the spelling system of Roman words is quite different from that of English words. Thus, it would almost perfectly perform for English writing without spelling errors.

The proposed methods further improve the performance of the rule-based method in all target corpora. Especially, the proposed method without iteration performs well. Indeed, it performs significantly better than the rule-based method does in both recall (99% confidence level, difference of proportion test) and precision (95% confidence level, difference of proportion test) in the whole corpus. They reinforce the rule-based method by overriding false positives and negatives via centroid identification as initially estimated from the results of the rule-based method as Fig. 1, Fig.2, and Fig. 3 illustrate in Sect. 5. This implies that the estimated centroids represent Roman and English words well. Because of this property, the proposed methods can distinguish mis-spelled Roman words from (often mis-spelled) English words. Interestingly, the proposed methods recognized mis-spelled Roman words that we would prove are difficult for even native speakers of the Japanese language to recognize as words; e.g., SHSHI, GZUUNOTOU, and MATHYA; correctly, SUSHI, GOZYUNOTOU (five-story pagoda), and MATTYA (strong green tea).

To see the property, we extracted characteristic trigrams of the Roman and English centroids. We sorted each trigram in descending and ascending orders by $\log \frac{r_i+\alpha}{e_i+\alpha}$ where r_i and e_i denote the feature values corresponding to the i-th trigram in the Roman and English centroids, respectively, and α is a parameter to assure that the value can always be calculated. Table 5 shows the top 20 characteristic trigrams that are extracted from the centroids of the proposed method without iteration; the whole target corpus was used and α was set to 0.001. It shows that trigrams such as *i$$*, associated with words ending with a vowel are characteristic of the Roman centroid. This is consistent with the first rule of the spelling system of Roman words. By contrast, it shows that trigrams associated with words ending with a consonant are characteristic of the English centroid. Indeed, some of these are morphological suffixes such as *ed$* and *ly$*. Others are associated with English syllables such as *ble* and *tion*.

Table 5: Characteristic trigram of centroids

Roman centroid	English centroid
i$$	y$$
u$$	s$$
ji$	d$$
aku	t$$
hi$	ed$
uji	r$$
ˆko	g$$
ˆka	l$$
ku$	ng$
ki$	ˆco
ou$	er$
kak	tio
nka	ati
zi$	ly$
uku	al$
ryu	nt$
dai	ble
ya$	abl
ika	es$
ri$	ty$

To our surprise, the proposed method without iteration outperforms the one with iteration in terms of F-measure. This implies that the proposed method performs better when each word is compared to an exemplar (centroid) based on the idealized Roman words, rather than one based on the Roman words actually observed. Like before, we extracted characteristic trigrams from the centroids of the proposed method with iteration. As a result, we found that trigrams such as *mpl* and *ˆkn* that violate the two rules of Roman words were ranked much higher. Similarly, trigrams that associate with Roman words were extracted as characteristic trigrams of the English centroid. This explains why the proposed method without iteration performs better.

Although the proposed methods perform well, there are still false positives and negatives. A major cause of false positives is mis-spelled English words, which suggests that spelling errors are problematic even in the proposed methods. It accounts for 94% of all false positives. The rest are foreign (excluding Japanese) words such as *pizza* that were not in the English word list and flow the two rules of Roman words. False negatives are mainly Roman words that partly consist of English syllables and/or English words. For example, OMIYAGE (souvenir) contains the English syllable *om* as in *omnipotent* as well as the English word *age*.

7 Conclusions

This paper described methods for recognizing Roman words in learner English. Experiments show that the described methods are effective in recognizing Roman words even in texts containing spelling errors which is often the case in learner English. One of the advantages of the described methods is that they only require the target text and an English word list that is easy to obtain. A tool based on the described methods is available at http://www.ai.info.mie-u.ac.jp/~nagata/tools/

For future work, we will investigate how to tag Roman words with POS tags; note that Roman words vary in POS as exemplified in Sect. 1. Also, we will explore to apply the described method to other languages, which will make it more useful in a variety of applications.

Acknowledgments

This research was partially supported by the Ministry of Education, Science, Sports and Culture, Grant-in-Aid for Young Scientists (B), 19700637.

References

Jan Aarts and Sylviane Granger. 1998. *Tag sequences in learner corpora: a key to interlanguage grammar and discourse*. Longman Pub Group.

Steven Abney. 2007. *Semisupervised Learning for Computational Linguistics*. Chapman & Hall/CRC.

Eric Brill, Gary Kacmarcik, and Chris Brockett. 2001. Automatically harvesting Katakana-English term pairs from search engine query logs. In *Proc. of 6th Natural Language Processing Pacific Rim Symposium*, pages 393–399.

Lou Burnard. 1995. *Users Reference Guide for the British National Corpus. version 1.0*. Oxford University Computing Services, Oxford.

Martin Chodorow and Claudia Leacock. 2000. An unsupervised method for detecting grammatical errors. In *Proc. of 1st Meeting of the North America Chapter of ACL*, pages 140–147.

Sylviane Granger. 1993. The international corpus of learner English. In *English language corpora: Design, analysis and exploitation*, pages 57–69. Rodopi.

Sylviane Granger. 1998. Prefabricated patterns in advanced EFL writing: collocations and formulae. In A. P. Cowie, editor, *Phraseology: theory, analysis, and application*, pages 145–160. Clarendon Press.

Na-Rae Han, Martin Chodorow, and Claudia Leacock. 2004. Detecting errors in English article usage with a maximum entropy classifier trained on a large, diverse corpus. In *Proc. of 4th International Conference on Language Resources and Evaluation*, pages 1625–1628.

Na-Rae Han, Martin Chodorow, and Claudia Leacock. 2006. Detecting errors in English article usage by non-native speakers. *Natural Language Engineering*, 12(2):115–129.

Emi Izumi, Kiyotaka Uchimoto, Toyomi Saiga, Thepchai Supnithi, and Hitoshi Isahara. 2003. Automatic error detection in the Japanese learners' English spoken data. In *Proc. of 41st Annual Meeting of ACL*, pages 145–148.

Kil S. Jeong, Sung H. Myaeng, Jae S. Lee, and Key-Sun Choi. 1999. Automatic identification and back-transliteration of foreign words for information retrieval. *Information Processing and Management*, 35:523–540.

Badam-Osor Khaltar, Atsushi Fujii, and Tetsuya Ishikawa. 2006. Extracting loanwords from Mongolian corpora and producing a Japanese-Mongolian bilingual dictionary. In *Proc. of the 44th Annual Meeting of ACL*, pages 657–664.

Kevin Knight and Jonathan Graehl. 1998. Machine transliteration. *Computational Linguistics*, 24(4):599–612.

Geoffrey Leech, Paul Rayson, and Andrew Wilson. 2001. *Word Frequencies in Written and Spoken English: based on the British National Corpus*. Longman.

Ryo Nagata, Takahiro Wakana, Fumito Masui, Atsuo Kawai, and Naoki Isu. 2005. Detecting article errors based on the mass count distinction. In *Proc. of 2nd International Joint Conference on Natural Language Processing*, pages 815–826.

Ryo Nagata, Astuo Kawai, Koichiro Morihiro, and Naoki Isu. 2006. A feedback-augmented method for detecting errors in the writing of learners of English. In *Proc. of 44th Annual Meeting of ACL*, pages 241–248.

Abdusalam F.A. Nwesri, Seyed M.M. Tahaghoghi, and Falk Scholer. 2006. Capturing out-of-vocabulary words in Arabic text. In *Proc. of 2006 Conference on EMNLP*, pages 258–266.

Yukio Tono. 2000. A corpus-based analysis of interlanguage development: analysing POS tag sequences of EFL learner corpora. In *Practical Applications in Language Corpora*, pages 123–132.

An Annotated Corpus Outside Its Original Context: A Corpus-Based Exercise Book

Barbora Hladká and Ondřej Kučera
Institute of Formal and Applied Linguistics, Charles University
Malostranské nám. 25
118 00 Prague
Czech Republic
hladka@ufal.mff.cuni.cz, ondrej.kucera@centrum.cz

Abstract

We present the STYX system, which is designed as an electronic corpus-based exercise book of Czech morphology and syntax with sentences directly selected from the Prague Dependency Treebank, the largest annotated corpus of the Czech language. The exercise book offers complex sentence processing with respect to both morphological and syntactic phenomena, i. e. the exercises allow students of basic and secondary schools to practice classifying parts of speech and particular morphological categories of words and in the parsing of sentences and classifying the syntactic functions of words. The corpus-based exercise book presents a novel usage of annotated corpora outside their original context.

1 Introduction

Schoolchildren can use a computer to chat with their friends, to play games, to draw, to browse the Internet or to write their own blogs - why should they not use it to parse sentences or to determine the morphological categories of words? We do not expect them to practice grammar as enthusiastically as they do what is mentioned above, but we believe that an electronic exercise book could make the practicing, which they need to do anyway, more fun.

We present the procedure of building an exercise book of the Czech language based on the Prague Dependency Treebank. First (in Section 2) we present the motivation for building an exercise book of Czech morphology and syntax based on an annotated corpus – the Prague Dependency Treebank (PDT). Then we provide a short description of the PDT itself in Section 3. Section 4 is the core of our paper. Section 4.1 is devoted to the filtering of the PDT sentences in such a way that the complexity of sentences included in the exercise book exactly corresponds to the complexity of sentences exercised in traditional Czech textbooks and exercise books. Section 4.2 documents the transformation of the sentences – more precisely a transformation of their annotations into the school analysis scheme as recommended by the official framework of the educational programme for general secondary education (Jeřábek and Tupý, 2005). The evaluation of the system is described in Section 4.3. Section 5 summarizes this paper and plans for the future work.

2 Motivation

From the very beginning, we had an idea of using an annotated corpus outside its original context. We recalled our experience from secondary school, namely from language lessons when we learned morphology and syntax. We did it "with pen and paper" and more or less hated it. Thus we decided to build an electronic exercise book to learn and practice the morphology and the syntax "by moving the mouse around the screen."

In principle, there are two ways to build an exercise book - manually or automatically. A manual procedure requires collecting sentences the authors usually make up and then process with regard to the chosen aspects. This is a very demanding, time-consuming task and therefore the authors manage to collect only tens (possibly hundreds) of sentences that simply cannot fully reflect the real usage of a language. An automatic procedure is possible when an annotated corpus of the language is available. Then the disadvantages of the manual procedure dis-

Proceedings of the Third ACL Workshop on Innovative Use of NLP for Building Educational Applications, pages 36–43,
Columbus, Ohio, USA, June 2008. ©2008 Association for Computational Linguistics

appear. It is expected that the texts in a corpus are already selected to provide a well-balanced corpus reflecting the real usage of the language, the hard annotation work is also done and the size of such corpus is thousands or tens of thousands of annotated sentences. The task that remains is to transform the annotation scheme used in the corpus into the sentence analysis scheme that is taught in schools. In fact, a procedure based on an annotated corpus that we apply is semi-automatic, since the annotation scheme transformation presents a knowledge-based process designed manually - no machine-learning technique is used.

We browsed the Computer-Assisted Language Learning (CALL) approaches, namely those concentrated under the teaching and language corpora interest group (e.g. (Wichmann and Fligelstone (eds.), 1997), (Tribble, 2001), (Murkherjee, 2004), (Schultze, 2003), (Scott, Tribble, 2006)). We realized that none of them actually employs manually annotated corpora – they use corpora as huge banks of texts without additional linguistic information (i.e. without annotation). Only one project (Keogh et al., 2004) works with an automatically annotated corpus to teach Irish and German morphology.

Reviewing the Czech electronic exercise books available (e.g. (Terasoft, Ltd., 2003)), none of them provides the users with any possibility of analyzing the sentence both morphologically and syntactically. All of them were built manually.

Considering all the facts mentioned above, we find our approach to be novel one. One of the most exciting aspects of corpora is that they may be used to a good advantage both in research and teaching. That is why we wanted to present this system that makes schoolchildren familiar with an academic product. At the same time, this system represents a challenge and an opportunity for academics to popularize a field with a promising future that is devoted to natural language processing.

3 The Prague Dependency Treebank

The Prague Dependency Treebank (PDT) presents the largest annotated corpus of Czech, and its second edition was published in 2006 (PDT 2.0, 2006). The PDT had arisen from the tradition of the successful Prague School of Linguistics. The dependency approach to syntactic analysis with the main role of a verb has been applied. The annotations go from the morphological layer through to the intermediate syntactic-analytical layer to the tectogrammatical layer (the layer of an underlying syntactic structure). The texts have been annotated in the same direction, i. e. from the simplest layer to the most complex. This fact corresponds with the amount of data annotated on each level – 2 million words have been annotated on the lowest morphological layer, 1.5 million words on both the morphological and the syntactic layer, and 0.8 million words on all three layers.

Within the PDT conceptual framework, a sentence is represented as a rooted ordered tree with labeled nodes and edges on both syntactic (Hajičová, Kirschner and Sgall, 1999) and tectogrammatical (Mikulová et al., 2006) layers. Thus we speak about syntactic and tectogrammatical trees, respectively. Representation on the morphological layer (Hana et al., 2005) corresponds to a list of (word token and morphological tag) pairs. Figure 1 illustrates the syntactic and morphological annotation of the sample sentence *Rozdíl do regulované ceny byl hrazen z dotací.* [The variation of the regulated price was made up by grants.] One token of the morphological layer is represented by exactly one node of the tree (*rozdíl* [variation], *do* [of], *regulované* [regulated], *ceny* [price], *byl* [was], *hrazen* [made up], *z* [by], *dotací* [grants], '.') and the dependency relation between two nodes is captured by an edge between them, i. e. between the dependent and its governor. The actual type of the relation is given as a function label of the edge, for example the edge (*rozdíl, hrazen*) is labeled by the function *Sb* (subject) of the node *rozdíl*. Together with a syntactic function, a morphological tag is displayed (*rozdíl, NNIS1-----A----*).

Since there is *m:n* correspondence between the number of nodes in syntactic and tectogrammatical trees, it would be rather confusing to display the annotations on those layers all together in one tree. Hence we provide a separate tree visualizing the tectogrammatical annotation of the sample sentence – see Figure 2. A tectogrammatical lemma and a functor are relevant to our task, thus we display them with each node in the tectogrammatical

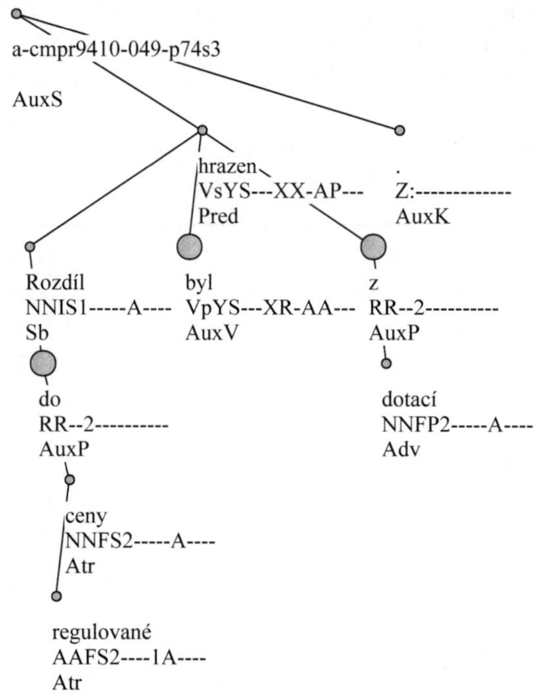

Figure 1: A PDT syntactic tree of the sentence *Rozdíl do regulované ceny byl hrazen z dotací.*

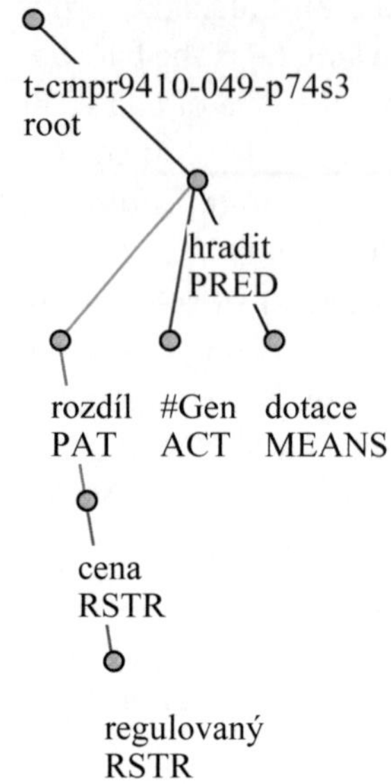

Figure 2: A PDT tectogrammatical tree of the sentence *Rozdíl do regulované ceny byl hrazen z dotací.*

tree, e. g. (*hradit*, *PRED*).

In the following text, we will be using the term the *PDT approach* when having in mind the conceptual framework of PDT annotation, and the *school approach* when having in mind the conceptual framework of a sentence analysis as it is taught in schools.

4 Exercise book composition

With regards to our idea, the electronic exercise book is an electronic system that consists of

- a database of sentences with their morphological and syntactic analyses automatically generated from an annotated corpus,
- a user interface
  - to select sentences from the database or, in other words, to compose the exercises,
  - to simultaneously analyze the selected sentences both morphologically and syntactically,
  - to check the analyses.

More specifically, the composition of the PDT-based exercise book of Czech morphology and syntax implies the selection of those sentences from PDT that are annotated morphologically and syntactically. However, there emerge some syntactic phenomena that are handled differently in the PDT approach than in the school approach. The data annotated tectogrammatically has to be taken into account to process these phenomena properly. Given that, the data annotated on all three layers (0.8 million words in 49,442 sentences) become the *candidate set* of sentences from which the exercise book is to be composed.

Unfortunately, the sentences from the candidate set cannot be merely taken as they are because of two factors:

- the complexity of sentences in the PDT goes

beyond the complexity of sentences in textbooks;

- some syntactic phenomena are handled differently in the PDT approach than in the school approach.

This means that some of the sentences have to be completely discarded (sentence filtering, see 4.1) and syntactic trees of the remaining sentences have to be transformed to match the school analysis of syntax (see 4.2). Luckily, the school approach to the morphology does not coincide with the PDT approach. Therefore the PDT morphological annotations do not need any special handling. It is impossible to browse the candidate set of sentences manually with regard to its volume. Both *sentence filtering* and *annotation transformation* must be done automatically. The whole process is shown in Figure 3.

To summarize, our work on the electronic exercise book covers the data and the software components ((Hladká, Kučera, 2005), (Kučera, 2006), (STYX, 2008)):

- *Annotated Sentence Database* Almost 12,000 annotated sentences generated by the *FilterSentences* component.

- *FilterSentences*. A component used to prepare the annotated sentence database suitable for usage in the exercise book. The end user will never have to use this.

- *Charon*. An administrative tool, used for viewing all of the available sentences and for composing the exercises. We assume that mostly teachers will use it.

- *Styx*. The electronic exercise book itself. It uses the exercises composed with Charon. An active sentence is analyzed both morphologically and syntactically as shown in Figure 4. During the morphological analysis, the user moves word by word, and for each word selects its part of speech. According to the selected part of speech, the combo boxes for the relevant morphological categories appear and let the user choose one of several choices they consider the proper one. During the syntactic analysis, the user moves nodes using the traditional drag and drop method to catch the dependent-governor relation. Afterwards, the syntactic functions are assigned, technically via pop-up menus. Once the analyses are finished, the correct answers are provided separately for morphology and syntax.

4.1 Sentence filtering

The candidate set consists of many sentences that are not appropriate for schoolchildren to analyze. They contain phenomena that authors of textbooks either do not consider at all or sometimes do not agree upon. The following seven filtering criteria have been formulated to exclude problematic sentences. For each filter, we provide a brief description.

1. *SimpleSentences*. The most complex filter that excludes compound and complex sentences.

2. *GraphicalSymbols*. Excludes sentences with various graphical symbols (except for the dot sign) because they imply more complex phenomena than the school analyses operate with.

3. *EllipsisApposition*. Excludes sentences containing an ellipsis or an apposition.

4. *OnePredicate*. Excludes sentences without a predicate (sentences with more than one predicate are already excluded by *SimpleSentences*).

5. *LessThanNWords*. Excludes sentences that are too long.

6. *MoreThanNWords*. Excludes sentences that are too short (usually simple headlines).

7. *AuxO*. Excludes sentences containing emotional, rhythmic particles carrying the *AuxO* syntactic function.

The filters were applied in the same order as they are listed above. First the filter *SimpleSentences* was applied on the candidate set of sentences. Then the sentences preserved by this filter were filtered by *GraphicalSymbols*, and so on. Table 1 provides an overall quantitative overview of sentence filtering – for illustration, the most complex filter *SimpleSentences* excluded the highest percentage of sentences

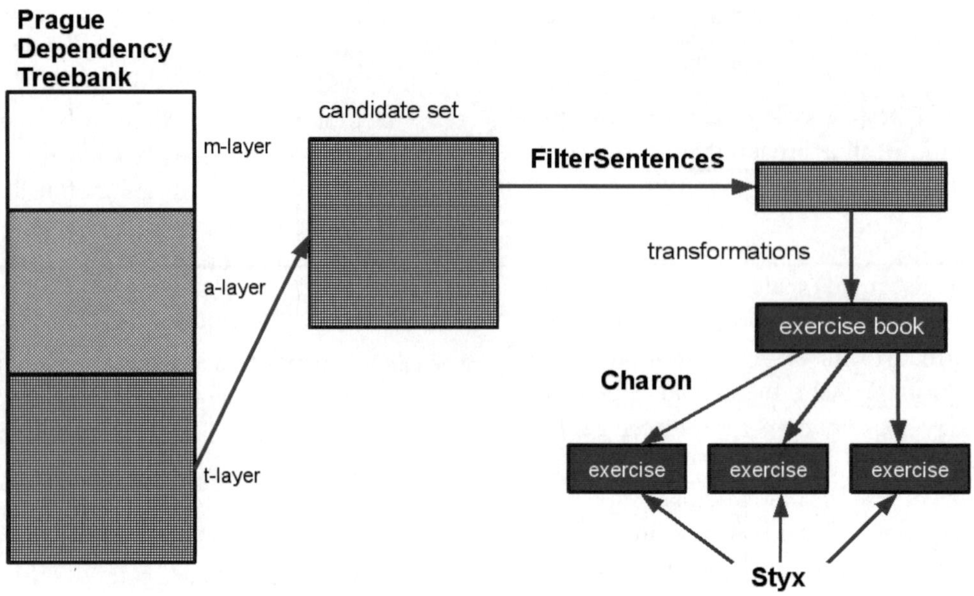

Figure 3: Exercise book composition

(54.4 %). As it is highlighted in the last row of the table, almost 12,000 sentences were preserved after processing the candidate set with all the filters.

Filter	# input sentences	# preserved sentences (%)
SimpleSentence	49,442	22,552 (45.6)
GraphicalSymbols	22,552	20,384 (90.4)
EllipsisAposition	20,383	13,633 (66.9)
OnePredicate	13,633	13,617 (99.9)
LessThanNWords	13,617	13,010 (95.5)
MoreThanNWords	13,010	11,718 (90.1)
AuxO	11,718	11,705 (99.9)
overall	**49,442**	**11,718 (23.7)**

Table 1: Quantitative overview of sentence filtering

4.2 Annotation transformation

In the school approach, a sentence is represented as a tree-like structure with labeled nodes. Unlike PDT syntactic trees, the structures of the school approach have no root node or, in another point of view have two roots: a subject and a predicate (see Figure 5 – *rozdíl, byl hrazen* respectively).

Besides the above-mentioned difference in analysis schemes, the PDT and the school approach differ in the following aspects:

- Many of the PDT syntactic functions do not have counterparts in the school approach.

- The school approach does not have the direct 1:1 correspondence between nodes of the morphological layer and the syntactic layer, i. e. a node can contain more than just one word as visible in Figure 5 – the pair of words *byl, hrazen* form one node as well as the pair *z, dotací*. The words inside each node are listed in accordance to the surface word order of the sentence.

With regards to the discussed differences, we systematically went through the PDT annotation guidelines (Hajičová, Kirschner and Sgall, 1999), analyzed all specified phenomena and designed their transformations into the school analysis scheme. Three elementary operations on syntactic trees and the rules mapping syntactic functions have been formulated. Then a transformation is understood as a sequence of these operations and mapping rules.

1. *JoinTheParentNode* The words at the node are moved up to the parent node and all child nodes of the given node become the child nodes of the parent node. The node is removed afterwards.

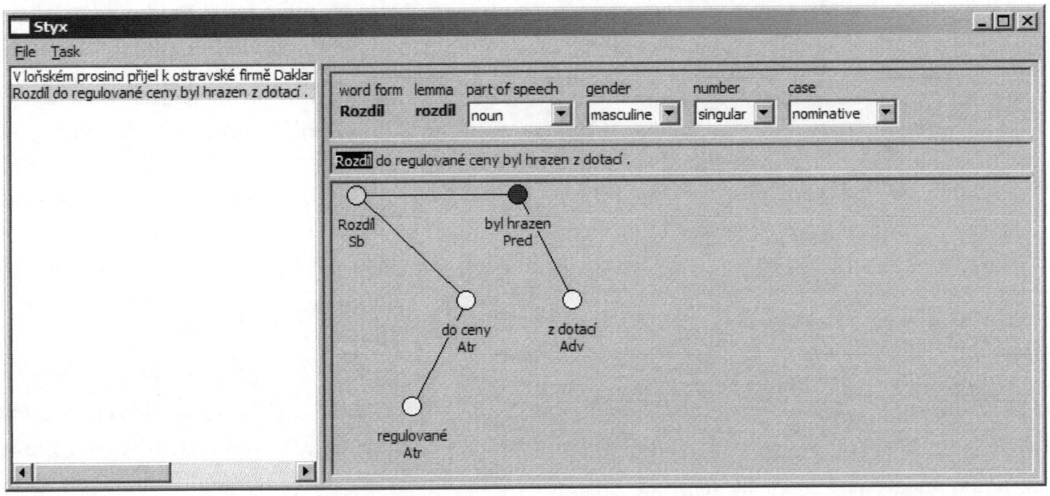

Figure 4: Styx—practicing

2. *AbsorbTheChildNodes* The words at all child nodes of the node are moved into the node. The child nodes are removed and their child nodes become the child nodes of the node. This operation is equivalent to the *JoinTheParentNode* operation applied to all child nodes of the node.

3. *RemoveTheNode* The node-leave is removed.

Mapping PDT syntactic functions follows these operations on trees. Given the complexity of syntactic phenomena and the differences between the approaches, it is not possible to map all functions in a straightforward way as is evident from Table 2. While the school approach works with seven syntactic functions (listed in the second column) the PDT approach labels with 25 functions[1] (listed in the first column). The PDT functions indicating the subject, the predicate, the attribute and the adverbial (in italics) are simply mapped to their school counterparts. The other functions are changed into the school functions in accordance with the type of operation the nodes they belong to pass. After the *AbsorbTheChildNodes* operation, the node is mostly labeled by the direct school counterpart of its "most important child node", i.e. the child node bearing one of the simply-mapped functions, vaguely noted. After the *JoinTheParentNode* operation, the parent node does not change its function in most cases.

[1]The total number of the PDT syntactic functions is actually higher. Here we list those functions that appear in sentences included in the exercise book.

PDT syntactic functions	school syntactic functions	description
Pred	Přs	predicate
Pnom	Přj	predicate nominal
Sb	Po	subject
Obj	Pt	object
Atr, AtrAdv, AdvAtr, AtrAtr, AtrObj, ObjAtr	Pk	attribute
Adv, Atv, AtvV	Pu	adverbial
Obj	D	complement
Coord	—	coordination
AuxC, AuxP, AuxZ, AuxO, AuxV, AuxR, AuxY, AuxK, AuxX, AuxG	—	auxiliary sentence members

Table 2: School vs. PDT syntactic functions

For illustration, a PDT syntactic tree in Figure 1 is transformed into a school structure displayed in Figure 5. Needed transformations include, for example, merging the nodes *(do, AuxP)* and *(ceny, Atr)* into the node *(do ceny, Pk)* or similarly merging *(byl, AuxV)* and *(hrazen, Pred)* into *(byl hrazen, Přs)*.

4.3 Evaluation

It is always difficult to evaluate such systems. It is impossible to express the quality of our system with

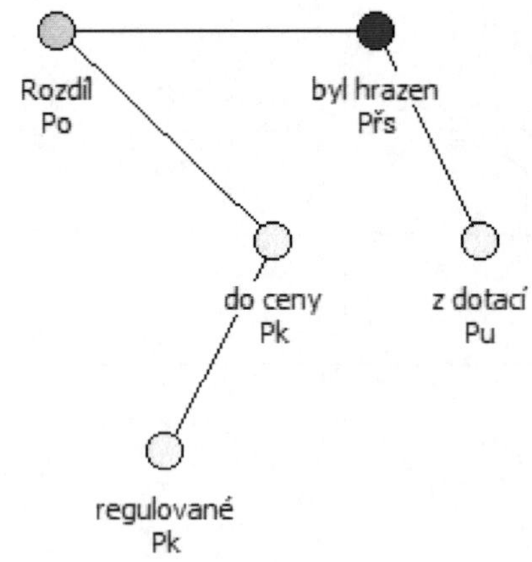

Figure 5: A school syntactic tree of the sentence *Rozdíl do regulované ceny byl hrazen z dotací.*

numerical figures only. The only number we can provide presents the sentence count included in the exercise book: We believe that almost 12,000 sentences bring enormous diversity to the practicing of morphology and syntax.

To find out the real value of our system, we presented it to two different audiences. First we presented it to academics, who really appreciated the idea of corpus assimilation for morphology and syntax learning in schools. Their discussions were mainly concerned with the transformation of annotations.

Then we presented the exercise book during Czech classes in secondary schools. We found out that both the teachers and the students were immediately able to use the system and they were excited about it. They agreed that such exercises would be a nice addition to their classes. Given the experience we acquired during the presentations, we created a sample class (a methodological guide) for teachers, and we collected some interesting ideas that may help us improve the system. These improvements concern i) the annotation transformations (1, 2, 3); ii) the variety of exercises (4); iii) the user interface (5):

1. We do not distinguish between the different types of adverbials. Thus we will provide the possibility of marking a node as being a place adverbial or time adverbial etc.

2. We do not distinguish concordant and discordant attributes yet.

3. Dealing with coordination needs revision, especially when it comes to a difference between dependents of the coordination as a whole and dependents of members of the coordination.

4.
   - During the morphological analysis, the user selects only the part of speech of the given word and STYX itself provides the relevant morphological categories to analyze. In this fashion, the exercises are too simplistic. To master the morphology, the user must know which categories are relevant to the given part of speech.
   - The Charon module will give the user the option of selecting sentences that contain some specific phenomena. Currently, an administrator goes through all the sentences "manually" and if they fulfill her/his selection criteria, (s)he includes them in the exercises.

5. The user interface has to be changed to be more "crazy," or dynamic, to attract not only the "A" pupils but the rest of them as well. Much more comfortable controls, for example by adding keyboard shortcuts for the most common actions, will be offered too.

5 Conclusion

The PDT-based exercise book has completed its initial steps. The theoretical aspects have been analyzed, the system has been implemented and demonstrated to schoolchildren. Their feedbacks motivates us to improve the system in such a way that it will become a real educational tool.

References

Hana Jiří and Dan Zeman and Hana Hanová and Jan Hajič and Barbora Hladká and Emil Jeřábek. 2005. A Manual for Morphological Annotation, 2nd edition. *ÚFAL Technical Report 27*, Prague, Czech Republic.

Hajičová Eva and Zdeněk Kirschner and Petr Sgall. 1999. A Manual for Analytic Layer Annotation of the Prague Dependency Treebank (English translation). *ÚFAL Technical Report*, Prague, Czech Republic.

Hladká Barbora and Ondřej Kučera. 2005. Prague Dependency Treebank as an exercise book of Czech. In *Proceedings of HLT/EMNLP 2005 Interactive Demonstrations*, pp. 14-15. Vancouver, British Columbia, Canada.

Jeřábek Jaroslav and Jan Tupý 2005. *The official framework educational programme for general secondary education.* Research pedagogical institute, Prague.

Keogh Katrina and Thomas Koller and Monica Ward and Elaine UíDhonnchadha and Josef van Genabith 2004. CL for CALL in the Primary School. In *Proceedings of the International Workshop in Association with COLING 2004*, Geneva, Switzerland.

Kučera Ondřej. 2006. Pražský závislostní korpus jako cvičebnice jazyka českého. *Master thesis.* Charles University, Prague, Czech Republic.

Mikulová Marie et al. 2006. A Manual for Tectogrammatic Layer Annotation of the Prague Dependency Treebank. *ÚFAL Technical Report*, Prague, Czech Republic.

Mukherjee, J. 2004. Bridging the gap between applied corpus linguistics and the reality of English language teaching in Germany. In U. Connor and T. Upton (eds.) *Applied Corpus Linguistics: A Multidimensional Perspective*. Amsterdam: Rodopi, pp. 239-250.

PDT 2.0 [online]. 2006. *Prague Dependency Treebank, 2nd edition.* http://ufal.mff.cuni.cz/pdt2.0

Scott Mike and Christopher Tribble 2006. *Textual Patterns: keyword and corpus analysis in language education*. Amsterdam: Benjamins.

Schultze Mathias 2003. AI in CALL: Artficially Inated or Almost Imminent? In *Proceedings of the World-CALL Conference*, Banff, Canada.

STYX [online]. 2008. *The STYX electronic exercise book of Czech* http://ufal.mff.cuni.cz/styx

Terasoft, Ltd. 2003. *TS Český jazyk 2 - jazykové rozbory*. http://www.terasoft.cz.

Tribble Christopher 2001 Corpora and teaching: adjusting the gaze. In *Proceedings of the ICAME 2001 Conference*, Louvain, Belgium.

Wichmann Anne and Steven Fligelstone (eds.) 1997. *Teaching and Language Corpora (Applied Linguistics and Language* London: Addison Wesley Longman.

Answering Learners' Questions by Retrieving Question Paraphrases from Social Q&A Sites

Delphine Bernhard and **Iryna Gurevych**
Ubiquitous Knowledge Processing Lab
Computer Science Department
Technische Universität Darmstadt, Hochschulstraße 10
D-64289 Darmstadt, Germany
{delphine|gurevych}@tk.informatik.tu-darmstadt.de

Abstract

Information overload is a well-known problem which can be particularly detrimental to learners. In this paper, we propose a method to support learners in the information seeking process which consists in answering their questions by retrieving question paraphrases and their corresponding answers from social Q&A sites. Given the novelty of this kind of data, it is crucial to get a better understanding of how questions in social Q&A sites can be automatically analysed and retrieved. We discuss and evaluate several pre-processing strategies and question similarity metrics, using a new question paraphrase corpus collected from the WikiAnswers Q&A site. The results show that viable performance levels of more than 80% accuracy can be obtained for the task of question paraphrase retrieval.

1 Introduction

Question asking is an important component of efficient learning. However, instructors are often overwhelmed with students' questions and are therefore unable to provide timely answers (Feng et al., 2006). Information seeking is also rendered difficult by the sheer amount of learning material available, especially online. The use of advanced information retrieval and natural language processing techniques to answer learners' questions and reduce the difficulty of information seeking is henceforth particularly promising. Question Answering (QA) systems seem well suited for this task since they aim at generating precise answers to natural language questions instead of merely returning documents containing answers. However, QA systems have to be adapted to meet learners' needs. Indeed, learners do not merely ask concrete or factoid questions, but rather open-ended, explanatory or methodological questions which cannot be answered by a single sentence (Baram-Tsabari et al., 2006). Despite a recent trend to render the tasks more complex at large scale QA evaluation campaigns such as TREC or CLEF, current QA systems are still ill-suited to meet these requirements.

A first alternative to full-fledged QA consists in making use of already available question and answer pairs extracted from archived discussions. For instance, Feng et al. (2006) describe an intelligent discussion bot for answering student questions in forums which relies on answers retrieved from an annotated corpus of discussions. This renders the task of QA easier since answers do not have to be generated from heterogeneous documents by the system. The scope of such a discussion bot is however inherently limited since it relies on manually annotated data, taken from forums within a specific domain.

We propose a different solution which consists in tapping into the wisdom of crowds to answer learners' questions. This approach provides the compelling advantage that it utilises the wealth of already answered questions available in online social Q&A sites. The task of Question Answering can then be boiled down to the problem of finding question paraphrases in a database of answered questions. Question paraphrases are questions which have identical meanings and expect the same answer while presenting alternate wordings. Several methods have already been proposed to identify question

Proceedings of the Third ACL Workshop on Innovative Use of NLP for Building Educational Applications, pages 44–52,
Columbus, Ohio, USA, June 2008.

paraphrases mostly in FAQs (Tomuro and Lytinen, 2004) or search engine logs (Zhao et al., 2007).

In this paper, we focus on the problem of question paraphrase identification in social Q&A sites within a realistic information seeking scenario: given a user question, we want to retrieve the best matching question paraphrase from a database of previously answered questions in order to display the corresponding answer. The use of social Q&A sites for educational applications brings about new challenges linked to the variable quality of social media content. As opposed to questions in FAQs, which are subject to editorial control, questions in social Q&A sites are often ill-formed or contain spelling errors. It is therefore crucial to get a better understanding of how they can be automatically analysed and retrieved. In this work, we focus on several pre-processing strategies and question similarity measures applied to the task of identifying question paraphrases in a social Q&A site. We chose WikiAnswers which has been ranked by comScore as the first fastest growing domain of the top 1,500 in the U.S. in 2007.

The remainder of the paper is organised as follows. Section 2 first discusses related work on paraphrase identification and question paraphrasing. Section 3 then presents question and answer repositories with special emphasis on social Q&A sites. Our methods to identify question paraphrases are detailed in section 4. Finally, we present and analyse the experimental results obtained in section 5 and conclude in section 6.

2 Related Work

The identification of question paraphrases in question and answer repositories is related to research focusing on sentence paraphrase identification (section 2.1) and query paraphrasing (section 2.2). The specific features of question paraphrasing have also already been investigated (section 2.3).

2.1 Sentence Paraphrase Identification

Paraphrases are alternative ways to convey the same information (Barzilay and McKeown, 2001). Paraphrases can be found at different levels of linguistic structure: words, phrases and whole sentences. While word and phrasal paraphrases can be assimilated to the well-studied notion of synonymy, sentence level paraphrasing is more difficult to grasp and cannot be equated with word-for-word or phrase-by-phrase substitution since it might entail changes in the structure of the sentence (Barzilay and Lee, 2003). In practice, sentence paraphrases are identified using various string and semantic similarity measures which aim at capturing the semantic equivalence of the sentences being compared. String similarity metrics, when applied to sentences, consist in comparing the words contained in the sentences. There exist many different string similarity measures: word overlap (Tomuro and Lytinen, 2004), longest common subsequence (Islam and Inkpen, 2007), Levenshtein edit distance (Dolan et al., 2004), word n-gram overlap (Barzilay and Lee, 2003) etc. Semantic similarity measures are obtained by first computing the semantic similarity of the words contained in the sentences being compared. Mihalcea et al. (2006) use both corpus-based and knowledge-based measures of the semantic similarity between words. Both string similarity and semantic similarity might be combined: for instance, Islam and Inkpen (2007) combine semantic similarity with longest common subsequence string similarity, while Li et al. (2006) make additional use of word order similarity.

2.2 Query Paraphrasing

In Information Retrieval, research on paraphrasing is dedicated to query paraphrasing which consists in identifying semantically similar queries. The overall objective is to discover frequently asked questions and popular topics (Wen et al., 2002) or suggest related queries to users (Sahami and Heilman, 2006). Traditional string similarity metrics are usually deemed inefficient for such short text snippets and alternative similarity metrics have therefore been proposed. For instance, Wen et al. (2002) rely on user click logs, based on the idea that queries and questions which result in identical document clicks are bound to be similar.

2.3 Question Paraphrasing

Following previous research in this domain, we define question paraphrases as questions which have all the following properties: (a) they have identical meanings, (b) they have the same answers, and (c) they present alternate wordings. Question paraphrases differ from sentence paraphrases by the additional condition (b). This definition encompasses the following questions, taken from the WikiAnswers web site: *How many ounces are there in a pound?, What's the number of ounces per pound?, How many oz. in a lb.?*

Question paraphrases share some properties both with declarative sentence paraphrases and query paraphrases. On the one hand, questions are complete sentences which differ from declarative sentences by their specific word order and the presence of question words and a question focus. On the other hand, questions are usually associated with answers, which makes them similar to queries associated with documents. Accordingly, research on the identification of question paraphrases in Q&A repositories builds upon both sentence and query paraphrasing.

Zhao et al. (2007) propose to utilise user click logs from the Encarta web site to identify question paraphrases. Jeon et al. (2005) employ a related method, in that they identify similar answers in the Naver Question and Answer database to retrieve semantically similar questions, while Jijkoun and de Rijke (2005) include the answer in the retrieval process to return a ranked list of QA pairs in response to a user's question. Lytinen and Tomuro (2002) suggest yet another feature to identify question paraphrases, namely question type similarity, which consists in determining a question's category in order to match questions only if they belong to the same category.

Our focus is on question paraphrase identification in social Q&A sites. Previous research was mostly based on question paraphrase identification in FAQs (Lytinen and Tomuro, 2002; Tomuro and Lytinen, 2004; Jijkoun and de Rijke, 2005). In FAQs, questions and answers are edited by expert information suppliers, which guarantees stricter conformance to conventional writing rules. In social Q&A sites, questions and answers are written by users and may hence be error-prone. Question paraphrase identification in social Q&A sites has been little investigated. To our knowledge, only Jeon et al. (2005) have used data from a Q&A site, namely the Korean Naver portal, to find semantically similar questions. Our work is related to the latter since it employs a similar dataset, yet in English and from a different social Q&A site.

3 Question and Answer Repositories

3.1 Properties of Q&A Repositories

Question and answer repositories have existed for a long time on the Internet. Their form has evolved from Frequently Asked Questions (FAQs) to Ask-an-expert services (Baram-Tsabari et al., 2006) and, even more recently, social Q&A sites. The latest, which include web sites such as Yahoo! Answers and AnswerBag, provide portals where users can ask their own questions as well as answer questions from other users. Social Q&A sites are increasingly popular. For instance, in December 2006 Yahoo! Answers was the second-most visited education/reference site on the Internet after Wikipedia according to the Hitwise company (Prescott, 2006). Even more strikingly, the Q&A portal Naver is the leader of Internet search in South Korea, well ahead of Google (Sang-Hun, 2007).

Several factors might explain the success of social Q&A sites:

- they provide answers to questions which are difficult to answer with a traditional Web search or using static reference sites like Wikipedia, for instance opinions or advice about a specific family situation or a relationship problem;
- questions can be asked anonymously;
- users do not have to browse a list of documents but rather obtain a complete answer;
- the answers are almost instantaneous and numerous, due to the large number of users.

Social Q&A sites record the questions and their answers online, and thus constitute a formidable repository of collective intelligence, including answers to complex questions. Moreover, they make it possible for learners to reach other people worldwide. The relevance of social Q&A sites for learning has been little investigated. To our knowledge, there has been only one study which has shown that Korean users of the Naver Question and Answer platform consider that social Q&A sites can satisfactorily and reliably support learning (Lee, 2006).

3.2 WikiAnswers

For our experiments we collected a dataset of questions and their paraphrases from the WikiAnswers web site. WikiAnswers[1] is a social Q&A site similar to Yahoo! Answers and AnswerBag. As of February 2008, it contained 1,807,600 questions, sorted in 2,404 categories (Answers Corporation, 2008).

Compared with its competitors, the main originality of WikiAnswers is that it relies on the *wiki* technology used in Wikipedia, which means that answers can be edited and improved over time by all contributors. Moreover, the Answers Corporation, which owns the WikiAnswers site, explicitly targets educational uses and even provides an educator toolkit.[2] Another interesting property of WikiAnswers is that users might manually tag question reformulations in order to prevent the duplication of questions asking the same thing in a different way. When a user enters a question which is not already part of the question repository, the web site displays a list of questions already existing on the site and similar to the one just asked by the user. The user may then freely select the question which paraphrases her question, if available, or choose to view one of the proposed alternatives without labelling it as a paraphrase. The user-labelled question reformulations are stored in order to retrieve the same answer when the question rephrasing is asked again. The wiki principle holds for the stored reformulations too, since they can subsequently be edited by other users if they consider that they correspond to another existing question or actually ask an entirely new question. It should be noted that contributors get not reward in terms of trust points for providing or editing alternate wordings for questions.

We use the wealth of question paraphrases available on the WikiAnswers website as the so called user generated gold standard in our question paraphrasing experiments. User generated gold standards have been increasingly used in recent years for research evaluation purposes, since they can be easily created from user annotated content. For instance, Mihalcea and Csomai (2007) use manually annotated keywords (links to other articles) in Wikipedia articles to evaluate their automatic keyword extraction and word sense disambiguation algorithms. Similarly, quality assessments provided by users in social media have been used as gold standards for the automatic assessment of post quality in forum discussions (Weimer et al., 2007). It should however be kept in mind that user generated gold standards are not perfect, as already noticed by (Mihalcea and Csomai, 2007), and thus constitute a trade-off solution.

For the experiments described hereafter, we randomly extracted a collection of 1,000 questions along with their paraphrases (totalling 7,434 question paraphrases) from 100 randomly selected FAQ files in the Education category of the WikiAnswers web site. In what follows, the corpus of 1,000 questions is called the *target questions* collection, while the 7,434 question paraphrases constitute the *input questions* collection. The objective of the task is to retrieve the corresponding target question for each input question. The target question selected is the one which maximises the question similarity value (see section 4.2).

4 Method

In order to rate the similarity of input and target questions, we have first pre-processed both the input and target questions and then experimented with several question similarity measures.

4.1 Pre-processing

We employ the following steps in pre-processing the questions:

Stop words elimination however, we keep question words such as *how*, *why*, *what*, etc. since these make it possible to implicitly identify the question type (Lytinen and Tomuro, 2002; Jijkoun and de Rijke, 2005)

Stemming using the Porter Stemmer[3]

Lemmatisation using the TreeTagger[4]

Spelling correction using a statistical system based on language modelling (Norvig, 2007).[5]

[1] http://wiki.answers.com/

[2] http://educator.answers.com/

[3] http://snowball.tartarus.org/

[4] http://www.ims.uni-stuttgart.de/projekte/corplex/TreeTagger/

[5] We used a Java implementation of the system, jSpellCorrect available at http://developer.gauner.org/jspellcorrect/, trained with the default English training data, to which we appended the myspell English dictionaries.

Stop words were eliminated in all the experimental settings, while stemming and lemmatisation were optionally performed to evaluate the effects of these pre-processing steps on the identification of question paraphrases. We added spelling correction to the conventional pre-processing steps, since we target paraphrasing of questions which often contain spelling errors, such as *When was indoor pluming invented?* or *What is the largest countery in the western Hemipher?* Other related endeavours at retrieving question paraphrases have identified spelling mistakes in questions as a significant source of errors in the retrieval process, but have not attempted to solve this problem (Jijkoun and de Rijke, 2005; Zhao et al., 2007).

4.2 Question Similarity Measures

We have experimented with several kinds of question similarity measures, belonging to two different families of measures: string similarity measures and vector space measures.

4.3 String Similarity Measures

Basic string similarity measures compare the words contained in the questions without taking word frequency into account.

Matching coefficient The matching coefficient of two questions q_1 and q_2 represented by the set of distinct words Q_1 and Q_2 they contain is computed as follows (Manning and Schütze, 1999):

$$\text{matching coefficient} = \mid Q_1 \cap Q_2 \mid$$

Overlap coefficient The overlap coefficient is computed according to the following formula (Manning and Schütze, 1999):

$$\text{overlap coefficient} = \frac{\mid Q_1 \cap Q_2 \mid}{min(\mid Q_1 \mid, \mid Q_2 \mid)}$$

Normalised Edit Distance The edit distance of two questions is the number of words that need to be substituted, inserted, or deleted, to transform q_1 into q_2. In order to be able to compare the edit distance with the other metrics, we have used the following formula (Wen et al., 2002) which normalises the minimum edit distance by the length of the longest question and transforms it into a similarity metric:

$$\text{normalised edit distance} = 1 - \frac{edit\_dist(q_1, q_2)}{max(\mid q_1 \mid, \mid q_2 \mid)}$$

Word Ngram Overlap This metric compares the word n-grams in both questions:

$$\text{ngram overlap} = \frac{1}{N} \sum_{n=1}^{N} \frac{\mid G_n(q_1) \cap G_n(q_2) \mid}{min(\mid G_n(q_1) \mid, \mid G_n(q_2) \mid)}$$

where $G_n(q)$ is the set of n-grams of length n in question q and N usually equals 4 (Barzilay and Lee, 2003; Cordeiro et al., 2007).

4.4 Vector Space Based Measures

Vector space measures represent questions as real-valued vectors by taking word frequency into account.

Term Vector Similarity Questions are represented as term vectors V_1 and V_2. The feature values of the vectors are the $tf.idf$ scores of the corresponding terms:

$$\text{tf.idf} = (1 + \log(tf)) * \log \frac{N+1}{df}$$

where tf is equal to the frequency of the term in the question, N is the number of target questions and df is the number of target questions in which the term occurs, computed by considering the input question as part of the target questions collection (Lytinen and Tomuro, 2002).

The similarity of an input question vector and a target question vector is determined by the cosine coefficient:

$$\text{cosine coefficient} = \frac{V_1 \cdot V_2}{\mid V_1 \mid \cdot \mid V_2 \mid}$$

Lucene's Extended Boolean Model The problem of question paraphrase identification can be cast as an Information Retrieval problem, since in real-world applications the user posts a question and the system returns the best matching questions from its database. We have therefore tested the results obtained using an Information Retrieval system, namely Lucene[6], which combines the Vector Space Model and the Boolean model. Lucene has already been successfully used by Jijkoun and de Rijke (2005) to retrieve answers from FAQ web pages by combining several fields: question text, answer text and the whole FAQ page. The target questions are indexed as documents and retrieved by transforming the input questions into queries.

[6] `http://lucene.apache.org/java/docs/`

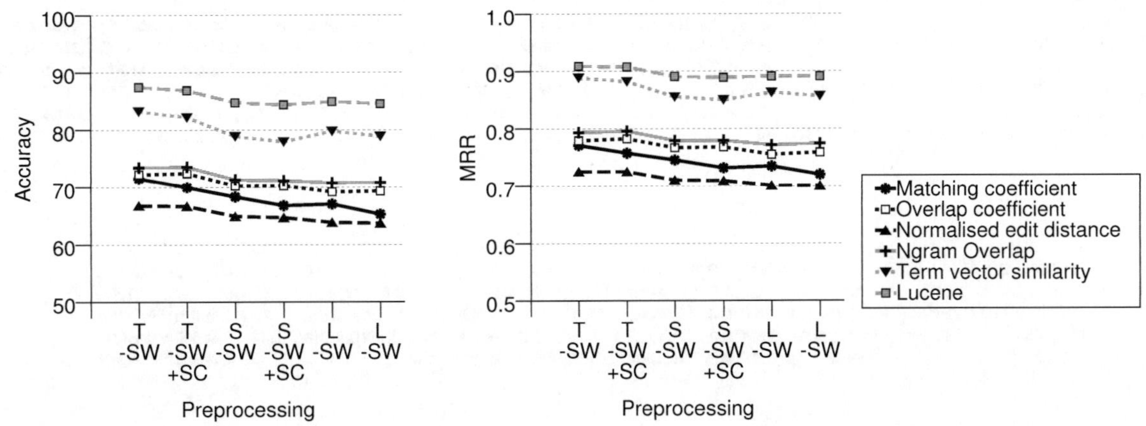

Figure 1: Accuracy (%) and Mean Reciprocal Rank obtained for different question similarity measures and pre-processing strategies: tokens (T), stemming (S), lemmatisation (L), stop words removal (-SW), spelling correction (+SC).

5 Evaluation and Experimental Results

5.1 Evaluation Measures

We use the following evaluation measures for evaluating the results:

Mean Reciprocal Rank For a question, the reciprocal rank RR is $\frac{1}{r}$ where r is the rank of the correct target question, or zero if the target question was not found. The Mean Reciprocal Rank (MRR) is the mean of the reciprocal ranks over all the input questions.

Accuracy We define accuracy as Success@1, which is the percentage of input questions for which the correct target question has been retrieved at rank 1.

5.2 Experimental Results

Figure 1 displays the accuracy and the mean reciprocal ranks obtained with the different question similarity measures and pre-processing strategies. As could be expected, vector space based similarity measures are consistently more accurate than simple string similarity measures. Moreover, both the accuracy and the MRR are rather high for vector space metrics (accuracy around 80-85% and MRR around 0.85-0.9), which shows that good results can be obtained with these retrieval mechanisms. Additional pre-processing, i.e. stemming, lemmatisation and spelling correction, does not ameliorate the tokens minus stop words (T -SW) baseline.

5.3 Detailed Error Analysis

Stemming and lemmatisation Morphological pre-processing brings about mitigated improvements over the tokens-only baseline. On the one hand, it improves paraphrase retrieval for questions containing morphological variants of the same words such as *What are analogies for mitochondria?* and *What is an analogy for mitochondrion?* On the other hand, it also leads to false positives, such has *How was calculus started?*, stemmed as *How was calculus start?* and lemmatised as *How be calculus start?*, which is mapped by Lucene to the question *How could you start your MA English studies?* instead of *Who developed calculus?*. The negative effect of stemming has already been identified by (Jijkoun and de Rijke, 2005) and our results are consistent with this previous finding.

Spelling correction We expected that spelling correction would have a positive impact on the results. There are indeed cases when spelling correction helps. For instance, given the question *How do you become an anestesiologist?*, it is impossible to retrieve the target question *How many years of medical school do you need to be an anesthesiolgist?* without spelling correction since *anesthesiologist* is ill-spelled both in the paraphrase and the target question.

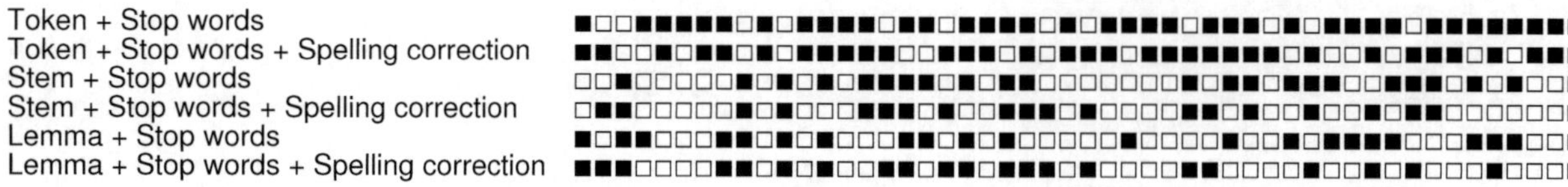

(a)

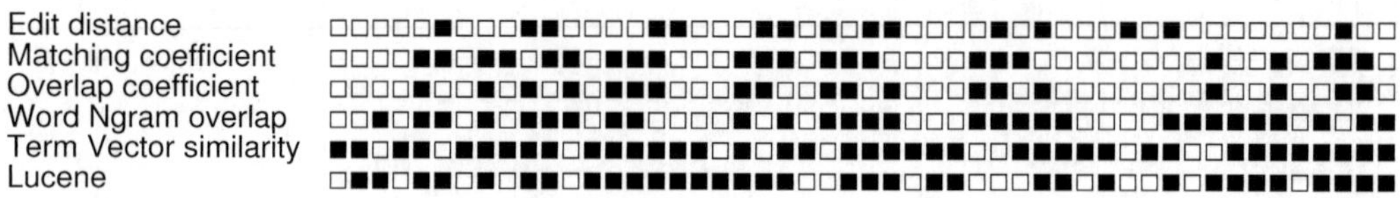

(b)

Figure 2: Comparison of the different pre-processing strategies 2(a) and methods 2(b) for 50 input questions. For the pre-processing comparison, the Lucene retrieval method has been used, while the methods have been compared using baseline pre-processing (tokens minus stop words). A filled square indicates that the target question has been retrieved at rank 1, while a blank square indicates that the target question has not been retrieved at rank 1.

There are however cases when spelling correction induces worse results, since it is accurate in only approximately 70% of the cases (Norvig, 2007). A major source of errors lies in named entities and abbreviations, which are recognised as spelling errors when they are not part of the training lexicon. For instance, the question *What are the GRE score required to get into top100 US universities?* (where GRE stands for Graduate Record Examination) is badly corrected as *What are the are score required to get into top100 US universities?*.

Spelling correction also induces an unexpected side effect, when the spelling error does not affect the question's focus. For instance, consider the following question, with a spelling error: *What events occured in 1919?*, which gets correctly mapped to the target question *What important events happened in 1919?* by Lucene; however, after spelling correction (*What events occurred in 1919?*), it has a bigger overlap with an entirely different question: *What events occurred in colonial South Carolina 1674-1775?*.

The latter example also points at another limitation of the evaluated methods, which do not identify semantically similar words, such as *occurred* and *happened*.

Errors in the gold standard Some errors can actually be traced back to inaccuracies in the gold standard: some question pairs which have been flagged as paraphrases by the WikiAnswers contributors are actually distantly related. For instance, the questions *When was the first painting made?* and *Where did leanardo da vinci live?* are marked as reformulations of the question *What is the secret about mona lisa?* Though these questions all share a common broad topic, they cannot be considered as relevant paraphrases.

We can deduce several possible improvements from what precedes. First, named entities and abbreviations play an important role in questions and should therefore be identified and treated differently from other kinds of tokens. This could be achieved by using a named entity recognition component during pre-processing and then assigning a higher weight to named entities in the retrieval process. This should also improve the results of spelling correction since named entities and abbreviations could be excluded from the correction. Second, semantic errors could be dealt with by using a semantic similarity metric similar to those used in declarative sentence paraphrase identification (Li et al., 2006; Mihalcea et al., 2006; Islam and Inkpen, 2007).

5.4 Comparison and Combination of the Methods

In a second part of the experiment, we investigated whether the evaluated methods display independent error patterns, as suggested by our detailed results analysis. Figure 2 confirms that the pre-processing techniques as well as the methods employed result in dissimilar error patterns. We therefore combined several methods and pre-processing techniques in order to verify if we could improve accuracy.

We obtained the best results by performing a majority vote combination of the following methods and pre-processing strategies: Lucene, Term Vector Similarity with stemming and Ngram Overlap with spelling correction. The combination yielded an accuracy of 88.3%, that is 0.9% over the best Lucene results with an accuracy of 87.4%.

6 Conclusion and Outlook

In this paper, we have shown that it is feasible to answer learners' questions by retrieving question paraphrases from social Q&A sites. As a first step towards this objective, we investigated several question similarity metrics and pre-processing strategies, using WikiAnswers as input data and user generated gold standard. The approach is however not limited to this dataset and can be easily applied to retrieve question paraphrases from other social Q&A sites.

We also performed an extended failure analysis which provided useful insights on how results could be further improved by performing named entity analysis and using semantic similarity metrics.

Another important challenge in using social Q&A sites for educational purposes lies in the quality of the answers retrieved from such sites. Previous research on the identification of high quality content in social Q&A sites has defined answer quality in terms of correctness, well-formedness, readability, objectivity, relevance, utility and interestingness (Jeon et al., 2006; Agichtein et al., 2008). It is obvious that all these elements play an important role in the acceptance of the answers by learners. We therefore plan to integrate quality measures in the retrieval process and to perform evaluations in a real educational setting.

Acknowledgments

This work was supported by the Emmy Noether Programme of the German Research Foundation (DFG) under grant No. GU 798/3-1.

References

Eugene Agichtein, Carlos Castillo, Debora Donato, Aristides Gionis, and Gilad Mishne. 2008. Finding high-quality content in social media. In *WSDM '08: Proceedings of the international conference on Web search and web data mining*, pages 183–194.

Answers Corporation. 2008. WikiAnswers Journalist Quick Guide. [Online; visited March 4, 2008]. `http://site.wikianswers.com/resources/WikiAnswers_1-pager.pdf`.

Ayelet Baram-Tsabari, Ricky J. Sethi, Lynn Bry, and Anat Yarden. 2006. Using questions sent to an Ask-A-Scientist site to identify children's interests in science. *Science Education*, 90(6):1050–1072.

Regina Barzilay and Lillian Lee. 2003. Learning to paraphrase: an unsupervised approach using multiple-sequence alignment. In *Proceedings of NAACL-HLT 2003*, pages 16–23. Association for Computational Linguistics.

Regina Barzilay and Kathleen R. McKeown. 2001. Extracting paraphrases from a parallel corpus. In *ACL '01: Proceedings of the 39th Annual Meeting of the Association for Computational Linguistics*, pages 50–57. Association for Computational Linguistics.

João Cordeiro, Gaël Dias, and Pavel Brazdil. 2007. Learning Paraphrases from WNS Corpora. In David Wilson and Geoff Sutcliffe, editors, *Proceedings of the Twentieth International Florida Artificial Intelligence Research Society Conference (FLAIRS)*, pages 193–198, Key West, Florida, USA, May 7-9. AAAI Press.

Bill Dolan, Chris Quirk, and Chris Brockett. 2004. Unsupervised construction of large paraphrase corpora: exploiting massively parallel news sources. In *COLING '04: Proceedings of the 20th international conference on Computational Linguistics*, pages 350–356. Association for Computational Linguistics.

Donghui Feng, Erin Shaw, Jihie Kim, and Eduard Hovy. 2006. An Intelligent Discussion-Bot for Answering Student Queries in Threaded Discussions. In *Proceedings of the 11th international conference on Intelligent user interfaces (IUI'06)*, pages 171–177.

Aminul Islam and Diana Inkpen. 2007. Semantic Similarity of Short Texts. In *Proceedings of the International Conference on Recent Advances in Natural Language Processing (RANLP 2007)*, Borovets, Bulgaria, September.

Jiwoon Jeon, W. Bruce Croft, and Joon Ho Lee. 2005. Finding similar questions in large question and answer archives. In *CIKM '05: Proceedings of the 14th ACM international conference on Information and knowledge management*, pages 84–90.

Jiwoon Jeon, W. Bruce Croft, Joon Ho Lee, and Soyeon Park. 2006. A framework to predict the quality of answers with non-textual features. In *SIGIR '06: Proceedings of the 29th annual international ACM SIGIR conference on Research and development in information retrieval*, pages 228–235.

Valentin Jijkoun and Maarten de Rijke. 2005. Retrieving answers from frequently asked questions pages on the web. In *CIKM '05: Proceedings of the 14th ACM international conference on Information and knowledge management*, pages 76–83.

Yu Sun Lee. 2006. Toward a New Knowledge Sharing Community: Collective Intelligence and Learning through Web-Portal-Based Question-Answer Services. Masters of arts in communication, culture & technology, Faculty of the Graduate School of Arts and Sciences of Georgetown University, May. [Online; visited February 15, 2008], http://hdl.handle.net/1961/3701.

Yuhua Li, David McLean, Zuhair A. Bandar, James D. O'Shea, and Keeley Crockett. 2006. Sentence Similarity Based on Semantic Nets and Corpus Statistics. *IEEE Transactions on Knowledge and Data Engineering*, 18(8):1138–1150.

Steven L. Lytinen and Noriko Tomuro. 2002. The Use of Question Types to Match Questions in FAQFinder. In *Proceedings of the 2002 AAAI Spring Symposium on Mining Answers from Texts and Knowledge Bases*, pages 46–53.

Christopher D. Manning and Hinrich Schütze. 1999. *Foundations of Statistical Natural Language Processing*. The MIT Press, Cambridge, Massachusetts.

Rada Mihalcea and Andras Csomai. 2007. Wikify!: linking documents to encyclopedic knowledge. In *CIKM '07: Proceedings of the sixteenth ACM conference on information and knowledge management*, pages 233–242.

Rada Mihalcea, Courtney Corley, and Carlo Strapparava. 2006. Corpus-based and Knowledge-based Measures of Text Semantic Similarity. In *Proceedings of AAAI 2006*, Boston, July.

Peter Norvig. 2007. How to Write a Spelling Corrector. [Online; visited February 22, 2008]. http://norvig.com/spell-correct.html.

Lee Ann Prescott. 2006. Yahoo! Answers Captures 96% of Q and A Market Share. Hitwise Intelligence [Online; visited February 26, 2008]. http://weblogs.hitwise.com/leeann-prescott/2006/12/yahoo_answers_captures_96_of_q.html.

Mehran Sahami and Timothy D. Heilman. 2006. A web-based kernel function for measuring the similarity of short text snippets. In *WWW '06: Proceedings of the 15th international conference on World Wide Web*, pages 377–386.

Choe Sang-Hun. 2007. To outdo Google, Naver taps into Korea's collective wisdom. International Herald Tribune, July 4. http://www.iht.com/articles/2007/07/04/technology/naver.php.

Noriko Tomuro and Steven Lytinen. 2004. Retrieval Models and Q&A Learning with FAQ Files. In Mark T. Maybury, editor, *New Directions in Question Answering*, pages 183–194. AAAI Press.

Markus Weimer, Iryna Gurevych, and Max Mühlhäuser. 2007. Automatically Assessing the Post Quality in Online Discussions on Software. In *Proceedings of the Demo and Poster Sessions of the 45th Annual Meeting of the Association for Computational Linguistics*, pages 125–128, Prague, Czech Republic, June. Association for Computational Linguistics.

Ji-Rong Wen, Jian-Yun Nie, and Hong-Jiang Zhang. 2002. Query clustering using user logs. *ACM Trans. Inf. Syst.*, 20(1):59–81.

Shiqi Zhao, Ming Zhou, and Ting Liu. 2007. Learning Question Paraphrases for QA from Encarta Logs. In *Proceedings of the 20th International Joint Conference on Artificial Intelligence*, pages 1795–1801, Hyderabad, India, January 6-12.

Learner Characteristics and Feedback in Tutorial Dialogue

Kristy Elizabeth Boyer[a] **Robert Phillips**[ab] **Michael D. Wallis**[ab] **Mladen A. Vouk**[a] **James C. Lester**[a]

[a]Department of Computer Science, North Carolina State University
[b]Applied Research Associates, Inc.
Raleigh, North Carolina, USA
{keboyer, rphilli, mdwallis, vouk, lester}@ncsu.edu

Abstract

Tutorial dialogue has been the subject of increasing attention in recent years, and it has become evident that empirical studies of human-human tutorial dialogue can contribute important insights to the design of computational models of dialogue. This paper reports on a corpus study of human-human tutorial dialogue transpiring in the course of problem-solving in a learning environment for introductory computer science. Analyses suggest that the choice of corrective tutorial strategy makes a significant difference in the outcomes of both student learning gains and self-efficacy gains. The findings reveal that tutorial strategies intended to maximize student motivational outcomes (e.g., self-efficacy gain) may not be the same strategies that maximize cognitive outcomes (i.e., learning gain). In light of recent findings that learner characteristics influence the structure of tutorial dialogue, we explore the importance of understanding the interaction between learner characteristics and tutorial dialogue strategy choice when designing tutorial dialogue systems.

1 Introduction

Providing intelligent tutoring systems (ITSs) with the ability to engage learners in rich natural language dialogue has been a goal of the ITS community since the inception of the field. Tutorial dialogue has been studied in the context of a number of systems devised to support a broad range of conversational phenomena. Systems such as CIRCSIM (Evens and Michael 2006), BEETLE (Zinn et al. 2002), the Geometry Explanation Tutor (Aleven et al. 2003), Why2/Atlas (VanLehn et al. 2002), ITSpoke (Litman et al. 2006), SCOT (Pon-Barry et al. 2006), ProPL (Lane and VanLehn 2005) and AutoTutor (Graesser et al. 2003) support research that has begun to the see the emergence of a core set of foundational requirements for mixed-initiative natural language interaction that occurs in the kind of tutorial dialogue investigated here. Moreover, recent years have witnessed the appearance of corpus studies empirically investigating speech acts in tutorial dialogue (Marineau et al. 2000), dialogues' correlation with learning (Forbes-Riley et al. 2005, Core et al. 2003, Rosé et al. 2003, Katz et al. 2003), student uncertainty in dialogue (Liscombe et al. 2005, Forbes-Riley and Litman 2005), and comparing text-based and spoken dialogue (Litman et al. 2006).

Recent years have also seen the emergence of a broader view of learning as a complex process involving both cognitive and affective states. To empirically explore these issues, a number of ITSs such as AutoTutor (Jackson et al. 2007), Betty's Brain (Tan and Biswas 2006), ITSpoke (Forbes-Riley et al. 2005), M-Ecolab (Rebolledo-Mendez et al. 2006), and MORE (del Soldato and Boulay 1995) are being used as platforms to investigate the impact of tutorial interactions on affective and motivational outcomes (e.g., self-efficacy) along with purely cognitive measures (i.e., learning gains). A central problem in this line of investigation is iden-

Proceedings of the Third ACL Workshop on Innovative Use of NLP for Building Educational Applications, pages 53–61,
Columbus, Ohio, USA, June 2008.

tifying tutorial strategies (e.g., Graesser et al. 1995) that can appropriately balance the tradeoffs between cognitive and affective student outcomes (Lepper et al. 1993). While a rich set of cognitive and affective tutorial strategies is emerging (e.g., Porayska-Pomsta et al. 2004), the precise nature of the interdependence between these types of strategies is not well understood. In addition, it may be the case that different populations of learners engage in qualitatively different forms of dialogue. Students with particular characteristics may have specific dialogue profiles, and knowledge of such profiles could inform the design of tutorial systems whose strategies leverage the characteristics of the target population. The extent to which different tutorial strategies, and specific instances of them in certain contexts, may be used to enhance tutorial effectiveness is an important question to designers of ITSs.

Given that human-human tutorial dialogue offers a promising model for effective communication (Chi et al. 2001), our methodology is to study naturally occurring tutorial dialogues in a task-oriented learning environment to investigate the relationship between the structure of tutorial dialogue, the characteristics of learners, and the impact of cognitive and motivational corrective tutorial strategies on learning and self-efficacy (Boyer et al. in press). A text-based dialogue interface was incorporated into a learning environment for introductory computer science. In the environment, students undertook a programming task and conversed with human tutors while designing, implementing, and testing Java programs.

The results of the study suggest that the choice of corrective tutorial strategy has a significant impact on the learning gains and self-efficacy of students. These findings reinforce those of other studies (e.g., Lepper et al. 1993, Person et al. 1995, Keller et al. 1983) that indicate that some cognitive and motivational goals may be at odds with one other because a tutorial strategy designed to maximize one set of goals (e.g., cognitive goals) can negatively impact the other. We contextualize our findings in light of recent results that learner characteristics such as self-efficacy influence the structure of task-oriented tutorial dialogue (Boyer et al. 2007), and may therefore produce important interaction effects when considered alongside tutorial strategy.

This paper is organized as follows. Section 2 describes the corpus study, including experimental design and tagging of dialogue and student problem-solving actions. Section 3 presents analysis and results. Discussion and design implications are considered in Section 4, and concluding remarks follow in Section 5.

2 Corpus Study

The corpus was gathered by logging text-based dialogues between tutors and novice computer science students. The learning task was to complete a Java programming problem that required students to apply fundamental concepts such as iteration, modularization, and sequential-access data structures. This study was conducted to compare the impact of certain corrective cognitive and motivational tutorial strategies on student learning and self-efficacy in human-human tutoring. Specifically, the study considered the motivational strategies of praise and reassurance (Lepper et al. 1993) and the category of informational tutorial utterances termed cognitive feedback (Porayska-Pomsta et al. 2004, Tan and Biswas 2006) that followed questionable student problem-solving action. Following the approach of Forbes-Riley (2005) and others (Marineau et al. 2000), utterances from a corpus of human-human tutorial dialogues were annotated with dialogue acts. Then, adopting the approach proposed by Ohlsson et al. (2007), statistical modeling techniques were employed to quantify the relative impact of these different tutorial strategies on the outcomes of interest (in this case, learning and self-efficacy gains).

2.1 Experimental Design

Subjects were students enrolled in an introductory computer science course and were primarily freshman or sophomore engineering majors in disciplines such as mechanical, electrical, and computer engineering.

The corpus was gathered from tutor-student interactions between 43 students and 14 tutors during a two-week study. Tutors and students were completely blind to each other's characteristics as they worked together remotely from separate labs. Tutors observed student problem-solving actions (e.g., programming, scrolling, executing programs) in real time. Tutors had varying levels of tutoring experience, and were not instructed about specific tutorial strategies.

Subjects first completed a pre-survey including items about self-efficacy, attitude toward computer science, and attitude toward collaboration. Subjects then completed a ten item pre-test over specific topic content. The tutorial session was controlled at 55 minutes for all subjects, after which subjects completed a post-survey and post-test containing variants of the items on the pre-versions.

2.2 Problem-Solving Tagging

The raw corpus contains 4,864 dialogue moves: 1,528 student utterances and 3,336 tutor utterances. As a chronology of tutorial dialogue interleaved with student problem-solving (programming) actions that took place during the tutoring sessions, the corpus contains 29,996 programming keystrokes and 1,277 periods of scrolling – all performed by students. Other problem-solving actions, such as opening and closing files or running the program, were sparse and were therefore eliminated from the analyses. Of the 3,336 tutor utterances, 1,243 occur directly after "questionable" student problem-solving action. (The notion of "questionable" is defined below.) This subset of tutorial utterances serves as the basis for the tutorial strategy comparison.

Student problem-solving actions were logged throughout tutoring sessions. Two actions were under consideration for the analysis: typing in the programming interface and scrolling in the program editor window. To interpret the raw logged student problem-solving actions, these events were automatically tagged using a heuristic measure for correctness: if a problem-solving action was a programming keystroke (character) that survived until the end of the session, this event was tagged *promising*, to indicate it was probably correct. If a problem-solving act was a programming keystroke (character) that did not survive until the end of the session, the problem-solving act was tagged *questionable*. Both these heuristics are based on the observation that in this tutoring context, students solved the problem in a linear fashion and tutors did not allow students to proceed past a step that had incorrect code in place. Finally, periods of consecutive scrolling were also marked *questionable* because in a problem whose entire solution fits on one printed page, scrolling was almost uniformly undertaken by a student who was confused and looking for answers in irrelevant skeleton code provided to support the programming task.

2.3 Dialogue Act Tagging

Because utterances communicate through two channels, a cognitive channel and a motivational/affective channel, each utterance was annotated with both a required cognitive dialogue tag (Table 1) and an optional motivational/affective dialogue tag (Table 2). While no single standardized dialogue act tag set has been identified for tutorial dialogue, the tags applied here were drawn from several schemes in the tutorial dialogue and broader dialogue literature. A coding scheme for tutorial dialogue in the domain of qualitative physics influenced the creation of the tag set (Forbes-Riley et al. 2005), as did the four-category scheme (Marineau et al. 2000). A more expansive general dialogue act tag set also contributed commonly occurring acts (Stolcke et al. 2000). The motivational tags were drawn from work by Lepper (1993) on motivational strategies of human tutors.

Table 1 displays the cognitive subset of this dialogue act tag set, while Table 2 displays the motivational/affective tags. It should be noted that a cognitive tag was required for each utterance, while a motivational/affective tag was applied only to the subset of utterances that communicated in that channel. If an utterance constituted a strictly motivational/affective act, its cognitive channel was tagged with EX (EXtra-domain) indicating there was no relevant cognitive content. On the other hand, some utterances had both a cognitive component and a motivational/affective component. For example, a tutorial utterance of, "That looks great!" would have been tagged as positive feedback (PF) in the cognitive channel, and as praise (P) in the motivational/affective channel. In contrast, the tutorial move "That's right," would be tagged as positive feedback (PF) in the cognitive channel and would not be annotated with a motivational/affective tag. Table 3 shows an excerpt from the corpus with dialogue act tags applied.

Table 1: Cognitive Channel Dialogue Acts

	Act	Description	Tutor and Student Example Utterances	Average Count Per Session (Standard Deviation) Student	Tutor
Cognitive Channel Acts	Question (Q)	Questions about goals to pursue, domain concepts, etc.	"Where should we start?" "How do I declare an array?"	6.5 (4.2)	0.6 (0.8)
	Evaluative Question (EQ)	Questions that explicitly inquire about student knowledge state or correctness of problem-solving action.	"Do you know how to declare an array?" "Is that right?"	9.7 (7.1)	7.0 (5.0)
	Statement (S)	Declarative assertion.	"You need a closing bracket there." "I am looking for where this method is declared."	4.9 (4.1)	46.2 (21.0)
	Acknowledgement (ACK)	Positive acknowledgement of a previous statement.	"Okay." or "Yeah." "Alright."	3.8 (5.0)	2.5 (1.9)
	Extra Domain (EX)	A statement not related to the computer science discussion.	"Hello" or "You're Welcome" "Can I use my book?"	1.0 (2.1)	1.1 (2.4)
	Positive Feedback (PF)	Unmitigated positive feedback regarding problem solving action or student knowledge state.	"Yes, I know how to declare an array." "That is right."	2.7 (2.5)	12.0 (7.6)
	Lukewarm Feedback (LF)	Partly positive, partly negative feedback regarding student problem solving action or student knowledge state.	"Sort of." "You're close." or "Well, almost."	0.7 (1.2)	2.3 (2.5)
	Negative Feedback (NF)	Negative feedback regarding student problem solving action or student knowledge state.	"No." "Actually, that won't work."	2.1 (1.8)	1.3 (2.1)

The entire corpus was tagged by a single human annotator, with a second tagger marking 1,418 of the original 4,864 utterances. The resulting kappa statistics were 0.76 in the cognitive channel and 0.64 in the motivation channel.

3 Analysis and Results

Overall, these tutoring sessions were effective: they yielded learning gains (difference between posttest and pretest) with mean 5.9% and median 7.9%, which were statistically significant (p=0.038), and they produced self-efficacy gains

Table 2: Motivational/Affective Channel Dialogue Acts

	Act	Description	Tutor and Student Example Utterances	Average Count Per Session (Standard Deviation) Student	Tutor
Motivational/Affective Channel Acts	Confusion (C)	Explicit expression of confusion. Indicates disorientation beyond that indicated by negative feedback (which indicates the student lacks a particular piece of knowledge).	"I have no idea what to do." "I'm lost."	0.8 (1.2)	-
	Frustration (F)	Explicit expression of frustration.	"Grrr!" "This is so frustrating."	0.1 (0.4)	0.0 (0.3)
	Excitement (E)	Explicit expression of excitement.	"Sweet!" "Cool!"	0.4 (0.7)	0.3 (0.6)
	Praise (P)	Statement intended to emphasize a student's success. This goes beyond positive feedback, which serves as factual confirmation of correctness.	"Great job on that part!" "That's perfect."	-	4.2 (5.7)
	Reassurance (R)	Statement intended to minimize a student's failure.	"That part was hard." "Don't worry about it."	0.4 (0.6)	1.3 (1.6)
	Other Emotion (O)	Utterance that conveys affective or motivational content but for which there is no pre-defined tag.	"Ha ha." "I'm sorry."	0.7 (1.0)	1.5 (2.1)

(difference between pre-survey and post-survey scores) with mean 12.1% and median 12.5%, which were also statistically significant (p<0.0001). Analyses revealed that statistically significant relationships hold between tutorial strategy and learning, as well as between tutorial strategy and self-efficacy gains.

3.1 Analysis

First, the values of learning gain and self-efficacy gain were grouped into binary categories ("Low", "High") based on the median value. We then applied multiple logistic regression with the gain category as the predicted value. Tutorial strategy, incoming self-efficacy rating, and pre-test score were predictors in the model. The binarization approach followed by multiple logistic regression was chosen over multiple linear regression on a continuous response variable because the learning instruments (10 items each) and self-efficacy questionnaires (5 items each) yielded few distinct values of learning gain, meaning the response variable (learning gain and self-efficacy gain, respectively) would not have been truly continuous in nature. Logistic regression is used for binary response variables; it computes the odds of a particular outcome over another (e.g., "Having high learning gain versus low learning gain") given one value of the predictor variable over another (e.g., "The corrective tutorial strategy chosen was positive cognitive feedback instead of praise").

Table 3: Dialogue Excerpts

Utterance	Cognitive Tag	Motivational/ Affective Tag
Tutor: Is there a way you could only write the code to extract the digit once but have it go through each of the five digits?	EQ	
Student: Create a loop?	EQ	
Tutor: Yes!	PF	P
Student: Would a for loop be best?	EQ	
Tutor: Yes	PF	
Tutor: What are the three things we need for a loop?	EQ	
Student: Conditions, what we want it to do, then what increments you want it to increase by.	S	

3.2 Results

After accounting for the effects of pre-test score and incoming self-efficacy rating (both of which were significant in the model with $p<0.001$), observations containing tutorial encouragement were 56% less likely to result in high learning gain than observations without explicit tutorial encouragement ($p=0.001$). On the other hand, an analogous model of self-efficacy gain revealed that tutorial encouragement was 57% more likely to result in high self-efficacy gain compared to tutorial responses that had no explicit praise or reassurance ($p=0.054$). These models suggested that *the presence of tutorial encouragement in response to questionable student problem-solving action may enhance self-efficacy gain but detract from learning gain.*

Another significant finding was that observations in which the tutor used cognitive feedback plus praise were associated with 40% lower likelihood of high learning gain than observations in which the tutor used purely cognitive feedback. No impact was observed on self-efficacy gain. These results suggest that in response to questionable student problem-solving action, *to achieve learning gains, purely cognitive feedback is preferred over cognitive feedback plus praise, while self-efficacy gain does not appear to be impacted either way.*

Among students with low incoming self-efficacy, observations in which the tutor employed a standalone motivational act were 300% as likely to be in the high self-efficacy gain group as observations in which the tutor employed a purely cognitive statement or a cognitive statement combined with encouragement ($p=0.039$). In contrast, among students with high initial self-efficacy, a purely motivational tactic resulted in 90% lower odds of being in the high self-efficacy gain group. These results suggest that *standalone praise or reassurance may be useful for increasing self-efficacy gain among low initial self-efficacy students, but may decrease self-efficacy gain in high initial self-efficacy students.*

Considering strictly cognitive feedback, positive feedback resulted in 190% increased odds of high student self-efficacy gain compared to the other cognitive strategies ($p=0.0057$). Positive cognitive feedback did not differ significantly from other types of cognitive strategies in a Chi-square comparison with respect to learning gains ($p=0.390$). The models thus suggest when dealing with questionable student problem-solving action, *positive cognitive feedback is preferable to other types of cognitive feedback for eliciting self-efficacy gains, but this type of feedback is not found to be better or worse than other cognitive feedback for effecting learning gains.*

4 Discussion

The study found that the presence of direct tutorial praise or encouragement in response to questionable student problem-solving action increased the odds that the student reported high self-efficacy gain while lowering the odds of high learning gain. The study also found that, with regard to learning gains, purely cognitive feedback was preferable to cognitive feedback with an explicitly motivational component. These empirical findings are consistent with theories of Lepper et al. (1993) who found that some cognitive and affective goals in tutoring are "at odds." As would be predicted, the results also echo recent quantitative results from other tutoring domains such as qualitative physics (Jackson et al. 2007) and river ecosystems (Tan and Biswas 2006) that, in general, overt motivational feedback contributes to motivation but cognitive feedback matters more for learning.

Of the corrective tutorial strategies that were exhibited in the corpus, positive cognitive feedback emerged as an attractive approach for responding to plausibly incorrect student problem-solving actions. Responding positively (e.g., "Right") to questionable student actions is an example of indirect correction, which is recognized as a polite strategy (e.g., Porayska-Pomsta et al. 2004). A qualitative investigation of this phenomenon revealed that in the corpus, tutors generally followed positive feedback in this context with more substantive cognitive feedback to address the nature of the student's error. As such, the positive feedback approach seems to have an implicit, yet perceptible, motivational component while retaining its usefulness as cognitive feedback.

This study found that explicit motivational acts, when applied as corrective tutorial approaches, had different impacts on different student subgroups. Students with low initial self-efficacy appeared to benefit more from praise and reassurance than students with high initial self-efficacy. In a prior corpus study to investigate the impact of learner characteristics on tutorial dialogue (Boyer et al. 2007), we also found that learners from different populations exhibited significantly different dialogue profiles. For instance, high self-efficacy students made more declarative statements, or assertions, than low self-efficacy students. In addition, tutors paired with high self-efficacy students gave more conversational acknowledgments than tutors paired with low self-efficacy students, despite the fact that tutors were not made aware of any learner characteristics before the tutoring session. Additional dialogue profile differences emerged between high and low-performing students, as well as between males and females. Together these two studies suggest that learner characteristics influence the structure of tutorial dialogue, and that the choice of tutorial strategy may impact student subgroups in different ways.

5 Conclusion

The work reported here represents a first step toward understanding the effects of learner characteristics on task-oriented tutorial dialogue and the use of feedback. Results suggest that positive cognitive feedback may prove to be an appropriate strategy for responding to questionable student problem-solving actions in task-oriented tutorial situations because of its potential for addressing the sometimes competing cognitive and affective needs of students. For low self-efficacy students, it was found that direct standalone encouragement can be used to bolster self-efficacy, but care must be used in correctly diagnosing student self-efficacy because the same standalone encouragement does not appear helpful for high self-efficacy students. These preliminary findings highlight the importance of understanding the interaction between learner characteristics and tutorial strategy as it relates to the design of tutorial dialogue systems.

Several directions for future work appear promising. First, it will be important to explore the influence of learner characteristics on tutorial dialogue in the presence of surface level information about students' utterances. This line of investigation is of particular interest given recent results indicating that lexical cohesion in tutorial dialogue with low-performing students is found to be highly correlated with learning (Ward and Litman 2006). Second, while the work reported here has considered a limited set of motivational dialogue acts, namely praise and reassurance, future work should target an expanded set of affective dialogue acts to facilitate continued exploration of motivational and affective phenomena in this context. Finally, the current results reflect human-human tutoring strategies that proved to be effective; however, it remains to be seen whether these same strategies can be successfully employed in tutorial dialogue systems. Continuing to identify and empirically compare the effectiveness of alternative tutorial strategies will build a solid foundation for choosing and implementing strategies that consider learner characteristics and successfully balance the cognitive and affective concerns surrounding the complex processes of teaching and learning through tutoring.

Acknowledgments

The authors wish to thank Scott McQuiggan and the members of the Intellimedia Center for Intelligent Systems for their ongoing intellectual contributions, and the Realsearch Group at NC State University for extensive project development support. This work was supported in part by the National Science Foundation through Grant REC-0632450, an NSF Graduate Research Fellowship, and the STARS Alliance Grant CNS-0540523. Any opinions, findings, conclusions or recommendations expressed in this material are those of the author(s) and do not necessarily reflect the views of the National Science Foundation. Support was also provided by North Carolina State University through the Department of Computer Science and the Office of the Dean of the College of Engineering.

References

Kristy Elizabeth Boyer, Robert Phillips, Michael Wallis, Mladen Vouk, and James Lester. In press. Balancing cognitive and motivational scaffolding in tutorial dialogue. To appear in *Proceedings of the 9th International Conference on Intelligent Tutoring Systems*.

Kristy Elizabeth Boyer, Mladen Vouk, and James Lester. 2007. The influence of learner characteristics on task-oriented tutorial dialogue. *Proceedings of AIED*, pp. 127-134. IOS Press.

Vincent Aleven, Kenneth R. Koedinger, and Octav Popescu. 2003. A tutorial dialog system to support self-explanation: Evaluation and open questions. *Proceedings of the 11th International Conference on Artificial Intelligence in Education,* pp. 39-46. Amsterdam. IOS Press.

Vincent Aleven, Bruce McLaren, Ido Roll, and Kenneth Koedinger. 2004. Toward tutoring help seeking: Applying cognitive modeling to meta-cognitive skills. J. C. Lester, R. M. Vicari, and F. Paraguaçu (Eds.), *Proceedings of the 7th International Conference on Intelligent Tutoring Systems,* pp. 227-239. Berlin: Springer Verlag.

Albert Bandura. 2006. Guide for constructing self-efficacy scales. T. Urdan and F. Pajares (Eds.): *Self-Efficacy Beliefs of Adolescents*, pp. 307-337. Information Age Publishing, Greenwich, Connecticut.

Michelene T. H. Chi, Nicholas De Leeuw, Mei-Hung Chiu, and Christian LaVancher. 1994. Eliciting self-explanations improves understanding. *Cognitive Science,* 18:439-477.

Michelene T. H. Chi, Stephanie A. Siler, Heisawn Jeong, Takashi Yamauchi, and Robert G. Hausmann. 2001. Learning from human tutoring. *Cognitive Science,* 25(4):471-533.

Mark G. Core, Johanna D. Moore, and Claus Zinn. 2003. The role of initiative in tutorial dialogue. *Proceedings of the Tenth Conference on European Chapter of the Association for Computational Linguistics,* pp. 67-74.

Teresa del Soldato and Benedict du Boulay. 1995. Implementation of motivational tactics in tutoring systems. *Journal of Artificial Intelligence in Education,* 6(4):337-378. Association for the Advancement of Computing in Education, USA.

Martha Evens and Joel Michael. 2006. One-on-One Tutoring by Humans and Computers. Mahwah, New Jersey: Lawrence Erlbaum Associates.

Kate Forbes-Riley and Diane Litman. 2005. Using bigrams to identify relationships between student certainness states and tutor responses in a spoken dialogue corpus. *Proceedings of the 6th SIGdial Workshop on Discourse and Dialogue*. Lisbon, Portugal.

Kate Forbes-Riley, Diane Litman, Alison Huettner, and Arthur Ward. 2005. Dialogue-learning correlations in spoken dialogue tutoring. Looi, C-k., Mccalla, G., Bredeweg, B., Breuker, J. (Eds.): *Proceedings of AIED*, pp. 225-232. IOS Press.

Arthur C. Graesser, George T. Jackson, Eric Mathews, Heather H. Mitchell, Andrew Olney, Mathew Ventura, Patrick Chipman, Donald R. Franceschetti, Xiangen Hu, Max M. Louwerse, Natalie K. Person, and the Tutoring Research Group. 2003. Why/AutoTutor: A test of learning gains from a physics tutor with natural language dialog. *Proceedings of the Twenty-Fifth Annual Conference of the Cognitive Science Society,* pp. 474-479.

Arthur C. Graesser, Natalie K. Person, and Joseph P. Magliano. 1995. Collaborative dialogue patterns in naturalistic one-to-One tutoring. *Applied Cognitive Psychology*, 9(6):495-522. John Wiley & Sons, Ltd.

G. Tanner Jackson and Art Graesser. 2007. Content matters: An investigation of feedback categories within an ITS. Luckin, R., Koedinger, K. R., Greer, J. (Eds.): *Proceedings of AIED 2007*, 158:127-134. IOS Press.

Sandra Katz, David Allbritton, and John Connelly. 2003. Going beyond the problem given: How human tutors use post-solution discussions to support transfer. *International Journal of Artificial Intelligence in Education,* 13:79-116.

John M. Keller. 1983. Motivational design of instruction. Reigeluth, C.M. (Ed.): *Instructional-Design Theories and Models: An Overview of Their Current Status*, pp. 383-429. Lawrence Erlbaum Associates, Inc., Hillsdale, NJ.

H. Chad Lane and Kurt VanLehn. 2005. Teaching the tacit knowledge of programming to novices with natural language tutoring. *Computer Science Education,* 15:183-201.

Mark R. Lepper, Maria Woolverton, Donna L. Mumme, and Jean-Luc Gurtner. 1993. Motivational techniques of expert human tutors: Lessons for the design of computer-based tutors. Lajoie, S.P., Derry, S. J. (Eds.): *Computers as Cognitive Tools*, pp. 75-105. Lawrence Erlbaum Associates, Inc., Hillsdale NJ.

Jackson Liscombe, Julia Hirschberg, and Jennifer J. Venditti. 2005. Detecting certainness in spoken tutorial dialogues. *Proceedings of Interspeech,* 2005.

Diane J. Litman, Carolyn P. Rosé, Kate Forbes-Riley, Kurt VanLehn, Dumisizwe Bhembe, and Scott Silliman. 2006. Spoken versus typed human and computer dialogue tutoring. *International Journal of Artificial Intelligence in Education,* 16:145-170.

Johanna Marineau, Peter Wiemer-Hastings, Derek Harter, Brent Olde, Patrick Chipman, Ashish Karnavat, Victoria Pomeroy, Sonya Rajan, Art Graesser, and the Tutoring Research Group. 2000. Classification of speech acts in tutorial dialog. *Proceedings of the Workshop on Modeling Human Teaching Tactics and Strategies of ITS 2000*, pp. 65-71. Montreal, Canada.

Stellan Ohlsson, Barbara Di Eugenio, Bettina Chow, Davide Fossati, Xin Lu, and Trina C. Kershaw. 2007. Beyond the code-and-count analysis of tutoring dialogues. Luckin, R., Koedinger, K. R., Greer, J. (Eds.): *Proceedings of AIED 2007*, 158:349-356. IOS Press.

Natalie K. Person, Roger J. Kreuz, Rolf A. Zwaan, and Arthur C. Graesser. 1995. Pragmatics and pedagogy: Conversational rules and politeness strategies may inhibit effective tutoring. *Cognition and Instruction*, 13(2):161-188. Lawrence Erlbaum Associates, Inc., Hillsdale, NJ.

Heather Pon-Barry, Karl Schultz, Elizabeth Owen Bratt, Brady Clark, and Stanley Peters. 2006. Responding to student uncertainty in spoken tutorial dialogue systems. *International Journal of Artificial Intelligence in Education,* 16:171-194.

Kaśka Porayska-Pomsta and Helen Pain. 2004. Providing cognitive and affective scaffolding through teaching strategies: Applying linguistic politeness to the educational context. J.C. Lester, Vicari, R. M., Paraguaçu, F. (Eds.): *Proceedings of ITS 2004*, LNCS 3220:77-86. Springer-Verlag Berlin / Heidelberg.

Genaro Rebolledo-Mendez, Benedict du Boulay, and Rosemary Luckin. 2006. Motivating the learner: an empirical evaluation. Ikeda, M., Ashlay, K. D., Chan, T.-W. (Eds.): *Proceedings of ITS 2006*, LNCS 4053:545-554. Springer Verlag Berlin / Heidelberg.

Carolyn P. Rosé, Dumisizwe Bhembe, Stephanie Siler, Ramesh Srivastava, and Kurt VanLehn. 2003. The role of why questions in effective human tutoring. Hoppe, U., Verdejo, F., Kay, J. (Eds.): *Proceedings of AIED 2003*, pp. 55-62. IOS Press.

Andreas Stolcke, Klaus Ries, Noah Coccaro, Elizabeth Shriberg, Rebecca Bates, Daniel Jurafsky, Paul Taylor, Rachel Martin, Carol Van Ess-Dykema, and Marie Meteer. Dialogue act modeling for automatic tagging and recognition of conversational speech. 2000. *Computational Linguistics,* 26:339-373.

Jason Tan and Gautam Biswas. 2006. The role of feedback in preparation for future learning: A case study in learning by teaching environments. Ikeda, M., Ashley, K., Chan, T.-W. (Eds.): *Proceedings of ITS 2006*, LNCS 4053:370-381. Springer-Verlag Berlin / Heidelberg.

Kurt VanLehn, Pamela W. Jordan, Carolyn P. Rosé, Dumisizwe Bhembe, Michael Bottner, Andy Gaydos, Maxim Makatchev, Umarani Pappuswamy, Michael Ringenberg, Antonio Roque, Stephanie Siler, and Ramesh Srivastava. 2002. The architecture of Why2-Atlas: A coach for qualitative physics essay writing. *Proceedings of the 6th International Conference on Intelligent Tutoring Systems,* LNCS 2363:158-167.

Arthur Ward and Diane Litman. 2006. Cohesion and learning in a tutorial spoken dialog system. *Proceedings of the 19th International FLAIRS (Florida Artificial Intelligence Research Society) Conference.* Melbourne Beach, FL.

Claus Zinn, Johanna D. Moore, and Mark G. Core. 2002. A 3-tier planning architecture for managing tutorial dialogue. *Intelligent Tutoring Systems, Sixth International Conference.* LNCS 2363:574-584. Springer-Verlag, London, UK.

Automatic Identification of Discourse Moves in Scientific Article Introductions

Nick Pendar and **Elena Cotos**
Applied Linguistics and Technology Program
Iowa State University
Ames, IA 50011 USA
{pendar,ecotos}@iastate.edu

Abstract

This paper reports on the first stage of building an educational tool for international graduate students to improve their academic writing skills. Taking a text-categorization approach, we experimented with several models to automatically classify sentences in research article introductions into one of three rhetorical moves. The paper begins by situating the project within the larger framework of intelligent computer-assisted language learning. It then presents the details of the study with very encouraging results. The paper then concludes by commenting on how the system may be improved and how the project is intended to be pursued and evaluated.

1 Introduction and Background

Interest in automated evaluation systems in the field of language assessment has been growing rapidly in the last few years. Performance-based and high-stakes standardized tests (e.g., ACT, GMAT, TOEFL, etc.) have employed such systems due to their potential to yield evidence about the learners' language proficiency and/or subject matter mastery based on analyses of their constructed responses. Automated writing evaluation applications are also beginning to draw the attention of pedagogues who are much interested in assessment for learning, i.e., assessment used as a tool in gaining direction for remediation. Arguably, these technological innovations open up a wide range of possibilities for high-quality formative evaluation that can closely match teaching goals and tailor instruction to individual learners by providing them with feedback and direction on their attainment of knowledge.

Traditionally, automated evaluation has been used for essay grading, but its potential could be successfully extrapolated to other genres in both first language (L1) and second language (L2) academic contexts. Existing scoring systems can assess various constructs such as topical content, grammar, style, mechanics, syntactic complexity, and even deviance or plagiarism (Burstein, 2003; Elliott, 2003; Landauer et al., 2003; Mitchell et al., 2002; Page, 2003; Rudner and Liang, 2002). Because learner writing is generally highly erroneous, an emerging research trend has focused on automated error detection in L2 output finding novel approaches to develop intelligent ways to assess ill-formed learner responses (Burstein and Chodorow, 1999; Chodorow et al., 2007; Han et al., 2006; Leacock and Chodorow, 2003). Various NLP and statistical techniques also allow for the evaluation of text organization, which is however limited to recognizing the five-paragraph essay format, thesis, and topic sentences. At present, to our knowledge, there is only one automated evaluation system, AntMover (Anthony and Lashkia, 2003), that applies intelligent technological possibilities to the genre of research reports—a major challenge for new non-native speaker (NNS) members of academia. AntMover is able to automatically identify the structure of abstracts in various fields and disciplines.

Academic writing pedagogues have been struggling to find effective ways to teach academic writing. Frodesen (1995) argues that the writing instruction for non-native speaker students should "help

Proceedings of the Third ACL Workshop on Innovative Use of NLP for Building Educational Applications, pages 62–70,
Columbus, Ohio, USA, June 2008.

initiate writers into their field-specific research communities" (p. 333). In support of this opinion, (Kushner, 1997) reasons that graduate NNS courses have to combine language and discourse with the skill of writing within professional norms. Various pedagogical approaches have been attempted to achieve this goal. For instance, (Vann and Myers, 2001) followed the inductive analysis approach, in which students examined the format, content, grammatical, and rhetorical conventions of each section of research reports. Supplements to this approach were tasks that required students to write journal entries about the rhetorical conventions of prominent journals in their disciplines and tasks that placed the experience of writing up research "in the framework of an interactive, cooperative effort with cross-cultural interaction" (Vann and Myers, 2001, p. 82). Later, after having followed a primarily skill-based approach, in which students wrote field-specific literature reviews, summaries, paraphrases, data commentaries, and other discipline-specific texts, Levis and Levis-Muller (2003) reported on transforming the course into a project-based writing one. The project consisted of carrying out original research, the topic of which, for the purpose of coping with discipline diversity, was the same for all students and was determined by the instructor. From the start, the students were provided with a limited set of articles, for instance, on cross-cultural adjustment, with which they worked to identify potential research questions for a further investigation and to write the literature review. This approach placed a heavy emphasis on collaboration as students worked in small groups on developing data-collection instruments and on data analysis. Oral presentations on group-research projects wrapped up the course.

The academic writing course discussed in the paragraph above is corpus- and genre-based, combining a top-down approach to genre analysis and a bottom-up approach to the analysis of corpora (Cortes, 2006). Cortes (2006) explains that the course was designed to better address the issues of genre-specificity and disciplinarity since some students who took the previous form of the course claimed that, although they were taught useful things, they did not learn to write the way researchers in their disciplines generally do. In the present format of the course, each student is provided with a corpus of research articles published in top journals of his/her discipline. Students conduct class analyses of their corpus according to guidelines from empirical findings in applied linguistics about the discourse tendencies in research article writing. Their task is to discover organizational and linguistic patterns characteristic of their particular discipline, report on their observations, and apply the knowledge they gain from the corpus analyses when writing a research article for the final project in the course.

2 Motivation

Although each of the pedagogical approaches mentioned in the previous section has its advantages, they all fail to provide NNS students with sufficient practice and remediational guidance through extensive individualized feedback during the process of writing. An NLP-based academic discourse evaluation software application could account for this drawback if implemented as an additional instructional tool. However, an application with such capabilities has not yet been developed. Moreover, as mentioned above, the effects of automated formative feedback are not fully investigated. The long-term goal of this research project is the design and implementation of a new automated discourse evaluation tool as well as the analysis of its effectiveness for formative assessment purposes. Named IADE (Intelligent Academic Discourse Evaluator), this application will draw from second language acquisition models such as interactionist views and Systemic Functional Linguistics as well as from the Skill Acquisition Theory of learning. Additionally, it will be informed by empirical research on the provision of feedback and by Evidence Centered Design principles (Mislevy et al., 2006).

IADE will evaluate students' drafts of their academic writing in accordance with the course materials in terms of an adapted model of Swales' (Swales, 1990; Swales, 2004) move schema as partially presented in Table 1. IADE will achieve this by conducting a sentence-level classification of the input text for rhetorical shifts. Given a draft of a research article, IADE will identify the discourse moves in the paper, compare it with other papers in the same discipline and provide feedback to the user.

Move 1	**Establishing a Territory**
Step 1:	Claiming Centrality
Step 2:	Making topic generalization(s) and/or
Step 3:	Reviewing previous research
Move 2	**Establishing a niche**
Step 1A:	Indicating a gap or
Step 1B:	Highlighting a problem or
Step 1C:	Question-raising or
Step 1D:	Hypothesizing or
Step 1E:	Adding to what is known or
Step 1F:	Presenting justification
Move 3	**Occupying the niche**
Step 1A:	Announcing present research descriptively or
Step 1:	Announcing present research purposefully
Step 2A:	Presenting research questions or
Step 2B:	Presenting hypotheses
Step 3:	Definitional clarifications and/or
Step 4:	Summarizing methods and/or
Step 5:	Announcing principal outcomes and/or
Step 6:	Stating the value of the present research and/or
Step 7:	Outlining the structure of the paper

Table 1: Discourse move model for research article introductions based on (Swales, 1990; Swales, 2004)

	Discipline	**Files**
1.	Accounting	20
2.	Aero-space engineering	20
3.	Agronomy	21
4.	Applied linguistics	20
5.	Architecture	20
6.	Biology	20
7.	Business	20
8.	Chemical engineering	20
9.	Computer engineering	20
10.	Curriculum and instruction	20
11.	Economics	20
12.	Electrical engineering and power system	20
13.	Environmental engineering	20
14.	Food science & food service	20
15.	Health & human performance	20
16.	Industrial engineering	20
17.	Journalism	20
18.	Mechanical engineering	20
19.	Sociology	20
20.	Urban and regional planning	20

Table 2: Disciplines represented in the corpus for article introductions

The development of IADE is guided by the principles of Evidence Centered Design (ECD), "an approach to constructing and implementing educational assessments in terms of evidentiary arguments" (Mislevy et al., 2006, p. 15). This design allows the program to identify the discourse elements of students' work products that constitute evidence and to characterize the strength of this evidence about the writing proficiencies targeted for the purpose of formative assessment.

3 Discourse Move Identification

3.1 Data and Annotation Scheme

The discussions above imply that the first step in the development of IADE is automatic identification of discourse moves in research articles. We have approached this task as a classification problem. In other words, given a sentence and a finite set of moves and steps, what move/step does the sentence signify? This task is very similar to identifying the discourse structure of short argumentative essays discussed in (Burstein et al., 2003), the difference being in the genre of the essays and type of the discourse functions in question.

The corpus used in this study was compiled from an existing corpus of published research articles in 44 disciplines, used in an academic writing graduate course for international students. The corpus contains 1,623 articles and 1,322,089 words. The average length of articles is 814.09 words. We made a stratified sampling of 401 introduction sections representative of 20 academic disciplines (see Table 2) from this corpus of research articles. The size of this sub-corpus is 267,029 words; each file is on average 665.91 words long, resulting in 11,149 sentences as data instances.

The sub-corpus was manually annotated based on Swales' framework by one of the authors for moves and steps (see Figure 1 for an example). The markup scheme includes the elements presented in Table 1. Annotation was performed at sentence level, each sentence being assigned at least one move and almost always a step within that move as specified in the markup scheme.[1] The scheme allowed for multiple layers of annotation for cases when the same sentence signified more than one move or more than one step. This made it possible to capture an array of the semantic shades rendered by a given sentence.

```
<intro_m3 step="description">
<intro_m3 step="method">
<intro_m3 step="purpose">
  This paper presents an
  application of simulation,
  multivariate statistics,
  and simulation metamodels
  to analyze throughput of
  multiproduct batch chemical
  plants.
</intro_m3>
</intro_m3>
</intro_m3>
```

Figure 1: A sample annotated sentence

3.2 Feature Selection

In order to classify sentences correctly, we first need to identify features that can reliably indicate a move/step. We have taken a text-categorization approach to this problem.[2] In this framework each sentence is treated as a data item to be classified, and is represented as an n-dimensional vector in the $\mathcal{R}^n$ Euclidean space. More formally, a sentence s_i is represented as the vector $\bar{s}_i = \langle f_1, f_2, \ldots, f_n \rangle$ where each component f_j of the vector $\bar{s}_i$ represents a measure of feature j in the sentence s_i. The task of the learning algorithm is to find a function $F : S \to C$ that would map the sentences in the corpus S to classes in $M = \{m_1, m_2, m_3\}$ (where m_1, m_2, and m_3 stand for Move 1, Move 2, and Move 3, respectively). In this paper, for simplicity, we are assuming that F is a many-to-one function; however, it should be kept in mind that since sentences may signify multiple moves, in reality the relation may be many-to-many.

An important problem here is choosing features that would allow us to classify our data instances into the classes in question properly. In this study we focused on automatically identifying the major moves in the introduction section of research articles (i.e., m_1, m_2, m_3). Due to the sparseness of data, we have not attempted to identify the steps within the moves at this time.

We extracted word unigrams, bigrams and trigrams (i.e., single words, two word sequences, and three word sequences) from the annotated corpus. Subsection 3.5 reports the results of some of our experiments with these feature sets.

The following steps were taken in preprocessing:

1. All tokens were stemmed using the NLTK[3] port of the Porter Stemmer algorithm (Porter, 1980). This allows us to represent lexically related items as the same feature, thus reducing interdependence among features and also helping with the sparse data problem.

2. All numbers in the texts were replaced by the string `_number_`.

3. In case of bigrams and trigrams, the tokens inside each n-gram were alphabetized to capture the semantic similarity among n-grams containing the same words but in a different order. This tactic also reduces interdependence among features and helps with the sparse data problem.

4. All n-grams with a frequency of less than five were excluded. This measure was also taken to avoid overfitting the classifier to the training data.

The total number of each set of n-grams extracted is shown in Table 3.

To identify which n-grams are better indicators of moves, odds ratios were calculated for each as follows:

$$OR(t_i, m_j) = \frac{p(t_i|m_j) \cdot (1 - p(t_i|\bar{m}_j))}{(1 - p(t_i|m_j)) \cdot p(t_i|\bar{m}_j)} \qquad (1)$$

[1] Only in two instances a step was not assigned.

[2] For an excellent review, see (Sebastiani, 2002).

[3] http://www.nltk.org

n-gram	Number
unigrams	3,951
bigrams	8,916
trigrams	3,605

Table 3: Total number of n-grams extracted

where $OR(t_i, m_j)$ is the odds ratio of the term (n-gram) t_i occurring in move m_j; $p(t_i|m_j)$ is the probability of seeing the term t_i given the move m_j; and $p(t_i|\bar{m}_j)$ is the probability of seeing the term t_i given any move other than m_j. The above conditional probabilities are calculated as maximum likelihood estimates.

$$p(t_i|m_j) = \frac{\text{count}(t_i \text{ in } m_j)}{\sum_{k=1}^{N} \text{count}(t_k \text{ in } m_j)} \quad (2)$$

where N is the total number of n-grams in the corpus of sentences S.

Finally, we selected terms with maximum odds ratios as features. Subsection 3.5 reports on our experiments with classifiers using n-grams with highest odds ratios.

3.3 Sentence Representation

As mentioned in the previous subsection, each sentence is represented as a vector, where each vector component f_i represents a measure of feature i in the sentence. Usually, in text categorization this measure is calculated as what is commonly known as the tf.idf (term frequency times the inverse document frequency), which is a measure of the importance of a term in a document. However, since our "documents" are all sentences and therefore very short, we decided to only record the presence or absence of terms in the sentences as Boolean values; that is, a vector component will contain either a 0 for the absence of the corresponding term or a 1 for its presence in the sentence.

3.4 Classifier

We chose to use Support Vector Machines (SVM) for our classifier (Basu et al., 2003; Burges, 1998; Cortes and Vapnik, 1995; Joachims, 1998; Vapnik, 1995). SVMs are commonly used to solve classification problems by finding hyperplanes that best classify data while providing the widest margin possible between classes. SVMs have proven to be among the most powerful classifiers provided that the representation of the data captures the patterns we are trying to discover and that the parameters of the SVM classifier itself are properly set.

SVM learning is a supervised learning technique where the system is provided a set of labeled data for training. The performance of the system is then measured by providing the learned model a set of new (labeled) data, which were not present during the training phase. The system then applies the learned model on the new data and provides its own inferred labels. The labels provided by the system are then compared with the "true" labels already available. In this study, we used a common technique known as v-fold cross validation, in which data are divided into v equal-sized groups (either by random sampling or by stratified sampling). Then, the system is trained on all but one of the groups and tested on the remaining group. This process is repeated v times until all data items have been used in training and validation. This technique provides a fairly accurate view of how a model built on the whole data set will perform when given completely new data. All the results reported in the following subsection are based on five-fold cross validation experiments.

We predominantly used the machine learning environment RAPIDMINER (Mierswa et al., 2006) in the experimentation phase of the project. The SVMs were set to use the RBF kernel, which maps samples into a higher dimensional space allowing for capturing non-linear relationships among the data and labels. The RBF kernel has two parameters, C and γ. These parameters help against overfitting the classifier on the training data. The values of these parameters is not known before hand for each data set and may be found through an exhaustive search of different parameter settings (Hsu et al., 2008). In this study, we used $C = 2^3$ and $\gamma = 2^{-9}$, which were arrived at through a search of different parameter settings on the feature set with 3,000 unigrams. The search was performed by performing five-fold cross validation on the whole data set using models built with various combinations of C and γ values. Admittedly, these parameters are not necessarily the best parameters for the other feature sets on which exhaustive searches should be performed. This is the next step in our project.

3.5 Evaluation

We performed five-fold cross validation on 14 different feature sets as summarized in Table 4. The results of these experiments are summarized in Figures 2–4. Accuracy shows the proportion of classifications that agreed with the manually assigned labels. The other two performance measures, precision and recall, are commonly used in information retrieval, text categorization, and other NLP applications. For each category, precision measure what proportion of the items assigned to that category actually belonged to it, and recall measures what proportion of the items actually belonging to a category were labeled correctly. The measures reported here (macro-precision $\hat{\pi}^M$ and macro-recall $\hat{\rho}^M$) are weighted means of class precision and recall over the three moves.

$$\hat{\pi}^{\mu} = \frac{TP}{TP + FP} \quad (3)$$

$$\hat{\rho}^{\mu} = \frac{TP}{TP + FN} \quad (4)$$

$$\hat{\pi}^{M} = \frac{\sum_{i=1}^{|C|} w_i \hat{\pi}_i}{|C|} \quad (5)$$

$$\hat{\rho}^{M} = \frac{\sum_{i=1}^{|C|} w_i \hat{\rho}_i}{|C|} \quad (6)$$

The figures show that the unigram models result in the best recall and the trigram models, the best precision. Generally, we attribute lower recall to the sparseness of the data. Access to more training data will help improve recall. We should also note the behavior of the models with respect to bigram features. As seen on Figures 3 and 4, increasing the size of the bigram feature set causes a decline in model precision and a rise in model recall. Considering that there are far more frequent bigrams than unigrams or trigrams (cf. Table 4), this behavior is not surprising. Including more bigrams will increase recall because there are more possible phrases to indicate a move, but that will also result in a decline in precision because those bigrams may also frequently appear in other moves. It also seems that a model employing unigram, bigram and trigrams all will perform better than each individual model. We are planning to experiment with these feature sets, as well.

	Terms	N
1	Unigrams	1,000
2		2,000
3		3,000
4	Bigrams	1,000
5		2,000
6		3,000
7		4,000
8		5,000
9		6,000
10		7,000
11		8,000
12	Trigrams	1,000
13		2,000
14		3,000

Table 4: Feature sets used in experiments

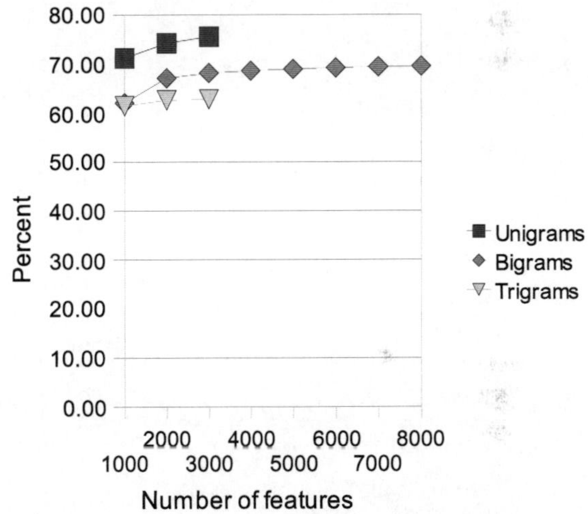

Figure 2: Model accuracy for different feature sets

Error analysis revealed that Move 2 is the hardest move to identify. It most frequently gets misclassified as Move 1. In the future, it might be helpful to make use of the relative position of the sentence in text in order to disambiguate the move involved. In addition, further investigation is needed to see what percentage of Move 2 sentences identified as Move 1 by the system also have been labeled Move 1 by the annotator. Recall that some of the sentences had multiple labels and in this study we are only considering single labels per sentence.

One question that might arise is how much infor-

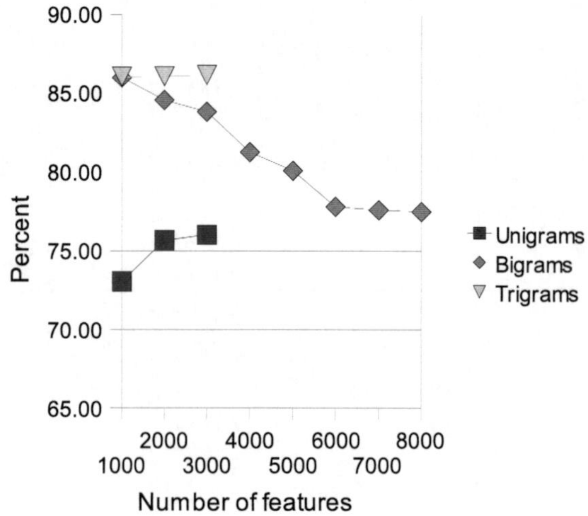

Figure 3: Model precision for different feature sets

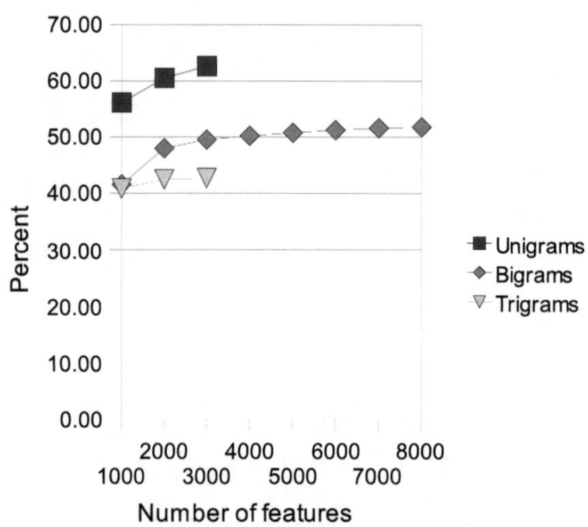

Figure 4: Model recall for different feature sets

mation about the discipline of the article contributes to classification accuracy. In other words, how discipline-dependent are our features? We also ran a set of experiments with the same features plus information about the scientific discipline in which each sentence was written. The change in system performance was not significant by any means, which suggests that our extracted features are not discipline-dependent.

3.6 Interannotator agreement

In order to get a clearer picture of the difficulty of the problem, we asked a second annotator to annotate a portion of the sub-corpus used in this study. The second annotations were done on a sample of files across all the disciplines adding up to 487 sentences. Table 5 contains a summary of the agreements between the two annotators.

	Move 1	Move 2	Move 3
No. agreed	457	452	480
$P(A)$	0.938	0.928	0.986
κ	0.931	0.919	0.984

Table 5: Interannotator agreement on 487 sentences.

Interannotator agreement κ, which is the probability of agreement minus chance agreement, is calculated as follows:

$$\kappa = \frac{P(A) - P(E)}{1 - P(E)} \quad (7)$$

where $P(A)$ represents observed probability of agreement, and $P(E)$ is the expected probability of agreement, i.e., chance agreement. Given three moves and uniform distribution among them, $P(E) = (\frac{1}{3})^2$. Therefore, the two annotators had an average κ of 0.945 over the three moves.

3.7 Limitations

This research is in its initial stages and naturally it has many limitations. One issue involves some of the choices we made in our experiments such as choosing to alphabetize the n-grams and choosing particular values for C and γ. We will be experimenting with non-alphabetized n-grams and also experimenting with different kernel parameters to find optimal models.

4 Discussion

This paper set out to identify rhetorical moves in research article introductions automatically for the purpose of developing IADE, an educational tool for helping international university students in the United States to improve their academic writing skills. The results of our models based on a relatively small data set are very encouraging, and research on improving the results is ongoing.

Apart from system accuracy, there are also some pedagogical issues that we need to keep in mind in the development of IADE. Warschauer and Ware (2006) call for the development of a classroom research agenda that would help evaluate and guide the application of automated essay scoring in the writing pedagogy. Based on a categorization developed by Long (1984), they propose three directions for research: product, process, and process/product, where "product refers to educational outcome (i.e., what results from using the software), process refers to learning and teaching process (i.e., how the software is used), and process/product refers to the interaction between use and outcome" (p. 10). On the level of evaluating technology for language learning in general, Chapelle (2007) specifies three targets for evaluation: "what is taught in a complete course", "what is taught through technology in a complete course", and "what is taught through technology" (p. 30). In the first case, an entire technology-based course is evaluated, in the second case, CALL materials used for learning a subset of course objectives, and in the third case, the use of technology as support and enhancement of a face-to-face course.

This project needs to pursue the third direction in both of these trends by investigating the potential of the IADE program specifically designed to be implemented as an additional component of a graduate course to improve non-native speaker students' academic writing skills. Since this program will represent a case of innovative technology, its evaluation, as well as the evaluation of any other new CALL applications, according to Chapelle (2007), is "perhaps the most significant challenge teachers and curriculum developers face when attempting to introduce innovation into language education" (p. 30). Therefore, the analysis of the effectiveness of IADE will be conducted based on Chapelle's (2001) framework, which has proven to provide excellent guidance for research of evaluative nature[4].

References

Laurence Anthony and George V. Lashkia. 2003. Mover: A machine learning tool to assist in the reading and writing of technical papers. *IEEE Transactions on Professional Communication*, 46(3):185–193.

A. Basu, C. Watters, and M. Shepherd. 2003. Support vector machines for text categorization. In *HICSS '03: Proceedings of the 36th Annual Hawaii International Conference on System Sciences (HICSS'03) - Track 4*, page 103.3, Washington, DC, USA. IEEE Computer Society.

Christopher J. C. Burges. 1998. A tutorial on support vector machines for pattern recognition. *Data Mining and Knowledge Discovery*, 2(2):121–167.

Jill C. Burstein and Martin Chodorow. 1999. Automated essay scoring for nonnative english. In *Proceedings of the ACL99 Workshop on Computer-Mediated Language Assessment and Evaluation of Natural Language Processing*, pages 68–75, Joint Symposium of the Association of Computational Linguistics and the International Association of Language Learning Technologies, College Park, Maryland.

Jill C. Burstein, Daniel Marcu, and Kevin Knight. 2003. Finding the WRITE stuff: automatic identification of discourse structure in student essays. *IEEE Intelligent Systems*, 18(1):32–39.

Jill C. Burstein. 2003. The e-rater text registered scoring engine: Automated essay scoring with natural language processing. In Shermis and Burstein (Shermis and Burstein, 2003), pages 113–121.

Carol Chapelle. 2001. *Computer applications in second language acquisition*. Cambridge University Press, New York.

Carol Chapelle. 2007. Challenges in evaluation of innovation: Observations from technology research. *Innovation in Language Learning and Teaching*, 1(1):30–45.

Martin Chodorow, Joel R. Tetreault, and Na-Rae Han. 2007. Detection of grammatical errors involving prepositions. In *Proceedings of the 4th ACL-SIGSEM Workshop on Prepositions*, pages 25–30.

Corinna Cortes and Vladimir Vapnik. 1995. Support-vector networks. *Machine Learning*, 20:273–297.

Viviana Cortes. 2006. Exploring genre and corpora in the English for academic writing class. *Manuscript submitted for publication*. Manuscript submitted for publication.

Scott Elliott. 2003. Intellimetric^{TM}: From here to validity. In Shermis and Burstein (Shermis and Burstein, 2003), pages 71–86.

Jan Frodesen. 1995. Negotiating the syllabus: A learning-centered, interactive approach to ESL graduate writing course design. In Diane Belcher and George Braine, editors, *Academic Writing in a Second Language: Essays on Research and Pedagogy*, pages 331–350. Ablex Publishing Corporation, NJ.

[4] see (Jamieson et al., 2005)

Na-Rae Han, Martin Chodorow, and Claudia Leacock. 2006. Detecting errors in English article usage by non-native speakers. *Natural Language Engineering*, 2(2):115–129.

Chih-Wei Hsu, Chih-Chung Chang, and Chih-Jen Lin. 2008. A practical guide to support vector classification. Unpublished manuscript.

Joanne Jamieson, Carol Chapelle, and Sherry Preiss. 2005. CALL evaluation by developers, a teacher, and students. *CALICO Journal*, 23(1):93–138.

T Joachims. 1998. Text categorization with support vector machines: Learning with many relevant features. In *In Proceedings of ECML-98, 10th European Conference on Machine Learning*.

Shimona Kushner. 1997. Tackling the needs of foreign academic writers: A case study. *IEEE Transactions on Professional Communication*, 40:20–25.

Thomas K. Landauer, Darrell Laham, and Peter W. Foltz. 2003. Automated scoring and annotation of essays with the Intelligent Essay Assessor. In Shermis and Burstein (Shermis and Burstein, 2003), pages 87–112.

Claudia Leacock and Martin Chodorow. 2003. Automated grammatical error detection. In Shermis and Burstein (Shermis and Burstein, 2003), pages 195–207.

John Levis and Greta Muller-Levis. 2003. A project-based approach to teaching research writing to nonnative writers. *IEEE Transactions on Professional Communication*, 46(3):210–220.

Michael Long. 1984. Process and product in ESL programme evaluation. *TESOL Quarterly*, 18(3):409–425.

I. Mierswa, M. Wurst, R. Klinkenberg, M. Scholz, and T. Euler. 2006. YALE (now: RAPIDMINER: Rapid prototyping for complex data mining tasks. In *Proceedings of the ACM SIGKDD International Conference on Knowledge Discovery and Data Mining (KDD 2006)*.

R. Mislevy, l. Steinberg, R. Almond, and J. Lukas. 2006. Concepts, terminology, and basic models of evidence-centered design. In D. Williamson, R. Mislevy, and I. Bejar, editors, *Automated scoring of complex tasks in computer-based testing*, pages 15–47. Lawrence Erlbaum Associates, Mahwah, NJ.

Tom Mitchell, Terry Russell, Peter Broomhead, and Nicola Aldridge. 2002. Towards robust computerised marking of free-text responses. In *Proceedings of the 6th International Computer Assisted Assessment Conference*, pages 233–249, Loughborough University.

Ellis Batten Page. 2003. Project Essay Grade. In Shermis and Burstein (Shermis and Burstein, 2003), pages 43–54.

Martin F. Porter. 1980. An algorithm for suffix stripping. *Program*, 14(3):130–137.

Lawrence M. Rudner and Tahung Liang. 2002. Automated essay scoring using Bayes' theorem. *The Journal of Technology, Learning and Assessment*, 1(2):3–21.

Fabrizio Sebastiani. 2002. Machine learning in automated text categorization. *ACM Computing Surveys*, 34(1):1–47.

Mark D. Shermis and Jill C. Burstein, editors. 2003. *Automated Essay Scoring: A cross-disciplinary perspective*. Lawrence Erlbaum Associates, Mahwah, NJ.

John Swales. 1990. *English in Academic and Research Settings*. Cambridge University Press, Cambridge.

John Swales. 2004. *Research Genres: Exploration and applications*. Cambridge University Press, Cambridge.

Roberta Vann and Cynthia Myers. 2001. Academic ESL options in a large research university. In Ilona Leki, editor, *Academic Writing Programs*, Case Studies in TESOL Practice Series. TESOL, Alexandria, VA.

Vladimir N. Vapnik. 1995. *The Nature of Statistical Learning Theory*. Springer, Berlin.

Mark Warschauer and Paige Ware. 2006. Automated writing evaluation: defining the classroom research agenda. *Language Teaching Research*, 10(2):1–24.

An Analysis of Statistical Models and Features for Reading Difficulty Prediction

Michael Heilman, Kevyn Collins-Thompson and **Maxine Eskenazi**
Language Technologies Institute
Carnegie Mellon University
Pittsburgh, PA 15213, USA
{mheilman,kct,max}@cs.cmu.edu

Abstract

A reading difficulty measure can be described as a function or model that maps a text to a numerical value corresponding to a difficulty or grade level. We describe a measure of readability that uses a combination of lexical features and grammatical features that are derived from subtrees of syntactic parses. We also tested statistical models for nominal, ordinal, and interval scales of measurement. The results indicate that a model for ordinal regression, such as the proportional odds model, using a combination of grammatical and lexical features is most effective at predicting reading difficulty.

1 Introduction

A reading difficulty, or readability, measure can be described as a function or model that maps a text to a numerical value corresponding to a difficulty or grade level. Inputs to this function are usually statistics for various lexical and grammatical features of the text. The output is one of a set of ordered difficulty levels, usually corresponding to grade levels for elementary school through high school. As such, reading difficulty prediction can be viewed as a regression of grade level on a set of textual features.

Early work on readability measures employed simple proxies for grammatical and lexical complexity, including sentence length and the number of syllables in a word. Fairly simple features were often employed because of a lack of computational power. Such features exhibit high bias because they rely on strong assumptions about what makes a text difficult to read. For example, the use of sentence length as a measure of grammatical complexity assumes that a longer sentence is more grammatically complex than a shorter one, which is often but not always the case. In one early model, the Dale-Chall model (Dale and Chall, 1948; Chall and Dale, 1995), reading difficulty is a linear function of the mean sentence length and the percentage of rare words, as defined by a list of 3,000 words commonly known by 4th grade. In this paper, sentence length is defined as the mean number of words in the sentences of a text.

Many early measures did not employ direct estimates of word frequency due to computational limitations (e.g., (Gunning, 1952; McLaughlin, 1969; Kincaid et al., 1975)). Instead, these measures relied on the strong relationship between the frequency of and the number of syllables in a word. More frequent words are more likely to have fewer syllables (e.g., "the") than less frequent words (e.g., "vocabulary"), an association that is related to Zipf's Law (Zipf, 1935). The Flesch-Kincaid measure (Kincaid et al., 1975) is probably the most common reading difficulty measure in use. It is implemented in common word processing programs. This measure is a linear function of the mean number of syllables per word and the mean number of words per sentence. Klare (1974) provides a summary of other early work on readability.

More recent approaches to reading difficulty employ more sophisticated models that make use of the growth in computational power. The Lexile Framework (e.g., (Stenner, 1996)) uses individual word frequency estimates as a measure of lexical difficulty. The word frequency estimates are derived

Proceedings of the Third ACL Workshop on Innovative Use of NLP for Building Educational Applications, pages 71–79,
Columbus, Ohio, USA, June 2008.

from a large, varied corpus of text. Lexile uses a Rasch model (Rasch, 1980) with the mean log word frequency as a lexical feature and the log of the mean sentence length as a grammatical feature. The Rasch model, related to logistic regression, is used to estimate the level of a student that would comprehend 75% of a given text. The converted log odds ratio called a "Lexile" that is used as part of this measure can be easily mapped to grade school levels.

A reading difficulty measure developed by Collins-Thompson and Callan (2005) uses smoothed unigram language modeling to capture the predictive ability of individual words based on their frequency at each reading difficulty level. Collins-Thompson and Callan found that certain words were very predictive of certain levels. For example, "grownup" was very predictive of grade 1, and "essay" was very predictive of grade 12. For a given text, this measure estimates the likelihood that the text was generated by each level's language model. The prediction is the level of the model with the highest likelihood of generating the text. There are no grammatical features.

Natural language processing techniques enable more sophisticated grammatical analysis for reading difficulty measures. Rather than using sentence length as a proxy, measures can employ tools for automatic analysis of the syntactic structure of texts (e.g., (Charniak, 2000)). A measure by Schwarm and Ostendorf (2005) incorporates syntactic analyses, among a variety of other types of features. It includes four grammatical features derived from syntactic parses of text: the mean parse tree height, the mean number of noun phrases, mean number of verb phrases, and mean number of "SBARs." "SBARs" are non-terminal nodes that are associated with subordinate clauses. Their system led to better predictions than the Flesch-Kincaid and Lexile measures, but the predictive value of the grammatical features is not entirely clear. In initial experiments using such course-grain grammatical features alone, rather than in conjunction with language modeling and other features as in Schwarm and Ostendorf's system, we found relatively poor prediction performance. Our final approach using subtrees of syntactic parses allows for a finer level of discrimination that may support the detection of differences in grade levels between texts that exhibit the same high level features.

A reading difficulty measure developed by Heilman, Collins-Thompson, Callan, and Eskenazi (2007) uses the frequency of grammatical constructions as a measure of grammatical difficulty. A set of approximately twenty constructions were selected from English as a Second Language grammar textbooks. This set includes grammatical constructions such as the passive voice, relative clauses, and various verb tenses. The frequencies are used as features for a nearest neighbor classification algorithm. The unigram language modeling approach of Collins-Thompson and Callan (2005) is used to estimate lexical difficulty in this measure. The final prediction is a linear function of the lexical and grammatical components. That model assumes that grammatical difficulty is adequately captured by a small number of constructions chosen according to detailed knowledge of English grammar. In that work, the constructions were selected from an English as a Second Language grammar textbook, a labor- and knowledge-intensive task that may be less practical for other languages.

We aim to identify the appropriate scale of measurement for reading difficulty–nominal, ordinal, or interval–by comparing the effectiveness of statistical models for each type of data. We also extend previous work combining lexical and grammatical features (Heilman et al., 2007) by making it possible to include a large number of grammatical features derived from syntactic structures without requiring significant linguistic or pedagogical content knowledge, such as a reference guide for the grammar of the language of interest.

2 Types of Features

2.1 Lexical Features

This section and the following section describe the lexical and grammatical features used in our reading difficulty models. The lexical features are the relative frequencies of word unigrams. The use of word unigrams is a standard approach in text classification (Yang and Pedersen, 1997), and has also been successfully used to predict reading difficulty (Collins-Thompson and Callan, 2005). Higher order n-grams such as bigrams and trigrams were not used as features because they did not improve predictions in preliminary tests. The specific set of lexical features was chosen based on the frequencies of words in the training corpus. The system performs morphological stemming and stopword removal. The remaining 5000 most common words comprised the lexical feature set.

2.2 Grammatical Features

Grammatical features are extracted from automatic context-free grammar parses of sentences. The system computes relative frequencies of partial syntactic derivations, which will be called 'subtrees' hereafter. The approach extends (Heilman et al., 2007), where frequencies of manually defined syntactic patterns were extracted from syntactic structures. In that approach, the features are defined manually using linguistic knowledge of the target language to implement tree search patterns, a labor- and knowledge-intensive process. The approach advocated in this paper, however, extracts frequencies for an automatically defined set of subtree patterns. The system considers all subtrees up to a given depth that occur in the training corpus. Examples of grammatical features at levels 0 through 2 are shown in Figure 1. The sentence for the parse tree shown was taken from a third grade text.

For depth 0, the system includes all subtrees consisting of just nonterminal nodes. This includes all parts of speech, as well as non-terminal nodes for noun phrases, adjective phrases, clauses, etc. For depth 1, the system includes subtrees corresponding to the application of a single context free grammar rule in the derivation of the tree. An example of a feature at this level would be a sentence node that dominates nodes for noun phrases and verb phrases. For deeper levels, the system includes subtrees corresponding to the successive application of rules on non-terminals symbols until either a terminal symbol is reached or the given depth is reached. An example feature for level 2 is a subtree in which a prepositional phrase node dominates a preposition node and noun phrase node, and the preposition node in turn dominates a preposition, and the noun phrase dominates determiner, adjective, and noun nodes.

We used a maximum depth of 3 in our experiments. Features of deeper levels occur less frequently in general, and deeper levels were avoided due to data sparseness. A depth first search algorithm extracts candidate grammatical features from the training corpus. First, a context-free grammar parser (Klein and Manning, 2003) derives parse trees for all texts in the training corpus. The algorithm traverses these parses, at each node counting all subtree features up to the given depth that are rooted at that node. The subtree features are sorted by their overall counts in the corpus. In our experiments, frequencies of the most common 1000 subtrees were chosen as the final features. These included 64 level 0 features corresponding to nonterminal symbols, 334 level 1 features, 461 level 2 features, and 141 level 3 features. Deeper levels have more possible features, but sparsity at level 3 resulted in fewer level 3 features being selected.

In our experiments, the subtrees included terminal symbols for stopwords. However, the system effectively removed content word terminals from parses before extracting features. The system could be modified to include terminal symbols for content words, or even to ignore all nodes for terminal symbols. Subtree features including terminal symbols for content words would, of course, occur with low frequency and not likely be included in the final feature set. Terminal symbols for content words were omitted so that lexical information was not included in the set of grammatical features. Similar to leaving higher order n-grams out of the lexical feature set, omitting terminal symbols for content words avoids confounding grammatical and lexical information in the grammatical feature set. Subtree counts are normalized by the number of words in a text to compute the relative frequencies. Normalization by the number of sentences in a text is also possible, but did not perform as well in preliminary tests. The Stanford Parser (Klein and Manning, 2003) version 1.5.1 was used to derive tree structures for sentences. We used the unlexicalized model included in the distribution which was trained on Wall Street Journal texts.

3 Statistical Models

3.1 Scales of Measurement for Reading Difficulty

Several statistical models were tested for effectiveness at predicting reading difficulty. The appropriateness of these models depends on the nature of

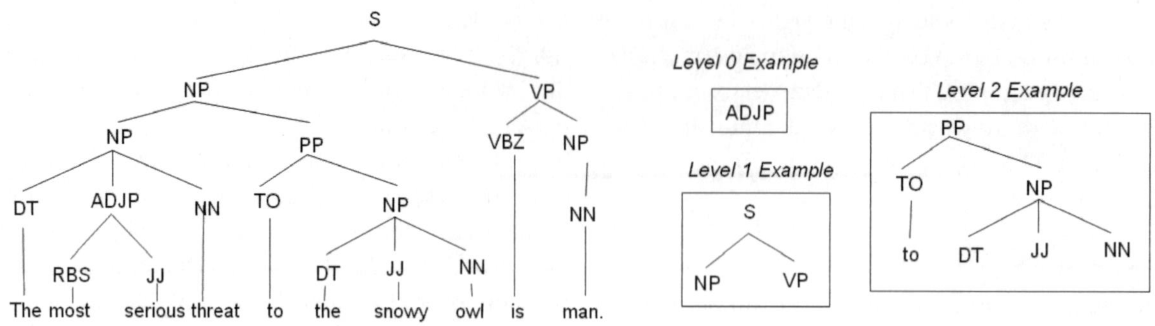

Figure 1: Parse Tree for Sentence from Third Grade Text with Example Subtree Features.

reading difficulty data, particularly the scale of measurement. The standard unit for reading difficulty is the grade level. First through twelfth grade levels in American schools have been used in previous work (e.g., (Heilman et al., 2007; Collins-Thompson and Callan, 2005)). English as a Second Language levels have also been used (Heilman et al., 2007), as well as grade levels for other languages such as French (Collins-Thompson and Callan, 2005). While these grades are assigned evenly spaced integers, the ranges of reading difficulty corresponding to these grades are not necessarily evenly spaced. It is possible, of course, that assuming even spacing between levels might produce more parsimonious and accurate statistical models. A more reasonable assumption is that the grade numbers assigned to each difficulty level denote an ordering: for example, that grade 1 is in some sense less than grade 2, which is less than grade 3, etc. Different statistical models handle this assumption more or less well.

Statistics generally distinguish four scales of measurement, which are, ordered by increasing assumptions about the relationships between values: nominal, ordinal, interval, and ratio (Stevens, 1946; Cohen et al., 2003). *Nominal* data involve no relationships between the labels or classes of the data. An example would be types of fruits, where a model might be used to make decisions between apples and oranges. This type of prediction is generally called classification in machine learning and related fields. *Ordinal* data have a natural ordering, but the values are not necessarily evenly spaced. For example, data about the severity of illnesses might have labels such as mild, moderate, severe, deceased, in which the transitions between consecutive classes all have the same direction but not the same magnitude. Making predictions about such data is generally called ordinal regression (McCullagh, 1980). *Interval data*, however, are both ordered and evenly spaced. An example would be temperature as measured in Fahrenheit degrees. Such data have an arbitrary zero point, and negative values may occur. *Ratio* data, of which annual income is an example, do have a meaningful zero point. We will not discuss ratio data further since its distinction from interval data is not relevant to this paper. It is not clear to which scale reading difficulty corresponds. The assumption of an interval scale allows for simpler models with fewer parameters. However, models for ordinal or even nominal data might be more appropriate if the strong assumption of an interval scale does not hold.

We experimented with three linear and log-linear models corresponding to interval, ordinal, and nominal data. Parameters were estimated using L_2 regularization, which corresponds to a Gaussian prior distribution with zero mean and a user-specified variance over the parameters. We chose these models because they are commonly used in the statistics, machine learning, and behavioral science communities, and aimed to set up meaningful comparisons among the scales of measurement. Other machine learning algorithms might also be employed. In fact, we briefly tested the maximum margin (Vapnik, 1995) approach, which led to comparable results and might be worth exploring in future work.

3.2 Linear Regression

Linear Regression (LIN) produces a linear model in which the dependent, or outcome, variable is a linear function of the values for predictor variables, or features. A prediction for a given text is the inner product of a vector of feature values for the text and a vector of regression coefficients estimated from training data. For the case of reading difficulty, the grade level is a linear combination of the lexical and/or grammatical feature values. LIN provides continuous estimates of reading difficulty, such that a prediction might fall between grade levels. The estimates were not rounded to whole numbers in the experiments. For rare cases of an LIN prediction falling outside the appropriate range of grade levels, the value was set to the maximum or minimum grade level. LIN implicitly assumes that the data fall on an interval scale, meaning that the levels are evenly spaced. The LIN model has relatively few parameters but makes strong assumptions about the scale of measurement. For details, see (Hastie et al., 2001).

3.3 Proportional Odds Model

The Proportional Odds (PO) model, also called the parallel regression model and the cumulative logit model, is a form of log-linear, or exponential, model for ordinal data (McCullagh, 1980). Given a new unlabeled instance as input, the model provides estimates of the probability that the instance belongs to a class at or above a particular level. In Equation (1), $P(y \geq j)$ is this estimated probability, α_j is an intercept parameter for the given level j, β is vector of regression coefficients, X_i is the vector of feature values for instance i, and y_i is the predicted reading difficulty level.

$$P(y_i \geq j) = \frac{exp(\alpha_j + \beta^T X_i)}{1 + exp(\alpha_j + \beta^T X_i)} \quad (1)$$

$$ln\frac{P(y_i \geq j)}{1 - P(y_i \geq j)} = \alpha_j + \beta^T X_i \quad (2)$$

The PO model has a parameter α_j for the threshold, or intercept, at each level j, but only a single set β of parameters for the features. These two types of parameters correspond to an implicit assumption of ordinality. Having a single set of parameters for features across the levels means that changes in feature values proportionally affect the odds of transitioning from any one class to another.

The estimated probability of an instance belonging to a particular class is the difference between estimates for that class and the next highest class. For example, the estimated probability of a text being at the eighth grade level would be the estimate for being at or above eighth grade minus the estimate for being at or above ninth grade. As in binary logistic regression, the PO model estimates log odds ratios based on the values of features or predictor variables. The numerator of the odds ratio is the probability of being at or above a level, and the denominator is the probability of being below a level. Equation (2) shows the form of the model that is linear in the parameters.

3.4 Multi-class Logistic Regression

Multi-class Logistic Regression (LOG), or multinomial logit regression, is a log-linear model for nominal data. In contrast to the simpler PO model, the model maintains parameters for all of the features for every class except one category, which is used for comparison. Thus, for reading difficulty, there are about 11 times as many parameters to estimate compared to LIN and PO. The increased difficulty of parameter estimation for this model is offset for domains in which assumptions of ordinality or linearity do not hold. For more details, see (Hastie et al., 2001).

4 Evaluation

4.1 Web Corpus

The corpus of materials used for training and testing the models consists of the content text extracted from Web pages with reading difficulty level labels. Web pages were used because the system for predicting reading difficulty is being used as part of the REAP tutoring system, which finds authentic and appropriate Web pages for English vocabulary practice (Brown and Eskenazi, 2004; Heilman et al., 2006). Approximately half of these texts were authored by students at the particular grade level, and half were authored by teachers or writers and aimed at readers at a particular grade level. Texts were found for grade levels 1 through 12. The twelfth grade level also included some post-secondary level texts. Various genres and subjects were represented. In all cases, either the text itself or a link to it identified it as having a certain level. The content text was manually extracted from these Web pages so that noisy information such as navigation menus and advertisements were not included. Automatic content extraction may, however, be able to remove such noisy information without human intervention (e.g., (Gupta et al., 2003)). This Web corpus is adapted from the corpora used in prior work on reading difficulty predication (Collins-Thompson and Callan, 2005; Heilman et al., 2007). We modified that corpus because it contained a number of documents pertaining to mathematics and vocabulary practice. The majority of tokens in these texts were not part of well-formed, grammatical sentences suitable for reading practice. Since our goal is to measure the difficulty of reading passages, we removed these documents and added additional texts consisting of more suitable reading material. The corpus consisted of approximately 150,000 words, distributed among 289 texts. The number of texts for each grade level was approximately the same, with at least 28 texts at each level. The mean length in words of the texts was approximately 500 words, which corresponds to about a page. Texts for lower grades were necessarily shorter. We extracted excerpts for higher level texts so that texts were otherwise roughly equal in length across levels. For these excerpts, the first 500 or so words of text were extracted, while respecting sentence and paragraph boundaries.

4.2 Evaluation Metrics

Root mean square error (RMSE), Pearson's correlation coefficient, and accuracy within 1 grade level served as metrics for evaluating the performance of reading difficulty predictions. Multiple statistics were used because it is not entirely clear what the best measure of prediction quality is for reading difficulty. RMSE is the square root of the empirical mean of the squared error of predictions. It more strongly penalizes those errors that are further away from the true value. It can be interpreted as the average number of grade levels that predictions measure deviate from human-assigned labels.

Pearson's correlation coefficient measures the strength of the linear relationship, or similarity of trends, between two random variables. A high correlation would indicate that difficult texts would more likely receive high predicted difficulty values, and easier texts would be more likely to receive low predicted difficulty values. Correlations do not, however, measure the degree to which values match in absolute terms.

Adjacent accuracy is the proportion of predictions that were within one grade level of the human-assigned label for the given text. Exact accuracy is too stringent a measure because the human-assigned reading levels are not always perfect and consistent. For example, one school might read "Romeo and Juliet" in 9th grade while another school might read it in 10th grade. The drawback of this accuracy metric is that predictions that are two levels off are treated the same as predictions that are ten levels off.

4.3 Baselines

The performance of other algorithms for estimating reading difficulty was estimated using the same data. These comparison include Collins-Thompson and Callan's implementation of their language modeling approach (2005), an implementation of the Flesch-Kincaid reading level measure (Kincaid et al., 1975), and a measure using word frequency and sentence length similar to Lexile (Stenner et al., 1983). We did not directly test the approach described by (Heilman et al., 2007). We observe that its reported results for first language texts were not significantly different in terms of correlation and only slightly better in terms of mean squared error than the language modeling approach. Finally, a simple uniform baseline, which always chose the middle value of 6.5, was tested.

The Lexile-like measure (LX) used the same two features as the Lexile measure: mean log frequency or words and log mean sentence length. Instead of using a Rasch model and converting scores to "Lexiles," however, the PO model was used to directly predict grade levels. The log frequency values for words were estimated from the second release of the American National Corpus (Reppen et al., 2005), a 20 million word corpus with texts in American English from different genres on a variety of subjects. Using the proportional odds models is effectively equivalent to using Lexile's Rasch model and mapping its output to grade levels. The major difference between the Lexile measure and the implementation used in these experiments is the training data sets used to estimated word frequencies and model parameters.

4.4 Procedure

The Web Corpus was randomly split into training and test sets. The test set consisted of 25% of the individual texts at each level, a total of 84 texts. Ten-fold stratified cross-validation on the training set was employed to estimate the prediction performance according to the evaluation metrics. In cross-validation, data are partitioned randomly into a given number of folds, and each fold is used for testing while all others are used for training. For more details and a discussion of validation methods, see (Hastie et al., 2001). The regularization hyper-parameters were tuned on the training set during cross-validation by a simple grid search. After cross-validation, models were trained on the entire training set, and then evaluated using the held-out test data.

We tested whether each feature-set, algorithm pair or baseline performed significantly differently than our hypothesized best model, the PO model with the combined feature set. We employed the bias-corrected and accelerated (BC_a) Bootstrap (Efron and Tibshirani, 1993) with 50,000 replications of the held-out test data to generate confidence intervals for differences in evaluation results. If the $(1-\alpha)\%$ confidence intervals for the difference do not contain zero, which is the value corresponding to the null hypothesis, then that difference is significant at the α level. For example, the 99% confidence interval for the difference in adjacent accuracy between the language modeling baseline and the PO model with the combined feature set was (-1.86, -0.336), indicating that this difference is significant at the .01 level since it does not contain zero.

5 Results

Table 1 presents correlation coefficients, RMSE values, and accuracy values for cross-validation and held-out test data. Statistical significance was tested only for the held-out test data since the hyper-parameters were tuned during cross-validation. Our discussion of the results pertains mostly to the evaluation on the test-set.

Of the various statistical models, the PO model for ordinal data appears to provide superior performance over the LIN and LOG models. Compared to the LOG model, the PO model performs significantly better in terms of correlation and RMSE and comparably well in terms of adjacent accuracy. Compared to the LIN model, the PO model performs almost as well in terms of correlation, comparably well in terms of RMSE, and far better in terms of accuracy.

The performance of the methods when using different feature sets does not clearly indicate a best set of features to use for predicting reading difficulty. For the PO model, none of the feature sets lead to significant gains over the others in terms of any of the metrics. However, the combined feature set led to the best performance in terms of correlation and adjacent accuracy during cross-validation as well as RMSE on the test set, suggesting at the very least that including the extra features does not degrade performance.

The PO model with the combined feature set outperformed most of the baseline measures. LX had the same accuracy value on the test set. The LX method appears to perform the best in general of the baselines models. Interestingly, LX uses proportional odds logistic regression like PO, and thus assumes an ordinal but not interval scale of measurement. RMSE values were significantly lower for the PO model than for LX and the language modeling approach.

No statistically significant advantages are seen for PO model when compared to Flesch-Kincaid. We observe however, that for the sample of web pages which constitutes the evaluation corpus the PO model produced superior results across evaluation metrics. That is, PO performed better in terms of adjacent accuracy, RMSE, and correlation coefficients, both in cross-validation and testing with held-out data.

6 Discussion

In our tests, the PO model, which assumes ordinal data, lead to the most effective predictions of reading difficulty in general. This result indicates that the reading difficulty of texts, according to grade level, lies on an ordinal scale of measurement. That is,

Method	Features	Cross-Validation			Held-Out Test Set		
		Correl.	**RMSE**	**Adj. Acc.**	**Correl.**	**RMSE**	**Adj. Acc.**
LIN	Lexical	.629	2.73	.242	.779	2.42	.167**
	Grammatical	.767	2.26	.294	.753	2.33	.274*
	Combined	.679	2.57	.284	**.819****	**2.21**	.226**
PO	Lexical	.713	2.57	.498	.780	2.29	.464
	Grammatical	.762	**2.22**	.505	.734	2.42	**.560**
	Combined	**.773**	2.24	**.519**	.767	2.23	.440
LOG	Lexical	.517	3.24	.443	.619*	2.83*	.548
	Grammatical	.632	2.87	.443	.506**	3.38**	.464
	Combined	.582	2.94	.446	.652*	2.71*	.556
LX	-	.659	2.77	.467	.731	2.67*	.464
Lang. Modeling	-	.590	2.74	.370	.630	2.70**	.381
Flesch-Kincaid	-	.697	2.66	.388	.718	2.54	.369
Uniform	-	.000	3.39	.170	.000**	3.45**	.167**

Table 1: Results from Cross-Validation and Test Set Evaluations, as measured by Correlation Coefficients (Correl.), Root Mean Square Error (RMSE), and Adjacent Accuracy. The best result for each metric for each evaluation is given in bold. Asterisks indicate significant differences compared to the PO model with a Combined Feature Set. * = $p < .05$, ** = $p < .01$.

reading difficulty appears to increase steadily but not linearly with grade level. As such, the LIN approach that produces linear models was less effective, particularly in terms of adjacent accuracy. The LOG model, for nominal data, also led to inferior performance compared to the PO model, which can be attributed to the difficulty of accurately estimating a more complex model with many parameters for each level.

Our tests found that grammatical features alone can be effective predictors of readability. This finding disagrees with a previous result that found that a model using a combination of lexical and manually defined grammatical features (Heilman et al., 2007) outperformed a model using grammatical features alone. The superior predictive ability of the models we describe that use grammatical features can be attributed to the automatic derivation of a grammatical feature set that is more than an order of magnitude larger than in the previous approach. Our approach enables the use of much larger grammatical feature sets because it does not require the extensive linguistic knowledge and effort to manually define the grammatical features. The automatic approach also enables an easier transition to other languages, assuming a parser is available. Using the combined feature set did not hurt performance, however, and since regularized statistical models can avoid overfitting large numbers of parameters, a combined feature set still seems appropriate.

Acknowledgments

We thank Jamie Callan for his comments and suggestions. This research was supported in part by the Institute of Education Sciences, U.S. Department of Education, through Grant R305B040063 to Carnegie Mellon University; Dept. of Education grant R305G03123; the Pittsburgh Science of Learning Center which is funded by the National Science Foundation, award number SBE-0354420; and a National Science Foundation Graduate Research Fellowship awarded to the first author. Any opinions, findings, conclusions, or recommendations expressed in this material are the authors, and do not necessarily reflect those of the sponsors.

References

Jon Brown and Maxine Eskenazi. 2004. Retrieval of authentic documents for reader-specific lexical practice. *Proceedings of InSTIL/ICALL Symposium 2004.*

J. S. Chall and E. Dale. 1995. *Readability Revisited: The New Dale-Chall Readability Formula*. Brookline Books. Cambridge, MA.

Eugene Charniak. 2000. A maximum-entropy-inspired parser. *Proceedings of the NAACL.*

J. Cohen, P. Cohen, S. G. West, and L. S. Aiken. 2003. *Applied Multiple Regression/Correlation Analysis for the Behavioral Sciences, 3rd Edition*. Lawrence Erlbaum Associates, Inc.

Michael Collins and Nigel Duffy. 2002. Convolution Kernels for Natural Language. *Advances in Neural Information Processing Systems..*

Kevyn Collins-Thompson and Jamie Callan. 2005. Predicting reading difficulty with statistical language models. *Journal of the American Society for Information Science and Technology, 56(13). pp. 1448-1462..*

E. Dale and J. S. Chall. 1948. A Formula for Predicting Readability. *Educational Research Bulletin Vol. 27, No. 1.*

Bradley Efron and Robert J. Tibshirani. 1993. *An Introduction to the Bootstrap*. Chapman and Hall, New York.

R. Gunning. 1952. *The technique of clear writing..* McGraw-Hill, New York.

S. Gupta, G. Kaiser, D. Neistadt, and P. Grimm. 2003. *DOM-based content extraction of HTML documents.* ACM Press, New York.

Trevor Hastie, Robert Tibshirani, Jerome Friedman. 2003. *The Elements of Statistical Learning:Data Mining, Inference, and Prediction*. Springer.

Michael Heilman, Kevyn Collins-Thompson, Jamie Callan, and Maxine Eskenazi. 2007. Combining Lexical and Grammatical Features to Improve Readability Measures for First and Second Language Texts. *Proceedings of the Human Language Technology Conference*. Rochester, NY.

Michael Heilman, Kevyn Collins-Thompson, Jamie Callan, and Maxine Eskenazi. 2006. Classroom success of an Intelligent Tutoring System for lexical practice and reading comprehension. *Proceedings of the Ninth International Conference on Spoken Language Processing*. Pittsburgh, PA.

J. Kincaid, R. Fishburne, R. Rodgers, and B. Chissom. 1975. Derivation of new readability formulas for navy enlisted personnel. *Branch Report 8-75.* Chief of Naval Training, Millington, TN.

G. R. Klare. 1974. Assessing Readability. *Reading Research Quarterly, Vol. 10, No. 1. pp. 62-102..*

Dan Klein and Christopher D. Manning. 2003. Accurate Unlexicalized Parsing. *Proceedings of the 41st Meeting of the Association for Computational Linguistics, pp. 423-430.*

G. H. McLaughlin. 1969. SMOG grading: A new readability formula. *Journal of Reading.*

P. McCullagh. 1980. Regression Models for Ordinal Data. *Journal of the Royal Statistical Society. Series B (Methodological), Vol. 42, No. 2. pp. 109-142.*

G. Rasch. 1980. *Probabilistic Models for Some Intelligence and Attainment Tests.* MESA Press, Chicago, IL.

G. Rasch. 2005. *American National Corpus (ANC) Second Release..* Linguistic Data Consortium. Philadelphia, PA.

Sarah Schwarm and Mari Ostendorf. 2005. Reading level assessment using support vector machines and statistical language models. *Proceedings of the 43rd Annual Meeting on Association for Computational Linguistics.*

A. J. Stenner, M. Smith, and D. S. Burdick. 1983. Toward a Theory of Construct Definition. *Journal of Educational Measurement, Vol. 20, No. 4. pp. 305-316.*

A. J. Stenner. 1996. Measuring reading comprehension with the Lexile framework. *Fourth North American Conference on Adolescent/Adult Literacy.*

S. S. Stevens. 1946. On the theory of scales of measurement. *Science, 103, pp. 677-680.*

V. N. Vapnik. 1995. *The Nature of Statistical Learning Theory*. Springer.

Y. Yang and J. P. Pedersen. 1997. A Comparative Study on Feature Selection in Text Categorization. *Proceedings of the Fourteenth International Conference on Machine Learning (ICML'97), pp. 412-420.*

G. K. Zipf. 1935. *The Psychobiology off Language.* Houghton Mifflin, Boston, MA.

Retrieval of Reading Materials for Vocabulary and Reading Practice

Michael Heilman, Le Zhao, Juan Pino and **Maxine Eskenazi**
Language Technologies Institute
Carnegie Mellon University
Pittsburgh, PA 15213, USA
{mheilman,lezhao,jmpino,max}@cs.cmu.edu

Abstract

Finding appropriate, authentic reading materials is a challenge for language instructors. The Web is a vast resource of texts, but most pages are not suitable for reading practice, and commercial search engines are not well suited to finding texts that satisfy pedagogical constraints such as reading level, length, text quality, and presence of target vocabulary. We present a system that uses various language technologies to facilitate the retrieval and presentation of authentic reading materials gathered from the Web. It is currently deployed in two English as a Second Language courses at the University of Pittsburgh.

1 Introduction

Reading practice is an important component of first and second language learning, especially with regards to vocabulary learning (Hafiz and Tudor, 1989). Appropriating suitable reading material for the needs of a particular curriculum or particular student, however, is a challenging process. Manually authoring or editing readings is time-consuming and raises issues of authenticity, which are particularly significant in second language learning (Peacock, 1997). On the other hand, the Web is a vast resource of authentic reading material, but commercial search engines which are designed for a wide variety of information needs may not effectively facilitate the retrieval of appropriate readings for language learners.

In order to demonstrate the problem of finding appropriate reading materials, here is a typical example of an information need from a teacher of an English as a Second Language (ESL) course focused on reading skills. This example was encountered during the development of the system. It should be noted that while we describe the system in the context of ESL, we claim that the approach is general enough to be applied to first language reading practice and to languages other than English. To fit within his existing curriculum, the ESL teacher wanted to find texts on the specific topic of "international travel." He sought texts that contained at least a few words from the list of target vocabulary that his student were learning that week. In addition, he needed the texts to be within a particular range of reading difficulty, fifth to eighth grade in an American school, and shorter than a thousand words.

Sending the query "international travel" to a popular search engine did not produce a useful list of results[1]. The first result was a travel warning from the Department of State[2], which was at a high reading level (grade 10 according to the approach described by (Heilman et al., 2008)) and not likely to be of interest to ESL students because of legal and technical details. Most of the subsequent results were for commercial web sites and travel agencies. A query for a subset of the target vocabulary words for the course also produced poor results. Since the search engine used strict boolean retrieval methods, the top results for the query "deduce deviate hierarchy implicit undertake" were all long lists of ESL vocabulary words[3].

We describe a search system, called REAP Search, that is tailored to the needs of language

[1] www.google.com, March 5, 2008

[2] http://travel.state.gov/travel/cis_pa_tw/cis_pa_tw_1168.html

[3] e.g., www.espindle.org/university_word_list_uwl.html

Proceedings of the Third ACL Workshop on Innovative Use of NLP for Building Educational Applications, pages 80–88,
Columbus, Ohio, USA, June 2008.

teachers and learners. The system facilitates the retrieval of texts satisfying particular pedagogical constraints such as reading level and text length, and allows the user to constrain results so that they contain at least some, but not necessarily all, of the words from a user-specified target vocabulary list. It also filters out inappropriate material as well as pages that do not contain significant amounts of text in well-formed sentences. The system provides support for learners including an interface for reading texts, easy access to dictionary definitions, and vocabulary exercises for practice and review.

The educational application employs multiple language technologies to achieve its various goals. Information retrieval and web search technologies provide the core components. Automated text classifiers organize potential readings by general topic area and reading difficulty. We are also developing an approach to measuring reading difficulty that uses a parser to extract grammatical structures. Part of Speech (POS) tagging is used to filter web pages to maintain text quality.

2 Path of a Reading

In the REAP Search system, reading materials take a path from the Web to students through various intermediate steps as depicted in Figure 1. First, a crawling program issues queries to large-scale commercial search engines to retrieve candidate documents. These documents are annotated, filtered, and stored in a digital library, or corpus. This digital library creation process is done offline. A customized search interface facilitates the retrieval of useful reading materials by teachers, who have particular curricular goals and constraints as part of their information needs. The teachers organize their selected readings through a curriculum manager. The reading interface for students accesses the curriculum manager's database and provides the texts along with support in the form of dictionary definitions and practice exercises.

3 Creating a Digital Library of Readings

The foundation of the system is a digital library of potential reading material. The customized search component does not search the Web directly, but rather accesses this filtered and annotated database of Web pages. The current library consists of approximately five million documents. Construction of the digital library begins with a set of target vocabulary words that might be covered by a course or set of courses (typically 100-1,500 words), and a set of constraints on text characteristics. The constraints can be divided into three sets: those that can be expressed in a search engine query (e.g., target words, number of target words per text, date, Web domain), those that can be applied using just information in the Web search result list (e.g., document size), and those that require local annotation and filtering (e.g., reading level, text quality, profanity).

The system obtains candidate documents by query-based crawling, as opposed to following chains of links. The query-based document crawling approach is designed to download documents for particular target words. Queries are submitted to a commercial Web search engine[4], result links are downloaded, and then the corresponding documents are downloaded. A commercial web search engine is used to avoid the cost of maintaining a massive, overly general web corpus.

Queries consist of combinations of multiple target words. The system generates 30 queries for each target word (30 is a manageable and sufficient number in practice). These are spread across 2-, 3-, and 4-word combinations with other target words. Queries to search engines can often specify a date range. We employ ranges to find more recent material, which students prefer. The tasks of submitting queries, downloading the result pages, and extracting document links are distributed among a dozen or so clients running on desktop machines, to run as background tasks. The clients periodically upload their results to a server, and request a new batch of queries.

Once the server has a list of candidate pages, it downloads them and applies various filters. The final yield of texts is typically approximately one percent of the originally downloaded results. Many web pages are too long, contain too little well-formed text, or are far above the appropriate reading level for language learners. After downloading documents, the system annotates them as described in the next section. It then stores the pages in a full-

[4]www.altavista.com

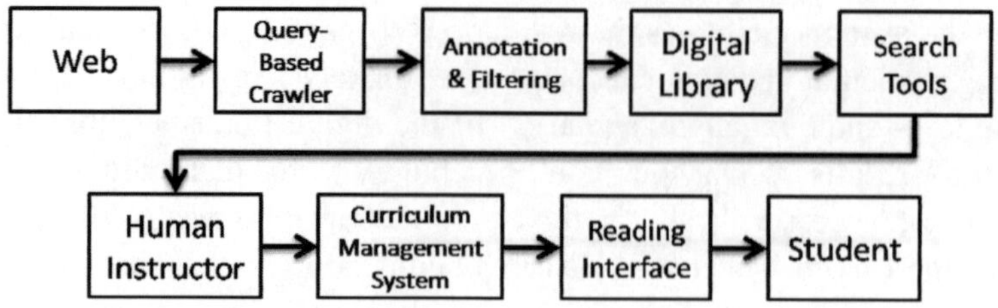

Figure 1: Path of Reading Materials from the Web to a Student.

text search engine called Indri, which is part of the Lemur Toolkit[5]. This index provides a consistent and efficient interface to the documents. Using Lemur and the Indri Query Language allows for the retrieval of annotated documents according to user-specified constraints.

4 Annotations and Filters

Annotators automatically tag the documents in the corpus to enable the filtering and retrieval of reading material that matches user-specified pedagogical constraints. Annotations include reading difficulty, general topic area, text quality, and text length. Text length is simply the number of word tokens appearing in the document.

4.1 Reading Level

The system employs a language modeling approach developed by Collins-Thompson and Callan (Collins-Thompson and Callan, 2005) that creates a model of the lexicon for each grade level and predicts reading level, or readability, of given documents according to those models. The readability predictor is a specialized Naive Bayes classifier with lexical unigram features. For web documents in particular, Collins-Thompson and Callan report that this language modeling-based prediction has a stronger correlation with human-assigned levels than other commonly used readability measures. This automatic readability measure allows the system to satisfy user-specified constraints on reading difficulty.

We are also experimenting with using syntactic features to predict reading difficulty. Heilman, Collins-Thompson, and Eskenazi (Heilman et al., 2008) describe an approach that combines predictions based on lexical and grammatical features. The grammatical features are frequencies of occurrence of grammatical constructions, which are computed from automatic parses of input texts. Using multiple measures of reading difficulty that focus on different aspects of language may allow users more freedom to find texts that match their needs. For example, a teacher may want to find grammatically simpler texts for use in a lesson focused on introducing difficult vocabulary.

4.2 General Topic Area

A set of binary topic classifiers automatically classifies each potential reading by its general topic, as described by Heilman, Juffs, and Eskenazi (2007). This component allows users to search for readings on their general interests without specifying a particular query (e.g., "international travel") that might unnecessarily constrain the results to a very narrow topic.

A Linear Support Vector Machine text classifier (Joachims, 1999) was trained on Web pages from the Open Directory Project (ODP)[6]. These pages effectively have human-assigned topic labels because they are organized into a multi-level hierarchy of topics. The following general topics were manually selected from categories in the ODP: Movies and Theater; Music; Visual Arts; Computers and Technology; Business; Math, Physics and Chemistry; Biology and Environment; Social Sciences; Health and Medicine; Fitness and Nutrition; Religion; Politics; Law and Crime; History; American Sports; and Outdoor Recreation.

Web pages from the ODP were used as gold-standard labels in the training data for the classifiers. SVM-Light (Joachims, 1999) was used as an implementation of the Support Vector Machines. In preliminary tests, the linear kernel produced slightly

[5] www.lemurproject.org

[6] dmoz.org

better performance than a radial basis function kernel. The values of the decision functions of the classifiers for each topic are used to annotate readings with their likely topics.

The binary classifiers for each topic category were evaluated according to the F1 measure, the harmonic mean of precision and recall, using leave-one-out cross-validation. Values for the $F1$ statistic range from .68 to .86, with a mean value of .76 across topics. For comparison, random guessing would be expected to correctly choose the gold-standard label only ten percent of the time. During an error analysis, we observed that many of the erroneous classifications were, in fact, plausible for a human to make as well. Many readings span multiple topics. For example, a document on a hospital merger might be classified as "Health and Medicine" when the correct label is "Business." In the evaluation, the gold standard included only the single topic specified by the ODP. The final system, however, assigns multiple topic labels when appropriate.

4.3 Text Quality

A major challenge of using Web documents for educational applications is that many web pages contain little or no text in well-formed sentences and paragraphs. We refer to this problem as "Text Quality." Many pages consist of lists of links, navigation menus, multimedia, tables of numerical data, etc. A special annotation tool filters out such pages so that they do not clutter up search results and make it difficult for users to find suitable reading materials.

The text quality filter estimates the proportion of the word tokens in a page that are contained in well-formed sentences. To do this it parses the Document Object Model structure of the web page, and organizes it into text units delineated by the markup tags in the document. Each new paragraph, table element, span, or divider markup tag corresponds to the beginning of a new text unit. The system then runs a POS tagger[7] over each text unit. We have found that a simple check for whether the text unit contains both a noun and a verb can effectively distinguish between content text units and those text units that are just part of links, menus, etc. The proportion of the total tokens that are part of content text units serves as a useful measure of text quality. We have found that a threshold of about 85% content text is appropriate, since most web pages contain at least some non-content text in links, menus, etc. This approach to content extraction is related to previous work on increasing the accessibility of web pages (Gupta et al., 2003).

[7]The OpenNLP toolkit's tagger was used (opennlp.sourceforge.net).

5 Constructing Queries

Users search for readings in the annotated corpus through a simple interface that appears similar to, but extends the functionality of, the interfaces for commercial web search engines. Figure 2 shows a screenshot of the interface. Users have the option to specify *ad hoc* queries in a text field. They can also use drop down menus to specify optional minimum and/or maximum reading levels and text lengths. Another optional drop-down menu allows users to constrain the general topic area of results. A separate screen allows users to specify a list of target vocabulary words, some but not all of which are required to appear in the search results. For ease of use, the target word list is stored for an entire session (i.e., until the web browser application is closed) rather than specified with each query. After the user submits a query, the system displays multiple results per screen with titles and snippets.

5.1 Ranked versus Boolean Retrieval

In a standard boolean retrieval model, with *AND* as the default operator, the results list consists of documents that contain all query terms. In conjunction with relevance ranking techniques, commercial search engines typically use this model, a great advantage of which is speed. Boolean retrieval can encounter problems when queries have many terms because every one of the terms must appear in a document for it to be selected. In such cases, few or no satisfactory results may be retrieved. This issue is relevant because a teacher might want to search for texts that contain some, but not necessarily all, of a list of target vocabulary words. For example, a teacher might have a list of ten words, and any text with five of those words would be useful to give as vocabulary and reading practice. In such cases, ranked retrieval models are more appropriate be-

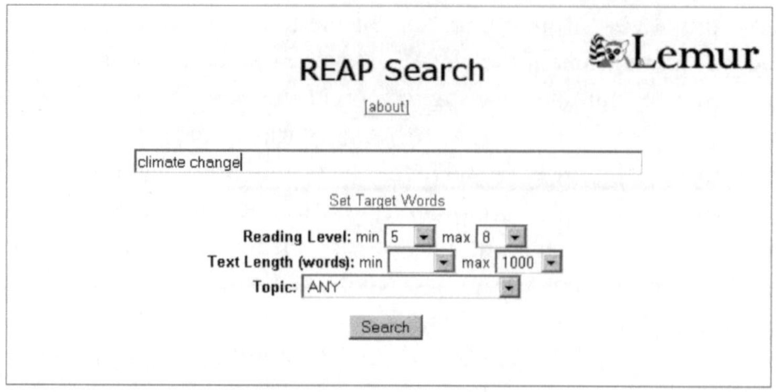

Figure 2: Screenshot of Search Interface for Finding Appropriate Readings.

cause they do not require that all of the query terms appear. Instead, these models prefer multiple occurrences of different word types as opposed to multiple occurrences of the same word tokens, allowing them to rank documents with more distinct query terms higher than those with distinct query terms. Documents that contain only some of the query terms are thus assigned nonzero weights, allowing the user to find useful texts that contain only some of the target vocabulary. The REAP search system uses the Indri Query Language's "combine" and "weight" operators to implement a ranked retrieval model for target vocabulary. For more information on text retrieval models, see (Manning et al., 2008).

5.2 Example Query

Figure 3 shows an example of a structured query produced by the system from a teacher's original query and constraints. This example was slightly altered from its original form for clarity of presentation. The first line with the *filrej* operator filters and rejects any documents that contain any of a long list of words considered to be profanity, which are omitted in the illustration for brevity and posterity. The *filreq* operator in line 2 requires that all of the constraints on reading level, text length and quality in lines 2-4 are met. The *weight* operator at the start of line 5 balances between the *ad hoc* query terms in line 5 and the user-specific target vocabulary terms in lines 6-8. The *uw10* operator on line 5 tells the system to prefer texts where the query terms appear together in an unordered window of size 10. Such proximity operators cause search engines to prefer documents in which query terms appear near each other. The implicit assumption is that the terms in queries such as "coal miners safety" are more likely to appear in the same sentence or paragraph in relevant documents than irrelevant ones, even if they do not appear consecutively. Importantly, query terms are separated from target words because there are usually a much greater number of target words, and thus combining the two sets would often result in the query terms being ignored. The higher weight assigned to the set of target words ensures they are not ignored.

6 Learner and Teacher Support

In addition to search facilities, the system provides extensive support for students to read and learn from texts as well as support for teachers to track students' progress. All interfaces are web-based for easy access and portability. Teachers use the search system to find readings, which are stored in a curriculum manager that allows them to organize their selected texts. The manager interface allows teachers to perform tasks such as specifying the order of presentation of their selected readings, choosing target words to be highlighted in the texts to focus learner attention, and specifying time limits for each text.

The list of available readings are shown to students when they log in during class time or for homework. Students select a text to read and move on to the reading interface, which is illustrated in Figure 4. The chosen web page is displayed in its original format except that the original hyperlinks and pop-ups are disabled. Target words that were

```
#filrej( #syn( PROFANITY HERE )
   #filreq( #band(#greater(textquality 85)
                  #greater(readinglevel 6) #less(readinglevel 9)
                  #greater(doclength 300) #less(doclength 1000))
                  #weight(1  #combine(business ethics) 1 #uw10(business ethics)
                         10 #combine(motive amend manipulate mutual pursue
                              equivalent sole implement exploit neutral
                              utilize primary sector framework extract))))
```

Figure 3: Example Structured Query. The line numbers on the left are for reference only.

chosen by the teacher are highlighted and linked to definitions. Students may also click on any other unknown words to access definitions. The dictionary definitions are provided from the Cambridge Advanced Learner's Dictionary[8], which is authored specifically for ESL learners. All dictionary access is logged, and teachers can easily see which words students look up.

The system also provides vocabulary exercises after each reading for additional practice and review of target words. Currently, students complete cloze, or fill-in-the-blank, exercises for each target word in the readings. Other types of exercises are certainly possible. For extra review, students also complete exercises for target words from previous readings. Students receive immediate feedback on the practice and review exercises. Currently, sets of the exercises are manually authored for each target word and stored in a database, but we are exploring automated question generation techniques (Brown et al., 2005; Liu et al., 2005). At runtime, the system selects practice and review exercises from this repository.

7 Related Work

A number of recent projects have taken similar approaches to providing authentic texts for language learners. WERTi (Amaral et al., 2006) is an intelligent automatic workbook that uses texts from the Web to increase knowledge of English grammatical forms and functions. READ-X (Miltsakaki and Troutt, 2007) is a tool for finding texts at specified reading levels. SourceFinder (Sheehan et al., 2007) is an authoring tool for finding suitable texts for standardized test items on verbal reasoning and reading comprehension.

The REAP Tutor (Brown and Eskenazi, 2004; Heilman et al., 2006) for ESL vocabulary takes a slightly different approach. Rather than teachers choosing texts as in the REAP Search system, the REAP Tutor itself selects individualized practice readings from a digital library. The readings contain target vocabulary words that a given student needs to learn based on a student model. While the individualized REAP Tutor has the potential to better match the needs of each student since each student can work with different texts, a drawback of its approach is that instructors may have difficulty coordinating group discussion about readings and integrating the Tutor into their curriculum. In the REAP Search system, however, teachers can find texts that match the needs and interests of the class as a whole. While some degree of individualization is lost, the advantages of better coordinated support from teachers and classroom integration are gained.

8 Pilot Study

8.1 Description

Two teachers and over fifty students in two ESL courses at the University of Pittsburgh used the system as part of a pilot study in the Spring of 2008. The courses focus on developing the reading skills of high-intermediate ESL learners. The target vocabulary words covered in the courses come from the Academic Word List (Coxhead, 2000), a list of broad-coverage, general purpose English words that frequently appear in academic writing. Students used the system once per week in a fifty-minute class for eight weeks. For approximately half of a session, students read the teacher-selected readings and worked through individualized practice exercises.

[8] dictionary.cambridge.org

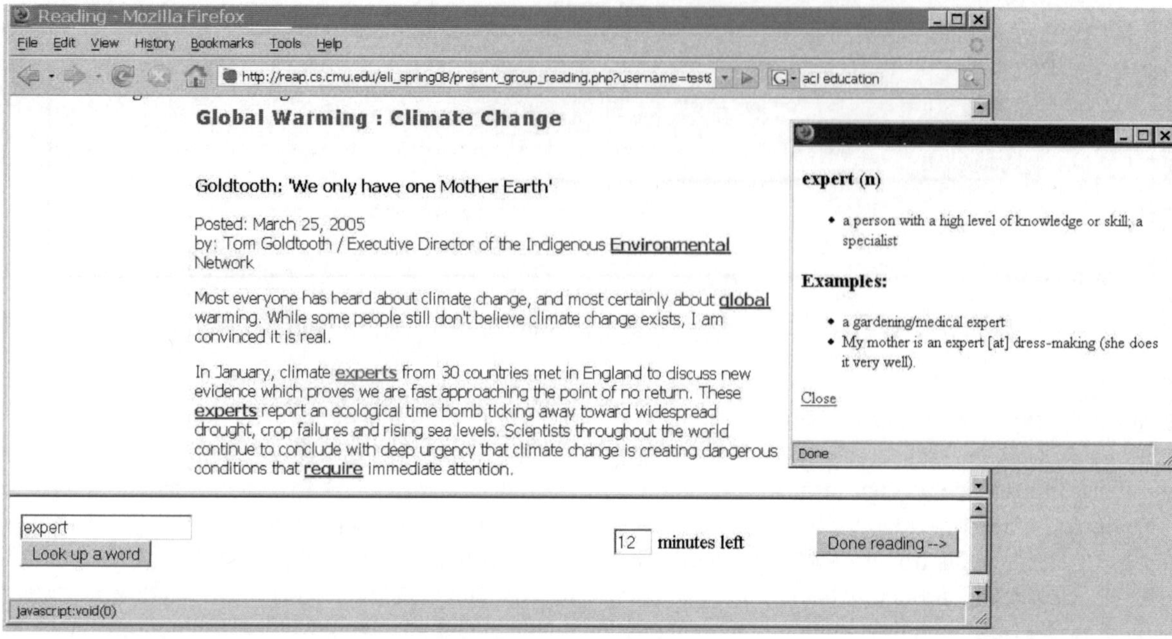

Figure 4: Screenshot of Student Interface Displaying a Reading and Dictionary Definition.

For the other half of each session, the teacher provided direct instruction on and facilitated discussion about the texts and target words, making connections to the rest of the curriculum when possible. For each session, the teachers found three to five readings. Students read through at least two of the readings, which were discussed in class. The extra readings allowed faster readers to progress at their own pace if they complete the first two. Teachers learned to use the system in a training session that lasted about 30 minutes.

8.2 Usage Analysis

To better understand the two teachers' interactions with the search system, we analyzed query log data from a four week period. In total, the teachers used the system to select 23 readings for their students. In the process, they issued 47 unique queries to the system. Thus, on average they issued 2.04 queries per chosen text. Ideally, a user would only have to issue a single query to find useful texts, but from the teachers' comments it appears that the system's usability is sufficiently good in general. Most of the time, they specified 20 target words, only some of which appeared in their selected readings. The teachers included *ad hoc* queries only some of the time. These were informational in nature and addressed a variety of topics. Example queries include the following: "surviving winter", "coal miners safety", "gender roles", and "unidentified flying objects". The teachers chose these topics because they matched up with topics discussed in other parts of their courses' curricula. In other cases, it was more important for them to search for texts with target vocabulary rather than those on specific topics, so they only specified target words and pedagogical constraints.

8.3 Post-test and Survey Results

At the end of the semester, students took an exit survey followed by a post-test consisting of cloze vocabulary questions for the target words they practiced with the system. In previous semesters, the REAP Tutor has been used in one of the two courses that were part of the pilot study. For comparison with those results, we focus our analysis on the subset of data for the 20 students in that course. The exit survey results, shown in 5, indicate that students felt it was easy-to-use and should be used in future classes. These survey results are actually very similar to previous results from a Spring 2006 study with the REAP Tutor (Heilman et al., 2006). However, responses to the prompt "My teacher helped me to learn by discussing the readings after I read

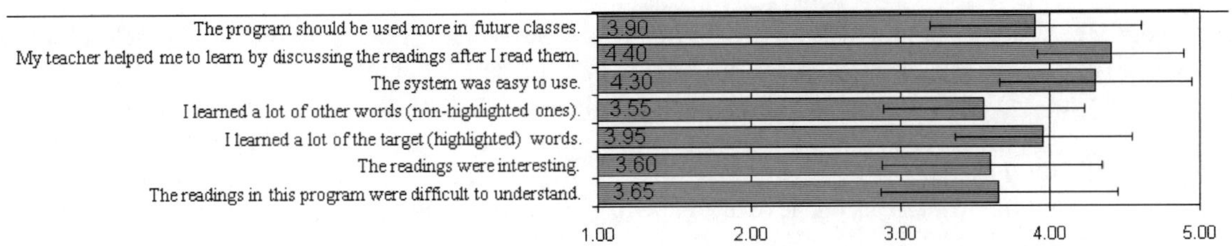

Figure 5: The results from the pilot study exit survey, which used a Likert response format from 1-5 with 1=Strongly Disagree, 3=Neither Agree nor Disagree, and 5=Strongly Agree. Error bars indicate standard deviations.

them" suggest that the tight integration of an educational system with other classroom activities, including teacher-led discussions, can be beneficial.

Learning of target words was directly measured by the post-test. On average, students answered 89% of cloze exercises correctly, compared to less than 50% in previous studies with the REAP Tutor. A direct comparison to those studies is challenging since the system in this study provided instruction on words that students were also studying as part of their regular coursework, whereas systems in previous studies did not.

9 Discussion and Future Work

We have described a system that enables teachers to find appropriate, authentic texts from the Web for vocabulary and reading practice. A variety of language technologies ranging from text retrieval to POS tagging perform essential functions in the system. The system has been used in two courses by over fifty ESL students.

A number of questions remain. Can language learners effectively and efficiently use such a system to search for reading materials directly, rather than reading what a teacher selects? Students could use the system, but a more polished user interface and further progress on filtering out readings of low text quality is necessary. Is such an approach adaptable to other languages, especially less commonly taught languages for which there are fewer available Web pages? Certainly there are sufficient resources available on the Web in commonly taught languages such as French or Japanese, but extending to other languages with fewer resources might be significantly more challenging. How effective would such a tool be in a first language classroom? Such an approach should be suitable for use in first language classrooms, especially by teachers who need to find supplemental materials for struggling readers. Are there enough high-quality, low-reading level texts for very young readers? From observations made while developing REAP, the proportion of Web pages below fourth grade reading level is small. Finding appropriate materials for beginning readers is a challenge that the REAP developers are actively addressing.

Issues of speed and scale are also important to consider. Complex queries such as the one shown in Figure 3 are not as efficient as boolean queries. The current system takes a few seconds to return results from its database of several million readings. Scaling up to a much larger digital library may require sophisticated distributed processing of queries across multiple disks or multiple servers. However, we maintain that this is an effective approach for providing texts within a particular grade level range or known target word list.

Acknowledgments

This research was supported in part by the Institute of Education Sciences, U.S. Department of Education, through Grant R305B040063 to Carnegie Mellon University; Dept. of Education grant R305G03123; the Pittsburgh Science of Learning Center which is funded by the National Science Foundation, award number SBE-0354420; and a National Science Foundation Graduate Research Fellowship awarded to the first author. Any opinions, findings, conclusions, or recommendations expressed in this material are the authors, and do not necessarily reflect those of the sponsors.

References

Luiz Amaral, Vanessa Metcalf and Detmar Meurers.

2006. Language Awareness through Re-use of NLP Technology. *Pre-conference Workshop on NLP in CALL – Computational and Linguistic Challenges. CALICO 2006.*

Jon Brown and Maxine Eskenazi. 2004. Retrieval of authentic documents for reader-specific lexical practice. *Proceedings of InSTIL/ICALL Symposium 2004*. Venice, Italy.

Jon Brown, Gwen Frishkoff, and Maxine Eskenazi. 2005. Automatic question generation for vocabulary assessment. *Proceedings of HLT/EMNLP 2005*. Vancouver, B.C.

Kevyn Collins-Thompson and Jamie Callan. 2005. Predicting reading difficulty with statistical language models. *Journal of the American Society for Information Science and Technology, 56(13). pp. 1448-1462.*

Averil Coxhead. 2000. A New Academic Word List. *TESOL Quarterly, 34(2).* pp. 213-238.

S. Gupta, G. Kaiser, D. Neistadt, and P. Grimm. 2003. *DOM-based content extraction of HTML documents.* ACM Press, New York.

F. M. Hafiz and Ian Tudor. 1989. Extensive reading and the development of language skills. *ELT Journal 43(1):4-13.* Oxford University Press.

Michael Heilman, Kevyn Collins-Thompson, Maxine Eskenazi. 2008. An Analysis of Statistical Models and Features for Reading Difficulty Prediction. *The 3rd Workshop on Innovative Use of NLP for Building Educational Applications*. Association for Computational Linguistics.

Michael Heilman, Alan Juffs, Maxine Eskenazi. 2007. Choosing Reading Passages for Vocabulary Learning by Topic to Increase Intrinsic Motivation. *Proceedings of the 13th International Conferenced on Artificial Intelligence in Education*. Marina del Rey, CA.

Michael Heilman, Kevyn Collins-Thompson, Jamie Callan, and Maxine Eskenazi. 2006. Classroom success of an Intelligent Tutoring System for lexical practice and reading comprehension. *Proceedings of the Ninth International Conference on Spoken Language Processing*. Pittsburgh, PA.

Thorsten Joachims. 1999. Making large-Scale SVM Learning Practical. *Advances in Kernel Methods - Support Vector Learning, B. Schlkopf and C. Burges and A. Smola (ed.)* MIT-Press.

Chao-Lin Liu, Chun-Hung Wang, Zhao-Ming Gao, and Shang-Ming Huang. 2005. Applications of Lexical Information for Algorithmically Composing Multiple-Choice Cloze Items *Proceedings of the Second Workshop on Building Educational Applications Using NLP*. Association for Computational Linguistics.

Christopher D. Manning, Prabhakar Raghavan and Hinrich Schtze. 2008. *Introduction to Information Retrieval.* Cambridge University Press. Draft available at http://www-csli.stanford.edu/~hinrich/information-retrieval-book.html.

Eleni Miltsakaki and Audrey Troutt. 2007. Read-X: Automatic Evaluation of Reading Difficulty of Web Text. *Proceedings of E-Learn 2007, sponsored by the Association for the Advancement of Computing in Education*. Quebec, Canada.

Matthew Peacock. 1997. The effect of authentic materials on the motivation of EFL learners. *ELT Journal 51(2):144-156.* Oxford University Press.

Kathleen M. Sheehan, Irene Kostin, Yoko Futagi. 2007. SourceFinder: A Construct-Driven Approach for Locating Appropriately Targeted Reading Comprehension Source Texts. *Proceedings of the SLaTE Workshop on Speech and Language Technology in Education.* Carnegie Mellon University and International Speech Communication Association (ISCA).

Real-Time Web Text Classification and Analysis of Reading Difficulty

Eleni Miltsakaki
Graduate School of Education
Universisty of Pennsylvania,
Philadelphia, PA 19104, USA.
elenimi@seas.upenn.edu

Audrey Troutt
Computer and Information Science
University of Pennsylvania
Philadelphia, PA 19104, USA
atroutt@seas.upenn.edu

Abstract

The automatic analysis and categorization of web text has witnessed a booming interest due to the increased text availability of different formats, content, genre and authorship. We present a new tool that searches the web and performs in real-time a) html-free text extraction, b) classification for thematic content and c) evaluation of expected reading difficulty. This tool will be useful to adolescent and adult low-level reading students who face, among other challenges, a troubling lack of reading material for their age, interests and reading level.

1 Introduction

According to the National Center for Education Statistics, 29% of high school seniors in public schools across America were below basic achievement in reading in 2005 (U.S. Department of Education 2005). Once these students enter high school, their reading problems, which began much earlier in their education, are compounded by many factors including a lack of suitable reading material for their age, interests and reading level. Most material written at a lower reading level is designed for much younger students; high-school students find it boring or embarrassing. On the other hand material designed for older students, while probably more interesting, is incomprehensible to such a student and leads to frustration and self-doubt. The internet is a vast resource for potential reading material and is often utilized by educators in the classroom, but it is not currently possible to filter the results of a search engine query by levels of readability. Instead, the software that some schools have adopted restricts students to lists and directories of hand-selected educational sites. This severely limits the content available to students and requires near-constant maintenance to keep current with new information available on the web.

We are developing a new system, Read-X, that searches the web and performs in real-time a) html-free text extraction, b) classification for thematic content and c) evaluation of expected reading difficulty. For the thematic classification task we collected a manually labeled corpus to train and compare three text classifiers. Our system is part of larger research effort to improve existing readability metrics by taking into account the profile of the reader. As a first step in this direction, we computed vocabulary frequencies per thematic area. We use these frequencies to predict unknown words for the reader relative to her familiarity with thematic areas (Toreador). These tools (Read-X and Toreador) will be useful to adolescent and adult low-level reading students who face, among other challenges, a troubling lack of reading material for their age, interests and reading level.

The remainder of the paper is organized as follows: first we will describe our motivation for creating Read-X and Toreador, which is based on studies that show that older struggling readers can make improvements in literacy and that those improvements can have a profound impact on their lives. Next we will describe existing technologies for literacy improvement and research related to our current project. Finally, we will give a detailed description

Proceedings of the Third ACL Workshop on Innovative Use of NLP for Building Educational Applications, pages 89–97,
Columbus, Ohio, USA, June 2008. ©2008 Association for Computational Linguistics

of Read-X and Toreador, including our methods of evaluating the readability of texts, thematically classifying the texts and modeling reader profiles into readability predictions, before concluding with an outline of future work.

2 Educational motivation

Low reading proficiency is a widespread problem evident in the performance of adolescents in U.S. schools. The National Center for Education Statistics (NCES) in 2005, the latest year for which data is available, reports that only 29% of eight graders in the United States achieved proficient or above reading, meaning the remaining 71% of students had only part of the reading skills needed for proficient work at their level or less (Snyder et al., 2006). (Hasselbring and Goin, 2004) reported that "as many as 20 percent of 17-year-olds have been estimated to be functionally illiterate, and 44 percent of all high-school students have been described as semi-literate". Reading below grade level is a serious problem for adolescents as it may hinder comprehension of textbooks and classroom materials in all fields. (Denti, 2004) mentions that "most high school textbooks are written at the tenth through twelfth grade levels with some textbooks used for U. S. government written at the seventeenth grade level". Reading skills are tied to academics success and are highly correlated with with "higher income and less unemployment, increased access to lifelong learning, greater amounts of personal reading for pleasure, and increased civic participation" (Strucker et al., 2007).

Recent research has shown that it is possible to identify adult literacy students on the brink of achieving reading fluency in order to provide them with concentrated instruction, dramatically improving their chances of attaining a high quality of life (Strucker et al., 2007). (Weinstein and Walberg, 1993) studied the factors related to achievement in reading and found that "frequent and extensive engagement in literacy-promoting activities as a young adult was associated with higher scores on literacy outcomes (independent of earlier-fixed characteristics and experiences)," which implies that through ample reading exercise students can achieve literacy regardless of their background.

The current and future versions of the system that we are developing uses natural language processing techniques to provide learning tools for struggling readers. The web is the single most varied resource of content and style, ranging from academic papers to personal blogs, and is thus likely to contain interesting reading material for every user and reading ability. The system presented here is the first to our knowledge which performs in real time a)keyword search, b)thematic classification and c)analysis of reading difficulty. We also present a second system which analyzes vocabulary difficulty according to reader's prior familiarity with thematic content.

3 Related work

In this section we discuss two main systems that are most closely related to our work on text classification and analysis of readability.

NetTrekker is a commercially available search tool especially designed for K-12 students and educators.[1] NetTrekker's search engine has access to a database of web links which have been manually selected and organized by education professionals. The links are organized thematically per grade level and their readability level is evaluated on a scale of 1-5. Level 1 corresponds to reading ability of grades 1-3 and 5 to reading ability of grades 11-13. Nettrekker has been adopted by many school districts in the U.S., because it offers a safe way for K-12 students to access only web content that is age appopriate and academically relevant. On the other hand, because the process of web search and classification is not automated, it is practically impossible for NetTrekker to dynamically update its database so that new material posted on the web can be included. However, Nettrekker's manual classification of web links is a valuable resource of manually labeled data. In our project, we use this resource to build labeled dataset for training statistical classifiers. We discuss the construction and use of this corpus in more detail in Section 5.1).

The REAP tutor, developed at the Language Technologies Institute at Carnegie Mellon, is designed to assist second language learners to build new vocabulary and facilitates student specific practice sessions (Collins-Thompson and Callan, 2004), (Heilman et

[1] Available at `http://www.nettrekker.com`.

al., 2006). The tutor allows the user to search for textual passages as well as other text retrieved from the web that contains specific vocabulary items. The educational gain for students practicing with the tutor has been shown in several studies (e.g., (Heilman et al., 2006)). Like NetTrekker, REAP retrieves and classifies web text off-line. Unlike, Nettrekker, however, textual analysis is automated. REAP's information retrieval system (Collins-Thompson and Callan, 2004) contains material from about 5 million pages gathered with web crawling methods. The data have been annotated and indexed off-line. Annotations include readability level computed with an earlier version of the method developed by (Heilman et al., 2007), (Heilman et al., 2006) described below, rough topic categorizations (e.g., fiction, nonfiction) and some elements of grammatical structure (e.g., part-of-speech tagging).

(Heilman et al., 2007) experiment with a system for evaluation of reading difficulty which employs both grammatical features and vocabulary. The grammatical features built in the model were identified from grammar books used in three ESL levels. (Heilman et al., 2007) find that while the vocabulary model alone outperformed the grammar-based model, the combined model performed best. All models performed better in English text and less well in ESL text. It would be very interesting to integrate this system with Read-X and evaluate its performance.

To address issues specific to struggling readers, (Hasselbring and Goin, 2004) developed the Peabody Literacy Lab (PLL), a completely computer-based program, using a variety of technologies to help students improve their ability to read. We will not elaborate further on this work because the PPL's focus in not in developing new technologies. PLL develops experimental programs using existing technologies.

4 Read-X project overview

In the Read-X project, we have developed two tools which are currently independent of each other. The first tool Read-X, performs a web search and classifies text as detailed in (5.1). The second tool Toreador, analyzes input text and predicts vocabulary difficulty based on grade or theme-specific vocabulary frequencies. The vocabulary predicted to be unfamiliar can be clicked on. This action activates a dictionary look-up search on Wordnet whose display is part of the tool's interface. More details and screenshots are given in (**??**).

5 Description of Read-X

Below we describe in detail the technical components of Read-X: internet search, text extraction and analysis of readability.

5.1 Read-X: Web search and text classification

Internet search. Read-X performs a search of the internet using the Yahoo! Web Services. When the search button is clicked or the enter key depressed after typing in a keyword, Read-X sends a search request to Yahoo! including the keywords and the number of results to return and receives results including titles and URLs of matching websites in an XML document. The Yahoo! Web Service is freely available for non-commercial use with a limit of 5000 requests per day. If Read-X is deployed for use by a wide number of users, it may be necessary to purchase the ability to process more requests with Yahoo or another search engine. Read-X is currently available at `http://net-read.blogspot.com`.

Text extraction. Read-X then retrieves the html, xml, doc or PDF document stored at each URL and extracts the human-readable text.[2] text is extracted from html and xml documents using the scraper provided by Generation Java by Henri Yandell, see www.generationjava.com. The Microsoft Word document scraper is part of the Apache Jakarta project by the Apache Software Foundation, see www.apache.org. The PDF scraper is part of the Apache Lucene project, see www.pdfbox.org. All three of these external tools are available under a common public license as open source software under the condition that any software that makes use of the tools must also make the source code available to users.

[2]Being able to identify appopriate web pages whose content is reading material and not "junk" is a non-trivial task. (Petersen and Ostendorf, 2006) use a classifier for this task with moderate success. We "read" the structure of the html text to decide if the content is appropriate and when in doubt, we err on the side of throwing out potentially useful content.

Readability analysis. For printed materials, there are a number of readability formulas used to measure the difficulty of a given text; the New Dale-Chall Readability Formula, The Fry Readability Formula, the Gunning-Fog Index, the Automated Readability Index, and the Flesch Kincaid Reading Ease Formula are a few examples. Usually these formulas count the number of syllables, long sentences, or difficult words in randomly selected passages of the text. To automate the process of readability analysis, we chose three Readability algorithms: Lix, Rix, see (Anderson, 1983), and Coleman-Liau, (Coleman and Liau, 1975), which were best suited for fast calculation and provide the user with either an approximate grade level for the text or a readability classification of very easy, easy, standard, difficult or very difficult. When each text is analyzed by Read-X the following statistics are computed: total number of sentences, total number of words, total number of long words (seven or more characters, and total number of letters in the text. Below we describe how each of the three readability scores are calculated using these statistics. Steps taken to develop more sophisticated measures for future implementations are presented in Section 7).

Lix readability formula: The Lix readability algorithm distinguishes between five levels of readability: very easy, easy, standard, difficult, or very difficult. If W is the number of words, LW is the number of long words (7 or more characters), and S is the number of sentences, them the Lix index is LIX = W/S + (100 * LW) / W. An index of 0-24 corresponds to a very easy text, 25-34 is easy, 35-44 standard, 45-54 difficult, and 55 or more is considered very difficult.

Rix readability formula: The Rix readability formula consists of the ratio of long words to sentences, where long words are defined as 7 or more characters. The ratio is translated into a grade level as indicated in Table (1).

Coleman-Liau readability formula: The Coleman-Liau readability formula is similar to the Rix formula in that it gives the approximate grade level of the text. Unlike the Lix and Rix formulas, the Coleman-Liau formula requires the random selection of a 100 word excerpt from the text. Before the grade level can be calculated, the cloze percent must be estimated for this selection. The cloze percent is the percent of words that, if deleted from the text, can be correctly filled in by a college undergraduate. If L is the number of letters in the 100 word sample and S is the number of sentences, then the estimated cloze percent is C = 141.8491 - 0.214590 * L + 1.079812 * S. The grade level can be calculated using the Coleman-Liau formula, where grade level is -27.4004 * C + 23.06395. In the SYS display we round the final result to the nearest whole grade level.

Ratio	GradelLevel
7.2 and above	College
6.2 and above	12
5.3 and above	11
4.5 and above	10
3.7 and above	9
3.0 and above	8
2.4 and above	7
1.8 and above	6
1.3 and above	5
0.8 and above	4
0.5 and above	3
0.2 and above	2
Below 0.2	1

Table 1: Rix translation to grade level

Classifier	Supercategories	Subcategories
Naive Bayes	66%	30%
MaxEnt	78%	66%
MIRA	76%	58%

Table 2: Performance of text classifiers.

6 Text classification

The automated classification of text into predefined categories has witnessed strong interest in the past ten years. The most dominant approach to this problem is based on machine learning techniques. Classifiers are built which learn from a prelabeled set of data the characteristics of the categories. The performance of commonly used classifiers varies depending on the data and the nature of the task. For the text classification task in Read-X, we a) built a corpus of prelabeled thematic categories and b)compared the performance of three classifiers to evaluate their performance on this task.

We collected a corpus of approximately 3.4 million words and organized it into two sets of labeling categories. We hand collected a subset of labels (most appropriate for a text classification task) from the set of labels used for the organization of web text in NetTrekker (see 3). We retrieved text for each category by following the listed web links in NetTrekker and manually extracting text from the sites. Our corpus is organized into a small hierarchy, with two sets of labels: a)labels for supercategories and b)labels for subcategories. There are 8 supercategories (Arts, Career and business, Literature, Philosophy and religion, Science, Social studies, Sports and health, Technology) and 41 subcategories (e.g., the subcategories for Literature are Art Criticism, Art History, Dance, Music, Theater). Subcategories are a proper subset of supercategories but in the classification experiments reported below the classifiers trained independently in the two data sets.

We trained three classifiers for this task: a Naive Bayes classifier, a Maximum Entropy classifier and MIRA, a new online learning algorithm that incorporates a measure of confidence in the algorithm(for details see (Crammer et al., 2008)). [3] The performance of the classifiers trained on the supercategories and subcategories data is shown in Table (2). All classifiers perform reasonably well in the supercategories classification task but are outperformed by the MaxEnt classifier in both the supercategories and subcategories classifications. The Naive Bayes classifiers performs worst in both tasks. As expected, the performance of the classifiers deteriorates substantially for the subcategories task. This is expected due to the large number of labels and the small size of data available for each subcategory. We expect that as we collect more data the performance of the classifiers for this task will improve. In an earlier implementation of Read-X, thematic classification was a coarser three-way classificaition task (literature, science, sports). In that implementation the MaxEnt classifier performed at 93% and the Naive Bayes classifier performed at 88% correct. In future implementations of the tool, we will make available all three levels thematic classification.

6.1 Runtime and interface

The first implementation of Read-X, coded in Java, has been made publicly available. The jar file is called from the web through a link and runs on Windows XP or Vista with Java Runtime Environment 6 and internet connection. Search results and analysis are returned within a few seconds to a maximum of a minute or two depending on the speed of the connection. The Read-X interface allows the user to constrain the search by selecting number of returned results and level of reading difficulty. A screenshot of Read-X (cropped for anonymity) is shown in Figure (1). The rightmost column is clickable and shows the retrieved html-free text in an editor. From this editor the text can be saved and further edited on the user's computer.

7 Description of Toreador

The analysis of reading difficulty based on standard readability formulas gives a quick and easy way to measure reading difficulty but it is problematic in several ways. First, readability formulas compute superficial features of word and sentence length. It is easy to show that such features fail to distinguish between sentences which have similar word and sentence lengths but differ in ease of interpretation. Garden path sentences, bountiful in the linguistic literature, demonstrate this point. Example (1) is harder to read than example (2) although the latter is a longer sentence.

(1) She told me a little white lie will come back to haunt me.

(2) She told me that a little white lie will come back to haunt me.

Secondly, it is well known that there are aspects of textual coherence such as topic continuity and rhetorical structure which are not captured in counts of words and sentences (e.g., (Higgins et al., 2004), (Miltsakaki and Kukich, 2004))

Thirdly, readability formulas do not take into account the profile of the reader. For example, a reader who has read a lot of literary texts will have less difficulty reading new literary text than a reader, with a similar educational background, who has never read

[3]We gratefully acknowledge MALLET, a collection of statistical NLP tools written in Java, publicly available at `http://mallet.cs.umass.edu` and Mark Dredze for his help installing and running MIRA on our data.

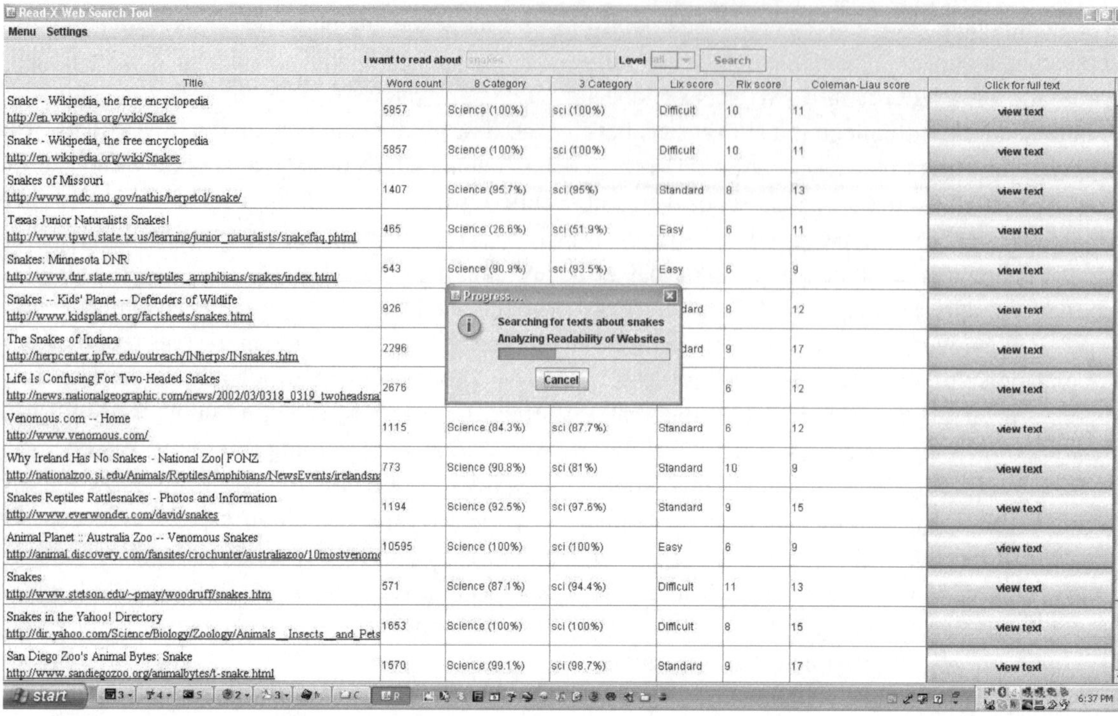

Figure 1: Search results and analysis of readability

any literature. In this section, we discuss the first step we have taken towards making more reliable predictions on text readability given the profile of the reader.

Readers who are familiar with specific thematic areas, are more likely to know vocabulary that is recurring in these areas. So, if we have vocabulary frequency counts per thematic area, we are in a better position to predict difficult words for specific readers given their reading profiles. Vocabulary frequency lists are often used by test developers as an indicator of text difficulty, based on the assumption that less frequent words are more likely to be unknown. However, these lists are built from a variety of themes and cannot be customized for the reader. We have computed vocabulary frequencies for all supercategories in the thematically labeled corpus. The top 10 most frequent words per supercategory are shown in Table (3). Vocabulary frequencies per grade level have also been computed but not shown here.

Toreador is a tool which runs independently of Read-X and it's designed to predict unknown vocabulary for specific reader and grade profiles currently specified by the user. A screenshot of Toreador is shown in Figure (2). The interface shows two tabs labeled "Enter text here" and "Read text here". The "Enter text here" tab allows the user to customize vocabulary difficulty predictions by selecting the desired grade or theme.[4] Then, text can be copied from another source and pasted in the window of the tool. The tool will analyze the text and in a few seconds return the results fo the analysis in the tab labeled "Read text here", shown in Figure (3). Toreador checks the vocabulary frequency of the words in the pasted text and returns the text highlighted with the words that do not rank high in the vocabulary frequency index for the chosen categories (grade or theme). The highlighted words are clickable. When they are clicked, they entry information from WordNet appears on the right panel. The system has not been evaluated yet so some tuning will be required to determine the optimal cut-off frequency point for highlighting words. An option is also available to deactivate highlights for ease of read or reading for global meaning. Words that the system has

[4]The screenshot in Figure (2) shows an earlier version of the tool where only three thematic categories were available.

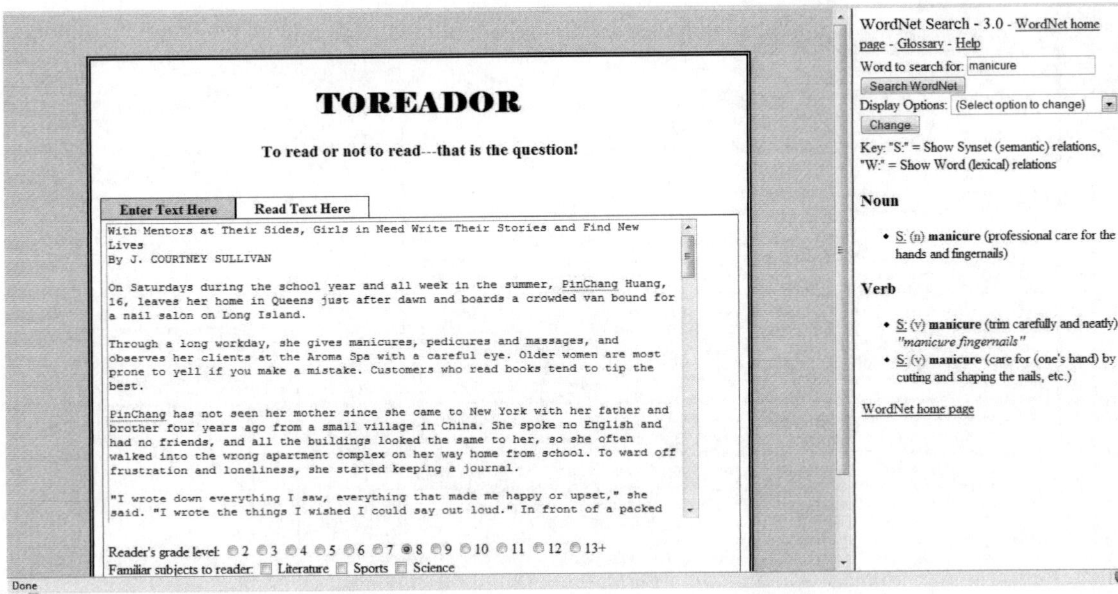

Figure 2: Text analysis of vocabulary difficulty

Arts	Career and Business	Literature	Philosophy	Science	Social Studies	Sports, Health	Technology
Word Freq	Word Freq	Word Freq	Word Freq	Word Freq	Word Freq	Word Freq	Word Freq
musical 166	product 257	seemed 1398	argument 174	trees 831	behavior 258	players 508	software 584
leonardo 166	income 205	myself 1257	knowledge 158	bacteria 641	states 247	league 443	computer 432
instrument 155	market 194	friend 1255	augustine 148	used 560	psychoanalytic 222	player 435	site 333
horn 149	price 182	looked 1231	belief 141	growth 486	social 198	soccer 396	video 308
banjo 128	cash 178	things 1153	memory 130	acid 476	clemency 167	football 359	games 303
american 122	analysis 171	caesar 1059	truth 130	years 472	psychology 157	games 320	used 220
used 119	resources 165	going 1051	logic 129	alfalfa 386	psychotherapy 147	teams 292	systems 200
nature 111	positioning 164	having 1050	things 125	crop 368	united 132	national 273	programming 174
artist 104	used 153	asked 1023	existence 115	species 341	society 131	years 263	using 172
wright 98	sales 151	indeed 995	informal 113	acre 332	court 113	season 224	engineering 170

Table 3: 10 top most frequent words per thematic category.

not seen before, count as unknown and can be erroneously highlighted (for example, the verb "give" in the screenshot example). We are currently running evaluation studies with a group of volunteers. While we recognize that the readability formulas currently implemented in Read-X are inadequate measures of expected reading difficulty, Toreador is not designed as an improvement over Read-X but as a component measuring expected vocabulary difficulty. Other factors contributing to reading difficulty such as syntactic complexity, propositional density and rhetorical structure will be modeled separately in the future.

8 Summary and future work

In this paper we presented preliminary versions of two tools developed to assist struggling readers identify text that is at the desired level of reading difficulty while at the same time interesting and relevant to their interests. Read-X is, to our knowledge, the first system designed to locate, classify and analyze reading difficulty of web text in real time, i.e., performing the web search and text analysis in seconds. Toreador analyzes the vocabulary of given text and predicts which words are likely to be difficult for the reader. The contribution of Toreador is that its predictions are based on vocabulary frequencies calculated per thematic area and are different depending on the reader's prior familiarity with the thematic areas.

We emphasize the shortcomings of the existing readability formulas, currently implemented in Read-X, and the need to develop more sophisticated measures of reading difficulty. We recognize that perceived difficulty is the result of many factors, which need to be analyzed and modeled separately.

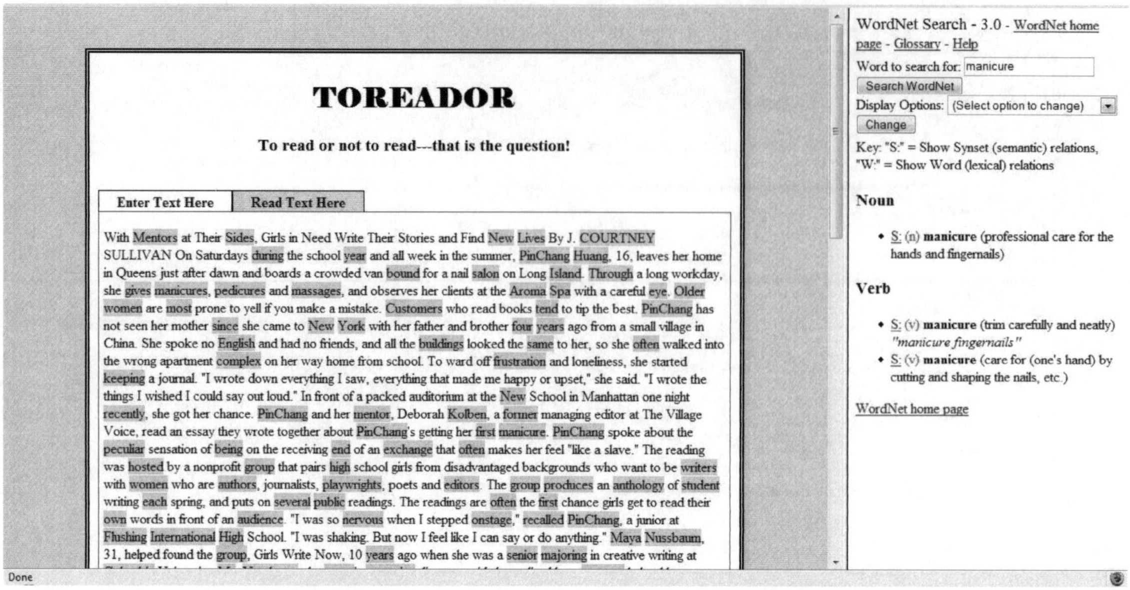

Figure 3: Text analysis of vocabulary difficutly

Our goal in this research project is not to provide a single readability score. Instead, we aim at buidling models for multiple factors and provide individual evaluation for each, e.g., measures of syntactic complexity, ambiguity, propositional density, vocabulary difficulty, required amount of inference to identify discourse relations and prior knowledge of the reader.

In future work, several studies are needed. To achieve satisfactory performance for the fine grained thematic categories, we are collecting more data. We also plan to run the subcategories classification not as an independent classificaition task but as subclassification task on supercategories. We expect that the accuracy of the classifier will improve but we also expect that for very fine thematic distinctions alternative approaches may be be required (e.g., give special weights for key vocabulary that will distinguish between sports subthemes) or develop new classification features beyond statistical analysis of word distributions.

More sophisticated textual, semantic and discourse organization features need to be explored which will reflect the perceived coherence of the text beyond the choice of words and sentence level structure. The recently released Penn Discourse Treebank 2.0 (Prasad et al., 2008)) [5] is a rich source with annotations of explicit and implicit discourse connectives and semantic labels which can be used to identify useful discourse features. Finally, more sophisticated models are needed of reader profiles and how they impact the perceived reading difficulty of the text.

9 Acknowledgments

We are grateful to Mark Dredze for his help running MIRA and Ani Nenkoca for useful discussions on readability. We thank the CLUNCH group at the Computer and Information Science department at the University of Pennsylvaniaand and two reviewers for their very useful feedback. This work is partially funded by the GAPSA/Provosts Award for Interdisciplinary Innovation to Audrey Troutt, University of Pennsylvania.

References

Jonathan Anderson. 1983. Lix and rix: Variations of a little-known readability index. *Journal of Reading*, 26(6):490–496.

M Coleman and T. Liau. 1975. A computer readability formula designed for machine scoring. *Journal of Applied Psychology*, 60:283–284.

[5]Project site, `http://www.seas.upenn.edu/~pdtb`

K. Collins-Thompson and J. Callan. 2004. Information retrieval for language tutoring: An overview of the REAP project. In *Proceedings of the Twenty Seventh Annual International ACM SIGIR Conference on Research and Development in Information Retrieval (poster descritpion.*

Koby Crammer, Mark Dredze, John Blitzer, and Fernando Pereira. 2008. Batch performance for an online price. In *The NIPS 2007 Workshop on Efficient Machine Learning.*

Lou Denti. 2004. Introduction: Pointing the way: Teaching reading to struggling readers at the secondary level. *Reading and Writing Quarterly*, 20:109–112.

Ted Hasselbring and Laura Goin. 2004. Literacy instruction for older struggling readers: What is the role of technology? *Reading and Writing Quarterly*, 20:123–144.

M. Heilman, K. Collins-Thompson, J. Callan, and M. Eskenazi. 2006. Classroom success of an intelligent tutoring system for lexical practice and reading comprehension. In *Proceedings of the Ninth International Conference on Spoken Language Processing.*

M. Heilman, K. Collins-Thompson, J. Callan, and M. Eskenazi. 2007. Combining lexical and grammatical features to improve readability measures for first and second language texts. In *Proceedings of the Human Language Technology Conference. Rochester, NY.*

Derrick Higgins, Jill Burstein, Daniel Marcu, and Claudia Gentile. 2004. Evaluating multiple aspects of coherence in student essays. In *Proceedings of the Human Language Technology and North American Association for Computational Linguistics Conference (HLT/NAACL 2004).*

Eleni Miltsakaki and Karen Kukich. 2004. Evaluation of text coherence for electronic essay scoring systems. *Natural Language Engineering*, 10(1).

Sarah Petersen and Mari Ostendorf. 2006. Assessing the reading level of web pages. In *Proceedings of Interspeech 2006 (poster)*, pages 833–836.

Rashmi Prasad, Nikhil Dinesh, Alan Lee, Eleni Miltsakaki, Livio Robaldo, Aravind Joshi, and Bonnie Webber. 2008. The penn discourse treebank 2.0. In *Proceedings of the 6th International Conference on Language Resources and Evaluation (LREC 2008).*

T. D. Snyder, A.G. Tan, and C.M. Hoffman. 2006. Digest of education statistics 2005 (nces 2006-030). In *U.S. Department of Education, National Center for Education Statistics. Washington, DC: U.S. Government Printing Office.*

John Strucker, Yamamoto Kentaro, and Irwin Kirsch. 2007. The relationship of the component skills of reading to ials performance: Tipping points and five classes of adult literacy learners. In *NCSALL Reports 29. Boston: National Center for the Study of Adult Learning and Literacy (NCSALL).*

Thomas Weinstein and Herbert J. Walberg. 1993. Practical literacy of young adults: educational antecedents and influences. *Journal of Research in Reading*, 16(1):3–19.

Towards Automatic Scoring of a Test of Spoken Language with Heterogeneous Task Types

Klaus Zechner and **Xiaoming Xi**
Educational Testing Service
Rosedale Road, Princeton, NJ 08541, USA
{kzechner,xxi}@ets.org

Abstract

This paper describes a system aimed at automatically scoring two task types of high and medium-high linguistic entropy from a spoken English test with a total of six widely differing task types.

We describe the speech recognizer used for this system and its acoustic model and language model adaptation; the speech features computed based on the recognition output; and finally the scoring models based on multiple regression and classification trees.

For both tasks, agreement measures between machine and human scores (correlation, kappa) are close to or reach inter-human agreements.

1 Introduction

As demand for spoken language testing and cost of human scoring have increased in recent years, there is a growing interest in building both research and industrial systems for automatically scoring non-native speech (Bernstein, 1999, Zechner and Bejar, 2006, Zechner et al, 2007).

However, past approaches have focused typically only on one type of spoken language, or on a range of types similar in linguistic entropy. Entropy in this context can be seen as a measure for how predictable the language in the expected spoken response is: Some tests, such as SET-10 (Bernstein 1999), are focused mostly on the lower entropy aspects of language, using tasks such as "reading" or "repetition", where the expected sequence of words is highly predictable. Other assessments, such as the TOEFL® Practice Online Speaking test, on the other hand, focus on more spontaneous, high-entropy responses (Zechner et al., 2007).

In this paper, we describe a spoken language test with heterogeneous task types, ranging from read speech to tasks that require candidates to give their opinions on an issue, whose goal is to assess communicative competence (Bachman, 1990; Bachman & Palmer, 1996); we call this test THT (Test with Heterogeneous Tasks). Communicative competence, in this context, refers to a speaker's ability to use the language for communicative purposes. The effectiveness of the communication typically consists of a few aspects including comprehensibility, accuracy, clarity, coherence and appropriateness, and is evident in a speaker's pronunciation, fluency, use of grammar and vocabulary, development of ideas, and sensitivity to the context of the communication.

This test has the advantage of being able to assess a wide range of non-native speakers' proficiencies by using tasks of varying difficulty levels to allow even low proficiency speakers some degree of success on easier task types.

We select two tasks from this test, one of higher and one of medium to high entropy, and first adapt a non-native English speech recognizer (trained on TOEFL® Practice Online data) to transcribed THT task responses, then compute a set of relevant speech features based on the recognition output, and finally build a scoring model using a subset of these features to predict trained human rater scores. In this paper, we will demonstrate that the machine-human score agreements on these two task types come close to or even exceed the level of inter-human agreement.

This paper is organized as follows: Section 2 discusses related work, Section 3 describes the test and the challenges for automatic scoring involved, Section 4 discusses the speech recognizer and the acoustic and language model adaptations per-

Proceedings of the Third ACL Workshop on Innovative Use of NLP for Building Educational Applications, pages 98–106,
Columbus, Ohio, USA, June 2008.

formed, and Section 5 describes the speech features selected for use in the scoring model. In Section 6, we report the construction of the scoring model and its results, Section 7 contains a general discussion and Section 8 concludes the paper with a brief discussion of future research.

2 Related work

There has been previous work to automatically characterize aspects of communicative competence such as fluency, pronunciation, and prosody. Franco et al. (2000) present a system for automatic evaluation of the pronunciation quality of both native and non-native speakers of English on a phone level and a sentence level (EduSpeak). Candidates read English texts and a forced alignment between the speech signal and the ideal path through the Hidden Markov Model (HMM) is computed. Next, the log posterior probabilities for pronouncing a certain phone at a certain position in the signal are computed to achieve a local pronunciation score. These scores are then combined with other automatically derived measures such as the rate of speech (number of words per second) or the duration of phonemes to yield global pronunciation scores.

Cucchiarini et al. (1997a, 1997b) describe a system for Dutch pronunciation scoring along similar lines. Their feature set, however, is more extensive and contains, in addition to log likelihood Hidden Markov Model scores, various duration scores, and information on pauses, word stress, syllable structure, and intonation. In an evaluation, correlations between four human scores and five machine scores range from 0.67 to 0.92.

Bernstein (1999) presents a test for spoken English (SET-10) that uses the following types of tasks: reading, sentence repetition, sentence building, opposites, short questions, and open-ended questions. All types except for the last are scored automatically and a score is reported that can be interpreted as an indicator of how native-like a speaker's speech is. In Bernstein et al. (2000), an experiment is performed to investigate the performance of the SET-10 test in predicting speakers' oral proficiency. It is shown that the SET-10 test scores can predict different levels on the Oral Interaction Scale of the Council of Europe's Framework (North, 2000) for describing oral proficiency of second/foreign language speakers with reasonable accuracy. This paper further reports on studies done to correlate the SET-10 automated scores with the human scores from two other tests of oral English communication skills. Correlations are found to be between 0.73 and 0.88.

Zechner and Bejar (2006) investigate the automated scoring of unrestricted, spontaneous speech of non-native speakers. They focus on exploring a number of different fluency features for the automated scoring of short (one minute) responses to test questions in a TOEFL-related program. They explore scoring models based on classification and regression trees (CART) as well as support vector machines (SVM). Their findings are that the SVM models are more useful for a quantitative analysis, whereas the CART models allow for a more transparent summary of the patterns underlying the data.

In this paper, we use CART to build the scoring model for one task type. We also adopt multiple regression for another task type which has the advantage of being more easily interpreted than, for example, SVMs. Another major difference between previous work and the work reported in this paper is that we use feature normalization and transformation to obtain statistically more meaningful input variables for the scoring model. In addition, we do not use the whole set of features in an exploratory fashion. Instead, we have carefully selected a subset of features that are both good predictors of human scores and maximize the representation of the concept of communicative competence.

3 The THT test

3.1 Task types and scoring rubrics of the THT Speaking test

There are six task types in the THT Speaking test, ranging from reading-aloud tasks to tasks that require short answers and tasks that require extended responses of one minute. The rubrics differ in both the dimensions of speaking skills measured and the possible score points. (Rubrics are characterizations of candidates' competence at given score levels and are used by human raters to determine the appropriate score for a response.) Below is a brief description of the task types and the rubrics.

Task type 1: Reading-aloud (Planning time: 45 seconds; Response time: 45 seconds; zero/very-low entropy)
There are two read-aloud tasks. Each task requires the test-taker to read a short paragraph of 40-60 words aloud. The reading materials include announcements, advertisements, introductions, etc. These two tasks are rated analytically on pronunciation and intonation and stress on a 3-point scale. That is to say, two separate scores are given on each task – one for pronunciation and one for intonation and stress.

Task type 2: Picture description (Planning time: 30 seconds; Response time: 45 seconds; medium-high entropy)
This task requires the test-taker to describe a picture in as much detail as possible.

This task is rated holistically on the combined impact of delivery (fluency, pronunciation etc.), use of structures, vocabulary, content relevance and fullness on a 3-point scale.

Task type 3: Open-ended short-answer questions (Planning time: none; Response time: 15-30 seconds; low/low-medium entropy)
The test-taker responds, without preparation, to three questions about familiar and accessible topics that draw on immediate personal experience. The first two questions each elicit a 15-second response that covers one or two pieces of information related to the specified topic. The third question requires a 30-second response that expresses an opinion or gives an explanation related to the topic. This task is rated holistically on the combined impact of delivery, use of structures, vocabulary, and task appropriateness on a 3-point scale.

Task type 4: Constrained short-answer questions (Planning time: none; Response time: 15-30 seconds; low/low-medium entropy)
The test-taker responds to three questions about a schedule/agenda that is provided in written form. All the information needed to answer the questions should be included on or easily inferred from the schedule. The test-taker has 15 seconds to respond to each of the first two questions. These questions ask for specific information on the schedule or easily inferred information about the schedule. The test-taker has 30 seconds to respond to the last question which requires a summary of multiple events or multiple pieces of information on the schedule. This task is rated holistically on the combined impact of delivery, use of structures, vocabulary, task appropriateness and content accuracy on a 3-point scale.

Task type 5: Respond to a voice mail (Planning time: 30 seconds; Response time: 60 seconds; high entropy)
In this task, the test-taker listens to a voicemail that describes a problem, question or situation and then assumes a particular role (bank teller, office assistant, etc.) to respond with a proposed solution or answer. This task is rated holistically on the combined impact of fluency, pronunciation, intonation and stress, grammar, vocabulary, register, content relevance, and cohesion and idea progression on a 5-point scale.

Task type 6: Opinion task (Planning time: 15 seconds; Response time: 60 seconds; high entropy)
In this task, the test-taker is expected to state an opinion or position on an issue that is familiar and accessible and to express support for the opinion or position with reasons, examples, arguments, etc. This task is rated holistically on the combined impact of fluency, pronunciation, intonation and stress, grammar, vocabulary, content relevance, and cohesion and idea progression on a 5-point scale.

3.2 Challenges of the THT test design to automatic scoring

1. Some of the tasks require responses that are expected to vary very little in vocabulary and content across examinees (e.g., Reading-aloud and Constrained short-answer questions) whereas others allow much more flexibility and variation in the use of vocabulary and grammatical structure and topical content (e.g. Respond to a voicemail and Opinion task). The predictability of the expected response will dictate what type of language modeling technique is preferable to optimize speech recognition results. Therefore, unlike in other systems focusing either on high or low entropy speech (e.g., Zechner and Bejar, 2006; Bernstein, 1999), in which a single speech recognizer is employed, it is anticipated that different types of speech recognizers are needed to suit different THT task types. This may increase both the amount of development

work and the complexity in integrating different types of recognizers into the real-time automated scoring system.

2. Furthermore, the scoring criteria of these six different task types are somewhat different. This suggests that different scoring models may need to be developed for different task types since the relevant speech features to be included in the scoring model for each task type may differ.

3. THT speaking tasks use two kinds of score scales: 0-3 and 0-5. Classification techniques, such as classification trees or cumulative logit models (Agresti, 2002; Menard, 2001), may be more appropriate for task types that use a 3-point scale. Prediction techniques such as multiple regression may be better suited for task types that are on a 5-point scale. Training different types of scoring models will certainly increase the complexity and the amount of scoring model development and evaluation work.

In summary, the complexity of the design of the THT Speaking test is expected to have a major impact on our efforts to develop an automated scoring system. Given these challenges and the research resources available, we decided on a strategy of starting with high entropy task types and proceeding to low entropy task types. For this paper, we selected the high entropy Opinion task and the medium-high entropy Picture tasks for system development.

4 Adaptation of the speech recognizer

For this work, we are using a state-of-the-art gender-independent Hidden Markov Model speech recognizer whose acoustic model was trained on about 30 hours of non-native speech and whose language model was built on several hundred hours of both native and non-native speech. The non-native data came from the TOEFL® Practice Online system, a web-based practice program for prospective takers of the Test Of English as a Foreign Language (TOEFL) (Zechner et al., 2007). This data is somewhat different from the THT, as there are only high-entropy tasks in TOEFL Speaking and as the speakers are generally more proficient. Due to this difference, the baseline word accuracy was fairly low (see Table 1).

Therefore, as a first step, we needed to adapt the automatic speech recognition engine to the THT speech data.

We had approximately 1,000 responses each from the Picture and Opinion tasks transcribed. As mentioned above, while the Opinion task responses are generally more spontaneous, the Picture task requires the candidate to accurately describe a picture and thus restricts the possible answer space considerably. Still, there is more room for individual choice and variation in the vocabulary, grammar and content produced than there is in the more restricted low-medium and low entropy task types in the THT Speaking test.

When using our baseline automatic speech recognition (ASR) engine without any adaptation to the THT speech data, we only obtained word accuracies between 25% and 33%, which was clearly inadequate, and far below a word accuracy where, at least for some speakers, meaningful information can be drawn from the ASR hypothesis.

Therefore, we undertook a series of adaptation and optimization steps with the goal of maximizing the word accuracy on the two task types for the THT Speaking test. We first adapted the acoustic model in batch mode with supervised maximum a-posteriori (MAP) adaptation using the combined data from both tasks, then the language model, optimized the filler cost parameter and finally conducted unsupervised maximum likelihood linear regression (MLLR) acoustic model adaptation based on individual speakers.

4.1 Acoustic model batch adaptation

We randomly selected about 90% of Picture and Opinion task response data for acoustic model (AM) adaptation, which contained 1,800 response files (over 25 hours of speech, adult speakers with typically low to intermediate English proficiency). Results are always reported on the held-out evaluation data containing 100 files for the Picture task and 80 files for the Opinion task.

We performed supervised maximum a posteriori (MAP) adaptation which is the method of choice for larger amounts of data and is typically performed in batch mode (Tomokiyo and Waibel, 2001; Wang et al., 2003). After one cycle of adaptation, word accuracy improved by about 8%, as is shown in Table 1. We also performed unsupervised maximum likelihood linear regression (MLLR) adaptation, which is discussed in Section 4.4 below.

	Picture task word accuracy		Opinion task word accuracy	
Method	Absolute	Increase from previous step	Absolute	Increase from previous step
Baseline recognizer	25.8%	NA	32.2%	NA
AM MAP adaptation	33.6%	7.8%	40.0%	7.8%
LM adaptation	50.4%	16.8%	51.0%	11.0%
Filler optimization	57.0%	6.6%	56.3%	5.3%
Ignoring fillers	60.5%	3.5%	59.2%	2.9%
MLLR Speaker adaptation	62.4%	1.9%	61.2%	2.0%

Table 1. Word accuracies after each incremental step of adaptation or optimization and performance improvement within each step for Picture and Opinion task types.

4.2 Language model adaptation

The second step was language model (LM) adaptation. The Picture and Opinion tasks were adapted separately using the same training sets as above. We built interpolated models between the task-specific LM and the baseline LM (from the original recognizer).

We obtained the best results using only the task-specific LM trained on the THT data set (given in Table 1). This indicates that the domain of each of the tasks is narrow enough that it can be sufficiently described with a set of about 900 transcribed examples each and it does not benefit from a larger LM such as our baseline LM.

4.3 Filler cost optimization

"Filler cost" is a recognizer-internal parameter that determines the likelihood of filler and noise words to be inserted into the hypothesis before or after "real" words. The higher the parameter's value, the less likely fillers will be inserted.

The experiments with the filler cost parameter grew out of an observation that the baseline recognizer has a tendency to hypothesize too many words when faced with different kinds of "uncertain" audio, such as mumbled words, noises or fillers. Therefore we conjectured that having the recognizer hypothesize more filler and noise words in these cases and be more restrictive with actual word hypotheses might increase the word accuracy overall.

We varied the filler cost parameter from its default, 3, down to its lowest meaningful value, 0. Our experiments show that for fillercost=0, a maximum word accuracy was achieved (given in Table 1), albeit at the cost of more than doubling the length of the recognizer's hypothesis by introducing a large amount of fillers (such as "um" or "uh", noises, mumbles etc.). We observe that using such a low filler cost parameter setting can negatively affect some speech features which are candidates for being used in a scoring model, such as "language model score". Therefore we have to carefully assess whether achieving a higher word accuracy is more beneficial to the overall performance of the feature set or whether it has too many negative effects on some important speech features. In future work we will attempt to tune the recognizer in such a way that it is not only optimized for a high word accuracy, but also for high accuracy in filler (and noise) prediction.

Word accuracy was computed with the fillers included or excluded. Since fillers are not real words, and in this round of scoring model development we did not use any features based on fillers, it was reasonable to compute the overall word accuracy with the fillers removed from the human and recognizer transcriptions, resulting in a moderate performance gain (see Table 1).

4.4 Unsupervised speaker adaptation

We used unsupervised maximum likelihood linear regression (MLLR) AM adaptation on top of the previous adaptation and optimization steps (Tomokiyo and Waibel, 2001; Wang et al., 2003). In this step, all words whose confidence score was higher than a pre-set threshold were collected and their acoustic information was used to adapt the acoustic model. All adaptations were done based on the utterances of a single speaker and pertained to that speaker only, i.e., it was not incremental or cumulative. Since a second decoding run is needed after the actual MLLR adaptations, the recognizer's response time more than doubles when this method is employed. The unsupervised speaker adaptation led to an additional increase of

Feature Number	Feature Name	Feature Class	Description	Used in
1	hmmscore	Pronunciation	Acoustic Model score: sum of the log probabilities of every frame, normalized for length	Opinion & Picture
2	typespersecond	Fluency & Vocabulary diversity	Number of unique words in response ("types") divided by length of response	Opinion & Picture
3	silencespersecond	Fluency	Number of silences per second	Opinion & Picture
4	repetitions	Fluency	Number of repetitions divided by number of words	Opinion
5	relevance-cos5	Vocabulary & Content	Cosine word vector product between a response and all responses in the training set that have the highest score (5 for the Opinion task)	Opinion
6	relevance-cos3	Vocabulary & Content	Cosine word vector product between a response and all responses in the training set that have the highest score (3 for the Picture task)	Picture

Table 2. Final features used for the scoring models for the Opinion and Picture tasks

approximately 2% for the Picture and Opinion tasks (see Table 1). There were large differences between different speakers in terms of the performance gain of MLLR adaptation on our data set, however. There was also a large variation of word accuracies between speakers (13-100%). The variation in accuracy across speakers can be due to many different factors, including the degree of accent, the grammaticality of the response, the voice quality and the recording quality.

5 Speech features

Based on the output of the ASR engine, a feature computation module computes a set of about 40 features for each response, mostly in the fluency domain (e.g. "average silence duration"), but also some features related to pronunciation, vocabulary diversity and content.

Instead of using all of these features in a scoring model, we used a process of iterative refinement and selection to narrow down the feature set, based on both the coverage of the concept of communicative competence and empirical performance (correlations with human scores) of the features. Following this process, five features were selected to be included in developing the scoring models for the Opinion task type and four for the Picture task type (see Table 2).

When we look at the correlations of these features to the human scores, we find that hmmscore, after being transformed to improve normality, was the strongest predictor of human scores for both the Opinion and Picture tasks with typespersecond as the second strongest (0.5 <= Pearson r <= 0.7).

6 Scoring models

All the responses were double scored by a randomly selected pair of raters who were trained for scoring this test. The agreements between the two ratings (both kappa and Pearson r correlation) were around 0.50 for the Picture and 0.72 for the Opinion task. (Note that the fewer points a scale has, the lower correlation we can expect due to less score variability, everything else being equal.)

While we use the same training sets for the scoring model experiments as for the above ASR experiments (sm-train), we add about 600 responses each to the evaluation sets (these responses were untranscribed) to yield a scoring model evaluation set size of about 700 responses each (sm-eval).

Scoring models were developed and evaluated for the Opinion and Picture task types separately. The Opinion tasks are on a 0-5 point scale whereas the Picture tasks are on a 0-3 point scale. There were only a handful of 0s on each task and they were excluded in building the scoring models.

For the Opinion tasks, multiple regression models employing different weights for the features were developed, namely an Equal Weights model, an Expert Weights model and an Optimal Weights model. In the Equal Weights model, each feature was assigned the same weight, indicating that all features are equally important in the prediction. In the Expert Weights model, different weights were assigned to different features that reflected our understanding of the different roles features play in indicating the overall speech quality. In the Optimal Weights model, weights were determined by the least squares optimization procedure using the sm-train data. All features were normalized to have a mean of 0 and a standard deviation of 1, such that their respective baseline influence on the model is comparable across features.

For the Picture task type, CART was used to predict the score class each response should be assigned to. CART 5.0 (Steinberg & Colla, 1997) was used to build the classification trees.

In addition, generic and task-specific models were developed for both task types. The task-specific models made use of task-specific vocabulary features (Features 5 and 6 in Table 2) which required using previous response data to each of the tasks within a particular task type. (Both task types had 4 different tasks each). The generic models, in contrast, used features that were the same across all tasks for a particular task type and did not use any task-specific vocabulary features. As it would be much more time-consuming and costly to build task-specific models, it is worthwhile to investigate how much more predictive power the task-specific vocabulary features could add over and beyond the features in the generic models.

6.1 Opinion task type

For the Opinion tasks, four features were used in building the generic models and five in developing the task-specific models. The following features Were used: hmmscore, typespersecond, silencespersecond, repetitions and relevancecos5 (the latter only in the task-specific model).

Table 3 shows the results on the sm-eval set. The Expert Weights model and the Optimal Weights models yielded very similar results (weighted kappa and correlation = 0.61-0.63) if we look at predicted scores that were rounded to the nearest integer. The agreements between regression model predicted scores and scores of human rater 1 were just a little below the agreements between two human raters (weighted kappa and correlation = 0.72). However, the results for the Equal Weights model were inferior.

The results for the task-specific models showed no improvement over the generic models, suggesting that the task-specific vocabulary feature did not contribute more predictive power beyond the four features already in the generic models.

Model	Multiple Regression (Equal Weights)	Multiple Regression (Expert Weights)	Multiple Regression (Optimal Weights)
Weighted κ	0.53	0.62	0.61
Pearson r Correlation (unrounded)	0.62	0.68	0.69
Pearson r Correlation (rounded)	0.56	0.63	0.63

Table 3. Performance of different weighting schemes on THT scoring model evaluation set for Opinion tasks (generic model)

6.2 Picture task type

As mentioned earlier, the Picture tasks are on a 0-3 point scale and we removed a small number of 0-scores from the analyses, making it a 3-point scale. Given this particular score scale, multiple regression may not be appropriate for this data as it requires a continuous or a quasi-continuous dependent variable (i.e. a variable that has at least 5 or more data points). Some classification techniques such as CART (Brieman et al., 1984) or logistic regression, which can take ordered score categories as the outcome variable, are better suited for this data. In this study, we analyzed the data with CART models.

CART 5.0 (Steinberg and Colla, 1997) was used to build the classification trees. We built two sets of CART models, one set with the task-specific vocabulary feature (relevancecos3) and one set without it. We explored different model configurations, i.e., different combinations of priors and splitting rules. For each combination, a 10-fold cross-validation was conducted. Subsequently, the optimal sub tree that was a relatively small tree with the highest or near-highest agreement with the human scores (weighted kappa) on the cross-validation sample was identified. Then the cases in the sm-eval data set were dropped down the optimal tree to obtain the evaluation results on the held-out data.

The results for the generic model vs. task-specific models are compared in Table 4. For both models, CART trees built using the Twoing[1] splitting rule combined with mixed priors (average of equal priors for different score classes and sm-train sample priors) yielded the best kappa values on the cross-validation data and were selected as the optimal trees. The agreements between the CART model predicted scores and first rater scores slightly exceeded that between two human raters on the sm-eval data set. Another observation from Table 4 was that for this task type, the task-specific CART model did not demonstrate an advantage over the generic model; actually, its performance was slightly worse than that of the generic model, a finding in line with the Opinion task.

	Generic	Task-specific	Inter-human agreement
Weighted κ	0.51	0.50	0.49
Pearson r Correlation	0.52	0.50	0.50

Table 4. Performance of CART models on THT scoring model evaluation set for Picture tasks (generic model vs. task-specific model)

7 Discussion

This paper investigates the feasibility of developing an automatic scoring system for the THT Speaking test, focusing on the particular challenges posed by the design of the test. The main challenge posed by the test design is the high variability in task types -- ranging from low-entropy Reading-aloud tasks to high-entropy Opinion tasks. While previous tests of spoken language have focused mainly on either high or low entropy tasks (Bernstein, 1999; Zechner and Bejar, 2006), we have made an attempt at starting to address the whole scale of entropy within a single test.

In this paper, we selected one high entropy task (Opinion) and one medium-high entropy task (Picture) to start our explorations. While we found that we could, for the most part, use a similar set of features for both tasks, we had to address the difference in score scales between these two task types. While we could use multiple regression for scoring the 5-point-scale Opinion task, we had to employ CART trees for the 3-point-scale Picture task, demonstrating that one can not necessarily use one type of scoring model for all tasks.

When moving to low and low-medium entropy tasks, we expect further adaptations, both in terms of the feature set (e.g., the higher importance of pronunciation features in Reading-aloud tasks), and in speech recognition, where more restrictive language models will be needed.

We have reported findings associated with the performance of the scoring models for the Opinion and Picture task types. Overall, the preliminary findings are quite promising: with a few key speech features, we were able to achieve prediction accuracies that could almost emulate or slightly exceed the agreements between two human raters at task level. Once we have developed scoring models for all task types, it is conceivable to aggregate the task level scores to produce a total summary score at the test level and it is very likely we would see a much stronger association between human scores and automated scores for the whole test.

The findings also suggest that task-specific modeling efforts did not seem to be necessary for the two task types investigated. This does not preclude the possibility, though, that task-specific scoring models are superior for other task types in which the expected content is much more restricted (such as the Constrained short-answer questions).

8 Conclusions and future work

We have demonstrated that by using a three-stage architecture of automatic speech recognition, feature computation, and scoring models, we are able to achieve some degree of success in generating automated scores for two task types of a spoken language test with a wide variation in entropy in its tasks. The agreement between machine scores and human scores comes close to or reaches the inter-human agreement levels for these two tasks.

In future work, we will switch our focus to task types that elicit more constrained speech (such as the Reading-aloud tasks and Constrained short-answer questions). In the meantime, we will continue to refine and evaluate the preliminary scoring models developed in this paper. In particular, we will explore cumulative logit models for tasks that are on a 0-3 point scale and compare the results to those of CART models.

[1] The Twoing rule divides the cases into two groups, gathers similar classes together, and attempts to separate the two groups in descendant nodes.

References

Agresti, A. (2002). Categorial data analysis (2nd ed.). New York: Wiley.

Bachman, L.F. (1990). *Fundamental Considerations in Language Testing.* New York: Oxford University Press.

Bachman, L. F., and Palmer, A. S. (1996). *Language testing in practice.* Oxford:OxfordUniversity Press.

Bernstein, J. (1999). PhonePass testing: Structure and construct. Menlo Park, CA: Ordinate Corporation.

Bernstein, J., DeJong, J., Pisoni, D., and Townshend, B. (2000). Two experiments in automatic scoring of spoken language proficiency. InSTILL2000, Dundee, Scotland.

Brieman, L., Jerome F., Olshen, R., and Stone, C. (1984). Classification and Regression Trees. Pacific Grove: Wadsworth.

Cucchiarini, C., Strik, H., & Boves, L. (1997a). Using speech recognition technology to assess foreign speakers' pronunciation of Dutch. Third international symposium on the acquisition of second language speech: NEW SOUNDS 97, Klagenfurt, Austria.

Cucchiarini, C., Strik, S., and Boves, L. (1997b). Automatic evaluation of Dutch pronunciation by using speech recognition technology. IEEE Automatic Speech Recognition and Understanding Workshop, Santa Barbara, CA.

Franco, H., Abrash, V., Precoda, K., Bratt, H., Rao, R., and Butzberger, J. (2000). The SRI EduSpeak system: Recognition and pronunciation scoring for language learning. InSTiLL-2000 (Intelligent Speech Technology in Language Learning), Dundee, Scotland.

Menard, S. (2001). Applied logistic regression analysis. Sage University Paper Series on Quantitative Applications in the Social Sciences 07-106, Thousand Oaks, CA: Sage.

North, B. (2000). The Development of a Common Framework Scale of Language Proficiency. New York, NY: Peter Lang.

Steinberg, D., and Colla, P. (1997). CART -- Classification and Regression Trees. San Diego, CA: Salford Systems.

Tomokiyo, L. M., and Waibel, A. (2001). Adaptation methods for non-native speech. Multilinguality in Spoken Language Processing, Aalborg.

Wang, Z., Schultz, T., and Waibel, A. (2003). Comparison of acoustic model adaptation techniques on non-native speech. IEEE International Conference on Acoustics, Speech, and Signal Processing (ICASSP-2003), Hong Kong, China.

Zechner, K., and Bejar, I. (2006). Towards Automatic Scoring of Non-Native Spontaneous Speech. HLT-NAACL-06, New York, NY.

Zechner, K., Higgins, D., and Xi, X. (2007). SpeechRater®: A Construct-Driven Approach to Score Spontaneous Non-Native Speech. Proceedings of the 2007 Workshop of the International Speech Communication Association (ISCA) Special Interest Group on Speech and Language Technology in Education (SLaTE), Farmington, PA, October.

Diagnosing meaning errors in short answers to reading comprehension questions

Stacey Bailey
Department of Linguistics
The Ohio State University
1712 Neil Avenue
Columbus, Ohio 43210, USA
s.bailey@ling.osu.edu

Detmar Meurers
Seminar für Sprachwissenschaft
Universität Tübingen
Wilhelmstrasse 19
72074 Tübingen, Germany
dm@sfs.uni-tuebingen.de

Abstract

A common focus of systems in Intelligent Computer-Assisted Language Learning (ICALL) is to provide immediate feedback to language learners working on exercises. Most of this research has focused on providing feedback on the form of the learner input. Foreign language practice and second language acquisition research, on the other hand, emphasizes the importance of exercises that require the learner to manipulate meaning.

The ability of an ICALL system to diagnose and provide feedback on the meaning conveyed by a learner response depends on how well it can deal with the response variation allowed by an activity. We focus on short-answer reading comprehension questions which have a clearly defined target response but the learner may convey the meaning of the target in multiple ways. As empirical basis of our work, we collected an English as a Second Language (ESL) learner corpus of short-answer reading comprehension questions, for which two graders provided target answers and correctness judgments. On this basis, we developed a Content-Assessment Module (CAM), which performs shallow semantic analysis to diagnose meaning errors. It reaches an accuracy of 88% for semantic error detection and 87% on semantic error diagnosis on a held-out test data set.

1 Introduction

Language practice that includes meaningful interaction is a critical component of many current language teaching theories. At the same time, existing research on intelligent computer-aided language learning (ICALL) systems has focused primarily on providing practice with grammatical forms. For most ICALL systems, although form assessment often involves the use of natural language processing (NLP) techniques, the need for sophisticated content assessment of a learner response is limited by restricting the kinds of activities offered in order to tightly control the variation allowed in learner responses, i.e., only one or very few forms can be used by the learner to express the correct content. Yet many of the activities that language instructors typically use in real language-learning settings support a significant degree of variation in correct answers and in turn require both form and content assessment for answer evaluation. Thus, there is a real need for ICALL systems that provide accurate content assessment.

While some meaningful activities are too unrestricted for ICALL systems to provide effective content assessment, where the line should be drawn on a spectrum of language exercises is an open question. Different language-learning exercises carry different expectations with respect to the level and type of linguistic variation possible across learner responses. In turn, these expectations may be linked to the learning goals underlying the activity design, the cognitive skills required to respond to the activity, or other properties of the activity. To develop adequate processing strategies for content assessment, it is important to understand the connection between exercises and expected variation, as conceptualized by the exercise spectrum shown in Figure 1, because the level of variation imposes re-

Proceedings of the Third ACL Workshop on Innovative Use of NLP for Building Educational Applications, pages 107–115,
Columbus, Ohio, USA, June 2008.

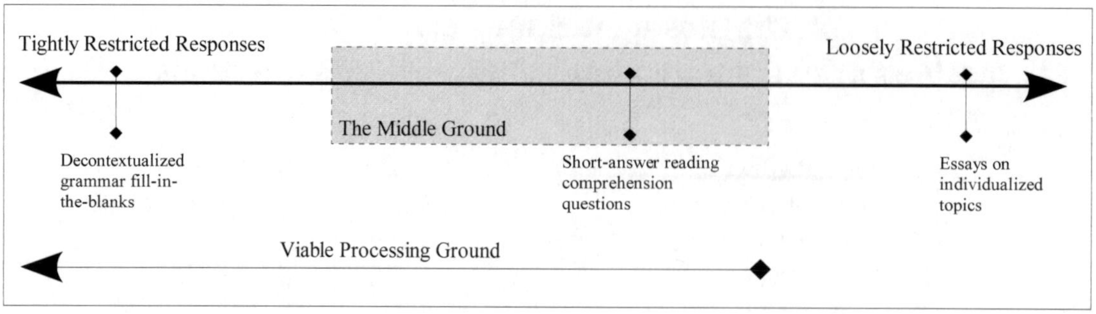

Figure 1: Language Learning Exercise Spectrum

quirements and limitations on different processing strategies. At one extreme of the spectrum, there are tightly restricted exercises requiring minimal analysis in order to assess content. At the other extreme are unrestricted exercises requiring extensive form and content analysis to assess content. In this work, we focus on determining whether shallow content-analysis techniques can be used to perform content assessment for activities in the space between the extremes. A good test case in this middle ground are loosely restricted reading comprehension (RC) questions. From a teaching perspective, they are a task that is common in real-life learning situations, they combine elements of comprehension and production, and they are a meaningful activity suited to an ICALL setting. From a processing perspective, responses exhibit linguistic variation on lexical, morphological, syntactic and semantic levels – yet the intended contents of the answer is predictable so that an instructor can define target responses.

Since variation is possible across learner responses in activities in the middle ground of the spectrum, we propose a shallow content assessment approach which supports the comparison of target and learner responses on several levels including token, chunk and relation. We present an architecture for a content assessment module (CAM) which provides this flexibility using multiple surface-based matching strategies and existing language processing tools. For an empirical evaluation, we collected a corpus of language learner data consisting exclusively of responses to short-answer reading comprehension questions by intermediate English language learners.

2 The Data

The learner corpus consists of 566 responses to short-answer comprehension questions. The responses, written by intermediate ESL students as part of their regular homework assignments, were typically 1-3 sentences in length. Students had access to their textbooks for all activities. For development and testing, the corpus was divided into two sets. The development set contains 311 responses from 11 students answering 47 different questions; the test set contains 255 responses from 15 students to 28 questions. The development and test sets were collected in two different classes of the same intermediate reading/writing course.

Two graders annotated the learner answers with a binary code for semantic correctness and one of several diagnosis codes to be discussed below. Target responses (i.e., correct answers) and keywords from the target responses were also identified by the graders.[1] Because we focus on content assessment, learner responses containing grammatical errors were only marked as incorrect if the grammatical errors impacted the understanding of the meaning.

The graders did not agree on correctness judgments for 31 responses (12%) in the test set. These were eliminated from the test set in order to obtain a gold standard for evaluation.

The remaining responses in the development and test sets showed a range of variation for many of the prompts. As the following example from the corpus illustrates, even straightforward questions based on

[1]Keywords refer to terms in the target response essential to a correct answer.

an explicit short reading passage yield both linguistic and content variation:

CUE: *What are the methods of propaganda mentioned in the article?*

TARGET: *The methods include use of labels, visual images, and beautiful or famous people promoting the idea or product. Also used is linking the product to concepts that are admired or desired and to create the impression that everyone supports the product or idea.*

LEARNER RESPONSES:

- *A number of methods of propaganda are used in the media.*
- *Bositive or negative labels.*
- *Giving positive or negative labels. Using visual images. Having a beautiful or famous person to promote. Creating the impression that everyone supports the product or idea.*

While the third answer was judged to be correct, the syntactic structures, word order, forms, and lexical items used (e.g., *famous person* vs. *famous people*) vary from the string provided as target. Of the learner responses in the corpus, only one was string identical with the teacher-provided target and nine were identical when treated as bags-of-words. In the test set, none of the learner responses was string or bag-of-word identical with the corresponding target sentence.

To classify the variation exhibited in learner responses, we developed an annotation scheme based on target modification, with the meaning error labels being adapted from those identified by James (1998) for grammatical mistakes. Target modification encodes how the learner response varies from the target, but makes the sometimes incorrect assumption that the learner is actually trying to "hit" the meaning of the target. The annotation scheme distinguishes *correct answers*, *omissions* (of relevant concepts), *overinclusions* (of incorrect concepts), *blends* (both omissions and overinclusions), and *non-answers*. These error types are exemplified below with examples from the corpus. In addition, the graders used the label *alternate answer* for responses that were correct given the question and reading passage, but that differed significantly in meaning from what was conveyed by the target answer.[2]

1. Necessary concepts left out of learner response.

   CUE: *Name the features that are used in the design of advertisements.*
   TARGET: *The features are eye contact, color, famous people, language and cultural references.*
   RESPONSE: *Eye contact, color*

2. Response with extraneous, incorrect concepts.

   CUE: *Which form of programming on TV shows that highest level of violence?*
   TARGET: *Cartoons show the most violent acts.*
   RESPONSE: *Television drama, children's programs and cartoons.*

3. An incorrect blend/substitution (correct concept missing, incorrect one present).

   CUE: *What is alliteration?*
   TARGET: *Alliteration is where sequential words begin with the same letter or sound.*
   RESPONSE: *The worlds are often chosen to make some pattern or play on works. Sequential works begins with the same letter or sound.*

4. Multiple incorrect concepts.

   CUE: *What was the major moral question raised by the Clinton incident?*[3]
   TARGET: *The moral question raised by the Clinton incident was whether a politician's personal life is relevant to their job performance.*
   RESPONSE: *The scandal was about the relationship between Clinton and Lewinsky.*

3 Method

The CAM design integrates multiple matching strategies at different levels of representation and various abstractions from the surface form to compare meanings across a range of response variations. The approach is related to the methods used in

[2]We use the term *concept* to refer to an entity or a relation between entities in a representation of the meaning of a sentence. Thus, a response generally contains multiple concepts.

[3]Note the incorrect presupposition in the cue provided by the instructor.

machine translation evaluation (e.g., Banerjee and Lavie, 2005; Lin and Och, 2004), paraphrase recognition (e.g., Brockett and Dolan, 2005; Hatzivassiloglou et al., 1999), and automatic grading (e.g., Leacock, 2004; Marín, 2004).

To illustrate the general idea, consider the example from our corpus in Figure 2.

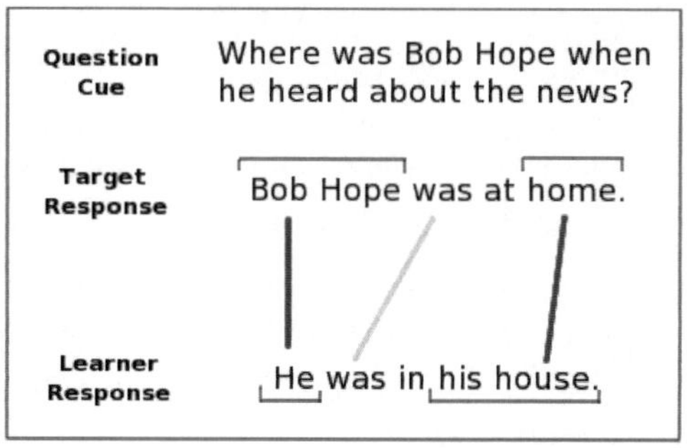

Figure 2: Basic matching example

We find one string identical match between the token *was* occurring in the target and the learner response. At the noun chunk level we can match *home* with *his house*. And finally, after pronoun resolution it is possible to match *Bob Hope* with *he*.

The overall architecture of CAM is shown in Figure 3. Generally speaking, CAM compares the learner response to a stored target response and decides whether the two responses are possibly different realizations of the same semantic content. The design relies on a series of increasingly complex comparison modules to "align" or match compatible concepts. Aligned and unaligned concepts are used to diagnose content errors. The CAM design supports the comparison of target and learner responses on token, chunk and relation levels. At the token level, the nature of the comparison includes abstractions of the string to its lemma (i.e., uninflected root form of a word), semantic type (e.g., date, location), synonyms, and a more general notion of similarity supporting comparison across part-of-speech.

The system takes as input the learner response and one or more target responses, along with the question and the source reading passage. The comparison of the target and learner input pair proceeds first with an analysis filter, which determines whether linguistic analysis is required for diagnosis. Essentially, this filter identifies learner responses that were copied directly from the source text.

Then, for any learner-target response pair that requires linguistic analysis, CAM assessment proceeds in three phases – Annotation, Alignment and Diagnosis. The Annotation phase uses NLP tools to enrich the learner and target responses, as well as the question text, with linguistic information, such as lemmas and part-of-speech tags. The question text is used for pronoun resolution and to eliminate concepts that are "given" (cf. Halliday, 1967, p. 204 and many others since). Here "given" information refers to concepts from the question text that are reused in the learner response. They may be necessary for forming complete sentences, but contribute no new information. For example, if the question is *What is alliteration?* and the response is *Alliteration is the repetition of initial letters or sounds*, then the concept represented by the word *alliteration* is given and the rest is new. For CAM, responses are neither penalized nor rewarded for containing given information.

Table 1 contains an overview of the annotations and the resources, tools or algorithms used. The choice of the particular algorithm or implementation was primarily based on availability and performance on our development corpus – other implementations could generally be substituted without changing the overall approach.

Annotation Task	**Language Processing Tool**
Sentence Detection, Tokenization, Lemmatization	MontyLingua (Liu, 2004)
Lemmatization	PC-KIMMO (Antworth, 1993)
Spell Checking	Edit distance (Levenshtein, 1966), SCOWL word list (Atkinson, 2004)
Part-of-speech Tagging	TreeTagger (Schmid, 1994)
Noun Phrase Chunking	CASS (Abney, 1997)
Lexical Relations	WordNet (Miller, 1995)
Similarity Scores	PMI-IR (Turney, 2001; Mihalcea et al., 2006)
Dependency Relations	Stanford Parser (Klein and Manning, 2003)

Table 1: NLP Tools used in CAM

After the Annotation phase, Alignment maps new (i.e., not given) concepts in the learner response to concepts in the target response using the annotated information. The final Diagnosis phase analyzes the alignment to determine whether the learner re-

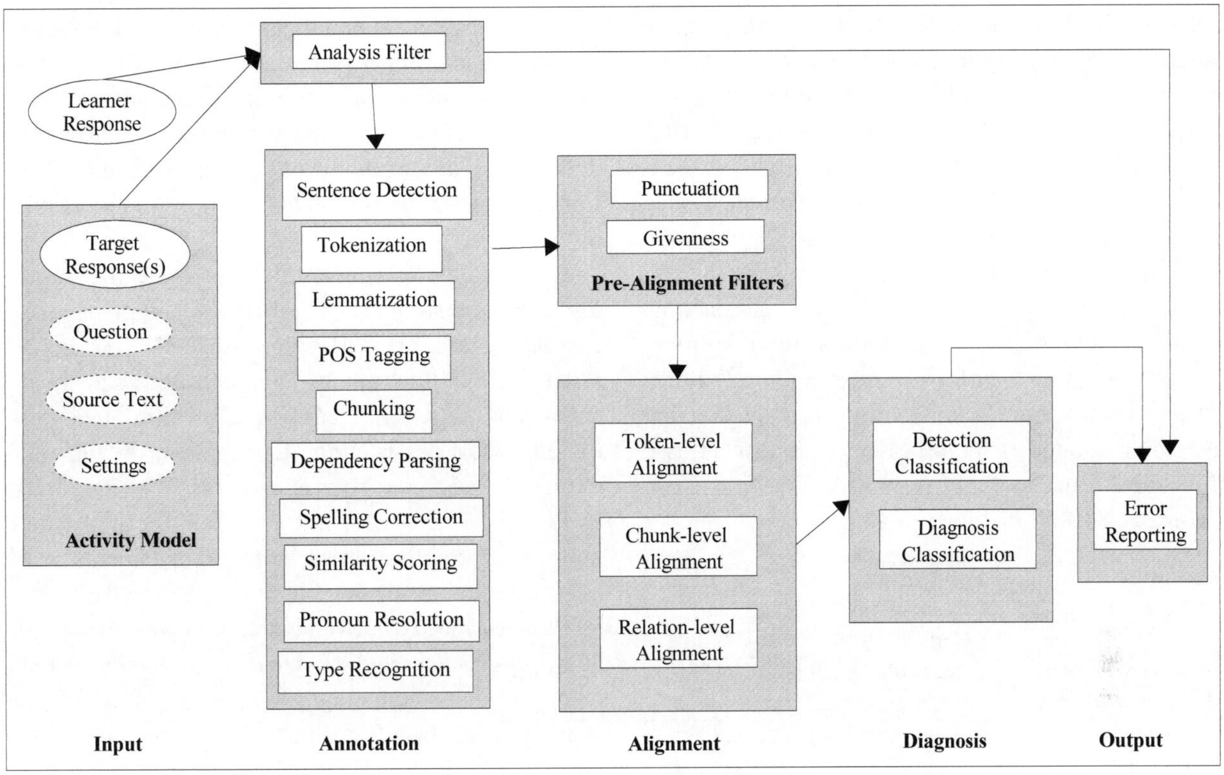

Figure 3: Architecture of the Content Assessment Module (CAM)

sponse contains content errors. If multiple target responses are supplied, then each is compared to the learner response and the target response with the most matches is selected as the model used in diagnosis. The output is a diagnosis of the input pair, which might be used in a number of ways to provide feedback to the learner.

3.1 Combining the evidence

To combine the evidence from these different levels of analysis for content evaluation and diagnosis, we tried two methods. In the first, we handwrote rules and set thresholds to maximize performance on the development set. On the development set, the hand-tuned method resulted in an accuracy of 81% for the semantic error detection task, a binary judgment task. However, performance on the test set (which was collected in a later quarter with a different instructor and different students) made clear that the rules and thresholds thus obtained were overly specific to the development set, as accuracy dropped down to 63% on the test set. The handwritten rules apparently were not general enough to transfer well from the development set to the test set, i.e., they relied on properties of the development set that where not shared across data sets. Given the variety of features and the many different options for combining and weighing them that might have been explored, we decided that rather than hand-tuning the rules to additional data, we would try to machine learn the best way of combining the evidence collected. We thus decided to explore machine learning, even though the set of development data for training clearly is very small.

Machine learning has been used for equivalence recognition in related fields. For instance, Hatzivassiloglou et al. (1999) trained a classifier for paraphrase detection, though their performance only reached roughly 37% recall and 61% precision. In a different approach, Finch et al. (2005) found that MT evaluation techniques combined with machine learning improves equivalence recognition. They used the output of several MT evaluation approaches based on matching concepts (e.g., BLEU) as features/values for training a support vector machine (SVM) classifier. Matched concepts and unmatched concepts alike were used as features for training the classifier. Tested against the Microsoft Research Paraphrase (MSRP) Corpus, the SVM classifier obtained 75% accuracy on identifying paraphrases. But it does not appear that machine learning techniques have so far been applied to or even discussed in the context of language learner corpora, where the available data sets typically are very small.

To begin to address the application of machine learning to meaning error diagnosis, the alignment data computed by CAM was converted into features suitable for machine learning. For example, the first feature calculated is the relative overlap of aligned keywords from the target response. The full list of features are listed in Table 2.

Features	Description
1. Keyword Overlap	Percent of keywords aligned (relative to target)
2. Target Overlap	Percent of aligned target tokens
3. Learner Overlap	Percent of aligned learner tokens
4. T-Chunk	Percent of aligned target chunks
5. L-Chunk	Percent of aligned learner chunks
6. T-Triple	Percent of aligned target triples
7. L-Triple	Percent of aligned learner triples
8. Token Match	Percent of token alignments that were token-identical
9. Similarity Match	Percent of token alignments that were similarity-resolved
10. Type Match	Percent of token alignments that were type-resolved
11. Lemma Match	Percent of token alignments that were lemma-resolved
12. Synonym Match	Percent of token alignments that were synonym-resolved
13. Variety of Match (0-5)	Number of kinds of token-level alignments

Table 2: Features used for Machine Learning

Features 1-7 reflect relative numbers of matches (relative to length of either the target or learner response). Features 2, 4, and 6 are related to the target response overlap. Features 3, 5, and 7 are related to overlap in the learner response. Features 8–13 reflect the nature of the matches.

The values for the 13 features in Table 2 were used to train the detection classifier. For diagnosis, a fourteenth feature – a detection feature (1 or 0 depending on whether the detection classifier detected an error) – was added to the development data to train the diagnosis classifier. Given that token-level alignments are used in identifying chunk- and triple-level alignments, that kinds of alignments are related to variety of matches, etc., there is clear redundancy and interdependence among features. But each feature adds some new information to the overall diagnosis picture.

The machine learning suite used in all the development and testing runs is TiMBL (Daelemans et al., 2007). As with the NLP tools used, TiMBL was chosen mainly to illustrate the approach. It was not evaluated against several learning algorithms to determine the best performing algorithm for the task, although this is certainly an avenue for future research. In fact, TiMBL itself offers several algorithms and options for training and testing. Experiments with these options on the development set included varying how similarity between instances was measured, how importance (i.e., weight) was assigned to features and how many neighbors (i.e., instances) were examined in classifying new instances. Given the very small development set available, making empirical tuning on the development set difficult, we decided to use the default learning algorithm (k-nearest neighbor) and majority voting based on the top-performing training runs for each available distance measure.

4 Results

Turning to the results obtained by the machine-learning based CAM, for the binary semantic error detection task, the system obtains an overall 87% accuracy on the development set (using the leave-one-out option of TiMBL to avoid training on the test item). Interestingly, even for this small development set, machine learning thus outperforms the accuracy obtained for the manual method of combining the evidence reported above. On the test set, the final TiMBL-based CAM performance for detection improved slightly to 88% accuracy. These results suggest that detection using the CAM design is viable, though more extensive testing with a larger corpus is needed.

Balanced sets Both the development and test sets contained a high proportion of correct answers – 71% of the development set and 84% of the test set were marked as correct by the human graders. Thus, we also sampled a balanced set consisting of 50% correct and 50% incorrect answers by randomly including correct answers plus all the incorrect answers to obtain a set with 152 cases (development subset) and 72 (test subset) sentences. The accuracy obtained for this balanced set was 78% (leave-one-out-testing with development set) and 67% (test set). The fact that the results for the balanced development set using leave-one-out-testing are comparable to the general results shows that the machine learner was not biased towards the ratio of correct and incorrect responses, even though there is a clear drop from development to test set, possibly related to the small size of the data sets available for training and testing.

Alternate answers Another interesting aspect to discuss is the treatment of alternate answers. Recall that alternate answers are those learner responses that are correct but significantly dissimilar from the given target. Of the development set response pairs, 15 were labeled as alternate answers. One would expect that given that these responses violate the assumption that the learner is trying to hit the given target, using these items in training would negatively effect the results. This turns out to be the case; performance on the training set drops slightly when the alternate answer pairs are included. We thus did not include them in the development set used for training the classifier. In other words, the diagnosis classifier was trained to label the data with one of five codes – *correct*, *omissions* (of relevant concepts), *overinclusions* (of incorrect concepts), *blends* (both omissions and overinclusions), and *non-answers*. Because it cannot be determined beforehand which items in unseen data are alternate answer pairs, these pairs were not removed from the test set in the final evaluation. Were these items eliminated, the detection performance would improve slightly to 89%.

Form errors Interestingly, the form errors frequently occurring in the student utterances did not negatively impact the CAM results. On average, a learner response in the test set contained 2.7 form errors. Yet, 68% of correctly diagnosed sentences included at least one form error, but only 53% of incorrectly diagnosed ones did so. In other words, correct responses had more form errors than incorrect responses. Looking at numbers and combinations of form errors, no clear pattern emerges that would suggest that form errors are linked to meaning errors in a clear way. One conclusion to draw based on these data is that form and content assessment can be treated as distinct in the evaluation of learner responses. Even in the presence of a range of form-based errors, human graders can clearly extract the intended meaning to be able to evaluate semantic correctness. The CAM approach is similarly able to provide meaning evaluation in the presence of grammatical errors.

Diagnosis For diagnosis with five codes, CAM obtained overall 87% accuracy both on the development and on the test set. Given that the number of labels increases from 2 to 5, the slight drop in overall performance in diagnosis as compared to the detection of semantic errors (from 88% to 87%) is both unsurprising in the decline and encouraging in the smallness of the decline. However, given the sample size and few numbers of instances of any given error in the test (and development) set, additional quantitative analysis of the diagnosis results would not be particularly meaningful.

5 Related Work

The need for semantic error diagnosis in previous CALL work has been limited by the narrow range of acceptable response variation in the supported language activity types. The few ICALL systems that have been successfully integrated into real-life language teaching, such as German Tutor (Heift, 2001) and BANZAI (Nagata, 2002), also tightly control expected response variation through deliberate exercise type choices that limit acceptable responses. Content assessment in the German Tutor is performed by string matching against the stored targets. Because of the tightly controlled exercise types and lack of variation in the expected input, the assumption that any variation in a learner response is due to form error, rather than legitimate variation, is a reasonable one. The recently developed TAGARELA system for learners of Portuguese (Amaral and Meurers, 2006; Amaral, 2007) lifts some of the restrictions on exercise types, while relying on shallow semantic processing. Using strategies inspired by our work, TAGARELA incorporates simple content assessment for evaluating learner responses in short-answer questions.

ICALL system designs that do incorporate more sophisticated content assessment include FreeText (L'Haire and Faltin, 2003), the Military Language Tutor (MILT) Program (Kaplan et al., 1998), and Herr Kommissar (DeSmedt, 1995). These systems restrict both the exercise types *and* domains to make content assessment feasible using deeper semantic processing strategies.

Beyond the ICALL domain, work in automatic grading of short answers and essays has addressed whether the students answers convey the correct meaning, but these systems focus on largely scoring rather than diagnosis (e.g., E-rater, Burstein and Chodorow, 1999), do not specifically address language learning contexts and/or are designed to work specifically with longer texts (e.g., AutoTutor, Wiemer-Hastings et al., 1999). Thus, the extent to which ICALL systems can diagnose meaning errors in language learner responses has been far from clear.

As far as we are aware, no directly comparable systems performing content-assessment on related language learner data exist. The closest related system that does a similar kind of detection is the C-rater system (Leacock, 2004). That system obtains 85% accuracy. However, the test set and scoring system were different, and the system was applied to responses from native English speakers. In addition, their work focused on detection of errors rather than diagnosis. So, the results are not directly comparable. Nevertheless, the CAM detection results clearly are competitive.

6 Summary

After motivating the need for content assessment in ICALL, in this paper we have discussed an approach for content assessment of English language learner responses to short answer reading comprehension questions, which is worked out in detail in Bailey (2008). We discussed an architecture which relies on shallow processing strategies and achieves an accuracy approaching 90% for content error detection on a learner corpus we collected from learners completing the exercises assigned in a real-life ESL class. Even for the small data sets available in the area of language learning, it turns out that machine learning can be effective for combining the evidence from various shallow matching features. The good performance confirms the viability of using shallow NLP techniques for meaning error detection. By developing and testing this model, we hope to contribute to bridging the gap between what is practical and feasible from a processing perspective and what is desirable from the perspective of current theories of language instruction.

References

Steven Abney, 1997. Partial Parsing via Finite-State Cascades. *Natural Language Engineering*, 2(4):337–344. http://vinartus.net/spa/97a.pdf.

Luiz Amaral, 2007. Designing Intelligent Language Tutoring Systems: Integrating Natural Language Processing Technology into Foreign Language Teaching. Ph.D. thesis, The Ohio State University.

Luiz Amaral and Detmar Meurers, 2006. Where does ICALL Fit into Foreign Language Teaching? Presentation at the 23rd Annual Conference of the Computer Assisted Language Instruction Consortium (CALICO), May 19, 2006. University of Hawaii. http://purl.org/net/icall/handouts/calico06-amaral-meurers.pdf.

Evan L. Antworth, 1993. Glossing Text with the PC-KIMMO Morphological Parser. *Computers and the Humanities*, 26:475–484.

Kevin Atkinson, 2004. Spell Checking Oriented Word Lists (SCOWL). http://wordlist.sourceforge.net/.

Stacey Bailey, 2008. Content Assessment in Intelligent Computer-Aided Language Learning: Meaning Error Diagnosis for English as a Second Language. Ph.D. thesis, The Ohio State University.

Satanjeev Banerjee and Alon Lavie, 2005. METEOR: An Automatic Metric for MT Evaluation with Improved Correlation with Human Judgments. In *Proceedings of Workshop on Intrinsic and Extrinsic Evaluation Measures for Machine Translation and/or Summarization at the 43th Annual Meeting of the Association of Computational Linguistics (ACL-2005)*. Ann Arbor, Michigan, pp. 65–72. http://aclweb.org/anthology/W05-0909.

Chris Brockett and William B. Dolan, 2005. Support Vector Machines for Paraphrase Identification and Corpus Construction. In *Proceedings of the Third International Workshop on Paraphrasing (IWP2005)*. pp. 1–8. http://aclweb.org/anthology/I05-5001.

Jill Burstein and Martin Chodorow, 1999. Automated Essay Scoring for Nonnative English Speakers. In *Proceedings of a Workshop on Computer-Mediated Language Assessment and Evaluation of Natural Language Processing, Joint Symposium of the Association of Computational Linguistics (ACL-99) and the International Association of Language Learning Technologies*. pp. 68–75. http://aclweb.org/anthology/W99-0411.

Walter Daelemans, Jakub Zavrel, Kovan der Sloot and Antal van den Bosch, 2007. *TiMBL: Tilburg Memory-Based Learner Reference Guide, ILK Technical Report ILK 07-03*. Induction of Linguistic Knowledge Research Group Department of Communication and Information Sciences, Tilburg University, P.O. Box 90153, NL-5000 LE, Tilburg, The Netherlands, version 6.0 edition.

William DeSmedt, 1995. Herr Kommissar: An ICALL Conversation Simulator for Intermediate German. In V. Melissa Holland, Jonathan Kaplan and Michelle Sams (eds.), *Intelligent Language Tutors: Theory Shaping Technology*, Lawrence Erlbaum Associates, pp. 153–174.

Andrew Finch, Young-Sook Hwang and Eiichiro Sumita, 2005. Using Machine Translation Evaluation Techniques to Determine Sentence-level Semantic Equivalence. In *Proceedings of the Third International Workshop on Paraphrasing (IWP2005)*. pp. 17–24. http://aclweb.org/anthology/I05-5003.

Michael Halliday, 1967. Notes on Transitivity and Theme in English. Part 1 and 2. *Journal of Linguistics*, 3:37–81, 199–244.

Vasileios Hatzivassiloglou, Judith Klavans and Eleazar Eskin, 1999. Detecting Text Similarity over Short Passages: Exploring Linguistic Feature Combinations via Machine Learning. In *Proceedings of Empirical Methods in Natural Language Processing and Very Large Corpora (EMNLP'99)*. College Park, Maryland, pp. 203–212. http://aclweb.org/anthology/W99-0625.

Trude Heift, 2001. Intelligent Language Tutoring Systems for Grammar Practice. *Zeitschrift für Interkulturellen Fremdsprachenunterricht*, 6(2). http://www.spz.tu-darmstadt.de/projekt_ejournal/jg-06-2/beitrag/heift2.htm.

Carl James, 1998. *Errors in Language Learning and Use: Exploring Error Analysis*. Longman Publishers.

Jonathan Kaplan, Mark Sobol, Robert Wisher and Robert Seidel, 1998. The Military Language Tutor (MILT) Program: An Advanced Authoring System. *Computer Assisted Language Learning*, 11(3):265–287.

Dan Klein and Christopher D. Manning, 2003. Accurate Unlexicalized Parsing. In *Proceedings of the 41st Meeting of the Association for Computational Linguistics (ACL 2003)*. Sapporo, Japan, pp. 423–430. http://aclweb.org/anthology/P03-1054.

Claudia Leacock, 2004. Scoring Free-Responses Automatically: A Case Study of a Large-Scale Assessment. *Examens*, 1(3).

Vladimir I. Levenshtein, 1966. Binary Codes Capable of Correcting Deletions, Insertions, and Reversals. *Soviet Physics Doklady*, 10(8):707–710.

Sébastien L'Haire and Anne Vandeventer Faltin, 2003. Error Diagnosis in the FreeText Project. *CALICO Journal*, 20(3):481–495.

Chin-Yew Lin and Franz Josef Och, 2004. Automatic Evaluation of Machine Translation Quality Using Longest Common Subsequence and Skip-Bigram Statistics. In *Proceedings of the 42nd Annual Meeting of the Association for Computational Linguistics (ACL-04)*. pp. 605–612. http://aclweb.org/anthology/P04-1077.

Hugo Liu, 2004. MontyLingua: An End-to-End Natural Language Processor with Common Sense. http://web.media.mit.edu/~hugo/montylingua, accessed October 30, 2006.

Diana Rosario Pérez Marín, 2004. Automatic Evaluation of Users' Short Essays by Using Statistical and Shallow Natural Language Processing Techniques. Master's thesis, Universidad Autónoma de Madrid. http://www.ii.uam.es/~dperez/tea.pdf.

Rada Mihalcea, Courtney Corley and Carlo Strapparava, 2006. Corpus-based and Knowledge-based Measures of Text Semantic Similarity. In *Proceedings of the National Conference on Artificial Intelligence*. American Association for Artificial Intelligence (AAAI) Press, Menlo Park, CA, volume 21(1), pp. 775–780.

George Miller, 1995. WordNet: A Lexical Database for English. *Communications of the ACM*, 38(11):39–41.

Noriko Nagata, 2002. BANZAI: An Application of Natural Language Processing to Web-Based Language Learning. *CALICO Journal*, 19(3):583–599.

Helmut Schmid, 1994. Probabilistic Part-of-Speech Tagging Using Decision Trees. In *International Conference on New Methods in Language Processing*. Manchester, United Kingdom, pp. 44–49.

Peter Turney, 2001. Mining the Web for Synonyms: PMI-IR Versus LSA on TOEFL. In *Proceedings of the Twelfth European Conference on Machine Learning (ECML-2001)*. Freiburg, Germany, pp. 491–502.

Peter Wiemer-Hastings, Katja Wiemer-Hastings and Arthur Graesser, 1999. Improving an Intelligent Tutor's Comprehension of Students with Latent Semantic Analysis. In Susanne Lajoie and Martial Vivet (eds.), *Artificial Intelligence in Education*, IOS Press, pp. 535–542.

Author Index

Association for Computational Linguistics
209 N. Eighth Street
Stroudsburg, Pennsylvania 18360